'Basak and Kitayama, experienced Indian and Japanese psychoanalysts, provide a brilliant model for the comparative study of psychoanalysis and culture. The themes they explore include mother-child dynamics; triadic relationships in the context of cultural practices; mythological symbolism as it relates to maternal sacrifice, guilt, and intense bonds between family members; shame culture; and the relationship between transience and resilience. A dialogue between Eastern and Western psychoanalytic traditions occurs that illuminates how family dynamics and cultural prohibitions differ, inform, and sometimes clash with each other. It is a profoundly interesting cross-cultural exploration for psychoanalysts, social scientists, and the general public.'

Harriet L. Wolfe, M.D., *President, International Psychoanalytical Association*

'The international psychoanalytic community will be both fascinated and deeply fertilised by this inspiring dialogue between an Indian and a Japanese analyst on fundamental issues of the human experience. Coming from two cultures so characterised, so rich in history, images and contents, they will contribute immensely to the future of psychoanalysis by opening up new scenarios and innovative ideas.'

Stefano Bolognini, *Past President International Psychoanalytical Association*

'This fascinating and historically important collection is an illuminating retrospective on the evolution of psychoanalysis in Japan and India. The artistic backgrounds of both authors brings their co-authorship together in an inspiring way. To read about some surprising convergences of the different cultures between India and Japan refreshes and advances both the practice and theory of psychoanalysis. Intriguing and stimulating I strongly recommend this book to all readers interested in the cultural impact on contemporary psychoanalysis.'

Jan Abram, *Author of The Surviving Object: psychoanalytic clinical essays on psychic survival-of-the-object (2022) New Library of Psychoanalysis, Routledge*

Psychoanalytic Explorations into the Primal Relationship in Japan and India

In this landmark collaboration, Osamu Kitayama and Jhuma Basak chronicle their long-standing collaboration and cultural exchange to survey the importance of familial relationships in Japan and India, exploring primal relations through a cross-cultural psychoanalytic lens.

Divided into three sections, *Psychoanalytic Explorations into the Primal Relationship in Japan and India* looks at each country's perception of parenthood and approach to raising children in turn before concluding in an illuminating dialogue between the two authors. Kitayama explores the maternal figure within the mother–child relationship, with a focus on the mother–son dyad, as well as relationships between parents. He considers, in depth, how Japanese culture can often exclude what is perceived as alien, delving into its rich tapestry of folklore to understand underlying 'mental scripts' which can shape collective perceptions, societal norms, and expectations, each of which can pose an issue to healthy familial relationships. Basak's response draws from Indian socio-cultural and mythological contexts, as well as clinical applications, to provide psychoanalytic insight into the stark differences and similarities between attitudes in Japan, India, and the Eastern culture at large. Both authors join together to highlight different child rearing practises such as co-sleeping and how they can shape human sexuality-subjectivity. Challenging the standardisation of the oedipal myth, the book draws from mythological and clinical examples in Japan and India to invite the reader into another world of parenting style and another idiom of psychoanalysis.

Uniquely positioned to develop understanding of how psychoanalysis has developed in non-Western countries, this book is an essential resource for psychoanalysts in training and in practice.

Osamu Kitayama is a Training and Supervising Analyst at the Japan Psychoanalytic Society, Professor Emeritus at Kyushu University, and President of Hakuoh University. He served as President of the Japan Psychoanalytic Society from 2016–2019 and continues to work with patients in private practice. He has authored numerous articles on culturally oriented psychoanalysis and books.

Jhuma Basak is a Training and Supervising Analyst at the Indian Psychoanalytical Society. She has published on culture and gender. Over the past 20 years, she has presented at IPA Congresses along with the first Keynote from Asia-Pacific, 4th IPA-region at the 53rd IPA Congress (*International Journal of Psychoanalysis*). A past Co-chair of COWAP Asia-Pacific, she co-edited *Psychoanalytic and Socio-Cultural Perspectives on Women in India: Violence, Safety and Survival* (2021).

Psychoanalysis and Women Series

Series Editor: Paula Ellman

For more information about this series, please visit: https://www.routledge.com/Psychoanalysis-and-Women-Series/book-series/KARNACPWS

Psychoanalytic Explorations into the Primal Relationship in Japan and India

Osamu Kitayama and Jhuma Basak

Routledge
Taylor & Francis Group

LONDON AND NEW YORK

Designed cover image: 'Yamaubato Kintaro' by Utamaro Kitagawa (1789-1804) from Kumon Institute of Education, Tokyo

First published 2025
by Routledge
4 Park Square, Milton Park, Abingdon, Oxon OX14 4RN

and by Routledge
605 Third Avenue, New York, NY 10158

Routledge is an imprint of the Taylor & Francis Group, an informa business

© 2025 Osamu Kitayama and Jhuma Basak

British Library Cataloguing-in-Publication Data
A catalogue record for this book is available from the British Library

Library of Congress Cataloging-in-Publication Data
A catalog record has been requested for this book

ISBN: 978-1-032-81901-3 (hbk)
ISBN: 978-1-032-75204-4 (pbk)
ISBN: 978-1-003-50193-0 (ebk)

DOI: 10.4324/9781003501930

Typeset in Times New Roman
by Taylor & Francis Books

Contents

Illustrations

Figures

Foreword by the Women and Psychoanalysis Book Series Editorial Board: Psychoanalytic Explorations into the Primal Relationship in Japan and India

Osamu Kitayama and Jhuma Basak

Worldwide, an interest in psychoanalysis' history has given way to a fascination with its geography. How psychoanalysis travels – the contours it has in locations distant from its origin – is beautifully illustrated in *Psychoanalytic Explorations into the Primal Relationship in Japan and India*. Co-authored by an Indian woman and a Japanese man, both psychoanalysts, the book traces the genesis of psychoanalysis in India and Japan illustrating how the field of psychoanalysis has evolved in tandem with the mythology, artwork, and parenting styles of the two countries.

Readers of *Psychoanalytic Explorations into the Primal Relationship in Japan and India* will find an introduction to the cultural specifics of these two geographies of psychoanalysis, in particular the effect of the cultural practice of long-term co-sleeping in India and Japan on the oedipal triangle. Via the dominant myths of these cultures, we begin to understand the experience of the self in "shame-based cultures" where the sovereignty of the ego is located not in the individual but in the group. The book equally illustrates how the aesthetic and imaginative vistas of cultural myths affect the reality of people's lives as they unfold in the analyst's clinic. For the reader who is familiar with European or North American psychoanalysis, the book offers a radical experience of difference within familiar psychoanalytic themes such as separation and individuation, dependence, gender, sexuality, and the primal scene. While they show the reader the unique configurations the oedipal drama takes in India and in Japan, the authors make the argument that in Japan and India the incest taboo is enforced over time rather than once and for all at a particular age. We are pleased to host this exciting work that showcases the extraordinary diversity that psychoanalysis holds as it travels.

About our book series: The Women and Psychoanalysis Book Series grew from the work of the International Psychoanalytical Association Committee on Women and Psychoanalysis (COWAP). The IPA–Routledge series furthers global perspectives and creativities on topics related to women, gender, and sexuality and psychoanalysis, including intersections with diversity and cross-cultural experience.

Acknowledgement

It has been a very enjoyable working process during the different stages of the development of the manuscript of the book in the past year. We are very thankful to the COWAP Book Series Editorial Board, and to Dr Paula Ellman, the Chair of the Editorial Board, for ardently participating with us in this journey.

Our heartfelt thanks and gratitude to the endorsees of this book – Drs Harriet Wolfe, Stefano Bolognini, and Jan Abram – who took out time from their commitments to share their precious thoughts with us.

We are thankful to Professor Jeffrey C. Miller, Ms Toko Igarashi, and Mr Eric Sheldon for their intensive translation works and for giving Kitayama invaluable support in English.

Introduction

Jhuma Basak

My interest in Japanese culture goes back to my youthful days as a contemporary dancer from Calcutta whose Indian artistic quest for soulful connections brought me to a visionary threshold of global aesthetics buried in the arts of the world. In that context, I came across Japan's concept of minimalism and its different art practices like the Noh, Kabuki, and Butoh. The loaded symbolic quality embedded in the arts and culture of Japan left a deep and lasting impression on me from my early days. My hunger for artistic folk traditions and cultural ethnology connected me to the rest of the world and its global literary and artistry realms. I found it to be most profound in Japan that, on one hand, it had its history of resilience, starting with its countless natural disasters in daily living (to date) to its rising from the atomic ashes of the Hiroshima–Nagasaki bombing; while, on the other hand, it resonated such constructive, refined, symbolic, abstract sensibility in its practice of the arts and culture. Its dichotomous quality is so enchanting, so venerable.

So, much later during my psychoanalytic odyssey closer to my midlife sojourn, when I learnt about the musical background of the Japanese psychoanalyst Osamu Kitayama, I was all the more intrigued to meet him and learn more about his psychoanalytic work on the prohibition of 'Don't Look' as well as about his musical experience. Coming from India where the sociocultural position of the male child in the family and society still reigns supreme, I found Kitayama's mother–son dyadic engagement in the prohibition of 'Don't Look' very captivating. Our first meeting and exchange on this enthralling concept was in 2004 at the 43rd IPA Congress in New Orleans. Thereafter, we had many more delightful occasions of attending and presenting together at different IPA congresses across the world. Though my initial journey with Kitayama was as a mentee where he was my PhD mentor, over the years it turned out to be a long and enriching passage of joint thinking and remains as a continuing dialogical exchange of psychoanalytic thoughts between each other as two collaborators.

This book is one such creation of that collaborative undertaking. The book takes up the aspect of maternal amalgamation in Eastern cultures, Japan and India, and exemplifies the Japanese theoretical conjecture of the prohibition of 'Don't Look' by Osamu Kitayama in view of its primal maternal prohibitions around the mother–child dyad (particularly for the mother–son symbiosis). Derived from mythological and cultural contexts of Japan (*The Crane Wife, Kojiki* 1968), Kitayama examines how breaking the prohibition, which is implanted in the mythological tale itself, brings about a tragic end to a happy dyadic pact between a husband–wife couple. The book further explores its clinical application, especially in view of the mother–son symbiotic relationship, both in Japan and India (Kitayama and Basak, respectively). The primal maternal prohibition (as exemplified by Kityama in Chapters 2 and 3, Part 1 of the book) is meant to be broken over time, distinct from the absolute paternal oedipal taboo of incest, thereby distinguishing a prohibition from a taboo. A major contrasting aspect in patricidal myths (of the West) from matricidal myths (of the East) is that while the former upholds the statement that '*he died for us*' (as in the death of Christ), the latter echoes the sentiment of '*she died for us*,' that is the mother (something that Kitayama distinguishes in his chapters and elaborates as a consequential intense survival guilt in the man).

Part 2 of the book initiates the discourse on the triadic tryst – i.e. the cultural growing up of the child amidst the primal triadic enthralment entrenched in the very site of the parental bed. At the heart of this triadic tryst is the notion of relationality that gets played out in the tripartite relationship between the mother–child and the father which gets provoked by the insinuations of the primal/parental bed itself. And this is what Kitayama refers to as 'the threesome way of thinking' ('this and that thinking'). Basak brings the Indian socio-cultural and clinical context into the study of the Japanese psychoanalytic theoretical construct of the prohibition of 'Don't Look,' thereby, adding a multi-layered, complex and expanded correlate to the application of the theoretical conjecture. It unlocks the parameters of its relevance to the Eastern culture at large, taking it beyond the Japanese cultural terrain into other Eastern cultures, like India. Different mythological semblances of maternal fusion ingrained in dyadic symbiotic relationships in India (like the 'Ganesha complex' conceptualised by Sudhir Kakar, Chapter 7), casts a reflection on cultural similarities and differences between Japan and India for the working of the prohibition of 'Don't Look,' carving its passageway to the triadic tryst as seen in the latter treatment of the book in Part 2. Altogether the book proposes to examine and establish a critical study of the cultural specificities and their clinical correlates, as well as to consider how they create an impact on the human subject, its culture-specific oedipal design, its related child-rearing processes, following its subsequent sexuality and gender development in life.

Part I The prohibition of 'Don't Look' in mythology, culture, and clinical contexts

Mythological tales carry the archaic fantasy of a culture, echoing a unified, interrelated voice of symbolic representation of its community. The quality of timelessness in these myths creates an omnipotent epic-presence of such

narratives in the culture and its collective psychic vault, the collective unconscious, that gets transported from generation to generation. Culturally speaking
India is rooted in the oral tradition where the travelogue of such tales is more
often in oral form which in its wandering course goes through many transmutations. Since culture is a continuum process of evolving and unfolding, the state of
a cultural flux may often equally tend to wash away much of the age-old oral
cultural wealth of a community. While change may essentially carry the hope of
an embryonic consequence, it can equally hold the potential of creating significant turmoil within the community as well. In the present age, the gap of
substantial mythological relevance in daily life, especially for the younger generation, may shake up the historically enduring cultural anchor of its community, creating a possible sense of instability and vacuum in modern-day living,
often invoking isolation amongst community members in their everyday living.
In an effort to metabolise such differences the playful infantile quality hidden in
the magical fables of the mythologies may seek a desperate outlet in external
environmental disharmony and even violence in contemporary times, as well as
seep into a present-day web of technological compulsive gameplays, gadgets, and
innovative devices. A sharp shift from the collective to individualisation may be
noticeable in this transition. One wonders if countries with ancient cultural histories, and oral traditions, are prepared to deal with such enormous socio-economic, technological and cultural conversion of the collective to the
individualistic plane. Perhaps it may be a direct impact of an engulfing capitalist
consumerism and its political socio-economic fragmentation of the community.

Mythologies have been like a legendary pillar of a society, as in both Japan
and India. As much as they have borne the dreamlike thrilling stories of community imagination, they have equally contained human intra-psychic intricacies
comprising painful, conflictual, ambivalent interrelational and intra-psychic
dynamism in the characters of the story. It may appear that these mythological
paradigms played out the paranoid–schizoid positions through the calamitous
narratives of its characters while it remained the task of the human agency in the
mortal world to learn from them to work out the depressive states in their real
life. That way it helped the community to find rapprochement and resilience in
daily living. In a sense, the myths seem to have acted as a 'guiding light' for the
community to follow. Perhaps modern-day psychic agony and disruption in the
humane foundation, its relationships, and ethical commitments, maybe interrelated to the loss of an ancient anchor of the community resulting in a volatile
shaking ground reality, especially for an oral tradition like India. There appears
to be no more a frame of reference for one to follow – an almost abandoned
state, lacking any parental guidance. As a result, life's journey becomes a lonesome, unknown erroneous expedition. In this section of the book the treatment
of the story of *The Crane Wife*, the Izanami–Izanaki myth, and the Ajase complex in Japanese psychoanalytic explorations unravel such an effort of human
learning and rapprochement that finds resonance in the cultural and clinical
elaborations by both Kitayama and Basak.

All mythological stories inherently endorse the dominant role of a 'hero' – symbolising the idealised hero of a community who serves as the intermediary connection between the mortal world and the divine realm. Be it Hercules in Greek mythology, Rama in Hindu epic, or Ajase (originally known as Ajatasatru) from Indian Buddhist legend which was later adapted into Japanese mythology – they are all tales of heroes that speak about their quests, trials, sacrifices and acquisitions. The story of Ajatasatru according to the Indian Buddhist fable takes us to the story of the son of King Bimbisara of Magadha (Ajatasatru) in ancient India who was well known for his ambitious expansion of the empire. It was prophesied that his birth would become the cause of his father's death. It is said that the Ajase story (the Japanese pronunciation of the Indian Sanskrit word Ajatasatru) first appeared in the scriptures of ancient India and entered Japan by way of China and Korea approximately between 700 to 1000 AD (Okonogi, 2022). After the death of Ajatasatru, around 459 BC, the Nandas came to power, followed by Alexander the Great in 327 BC. During this period Buddhism as a religion was very popular along with Jainism in that entire belt (Thapar, 1990; Avari, 2007).

In the 1950s, Heisaku Kosawa (2022) wrote his version of the Ajase story based on the *Kanmuryojukyo*, a Buddhist scripture, featuring the salvation of the mother. According to Kosawa, the wife of Binbasara (Bimbisara), Idaike (Vaidehi), feared the loss of her husband's love because of her fading beauty and hence she yearned to have a son. Experiencing deep anxiety, she consulted a soothsayer who told her that a certain sage living in the jungles would die in the next three years to be reborn as her son. In great impatience and plagued by anxiety Idaike killed the sage. However, in another version, it is said that the king and queen consulted the soothsayer due to their childlessness and learnt about their future son sealed in the body of the sage in the forest, following which the king ordered the killing of the sage. As the sage lay dying, he cursed Idaike who reincarnated as her son to one day kill his own father, the king. Fearing that the raging curse would come true Idaike gave birth to Ajase from the summit of a high tower desiring his death. But Ajase miraculously survived.

In Sanskrit (the ancient and classical Indian language), *Ajatasatru* means 'one who has no enemies' – *ajata* means the unborn; and *satru* meaning enemy. Both together is 'Ajatasatru,' who became the invincible king (Kapoor, 2018). Later, when Ajase learnt from *devavani* (the voice of God) that his mother tried to kill him, he was thoroughly disillusioned by his idealised love object, his mother, and attempted to kill her in anger. In another version of the Ajase story, Vaidehi's betrayal as a mother enrages Ajase, leaving him wanting to kill his mother. In the narrative of the betrayal of the mother, it is said that she would smear her body with honey and fill her jewelled crown with juice to offer to the imprisoned king, her husband. This oral temptation embedded in the honey-smeared body of the wife/mother may indicate a secret element of seductive, both passionate and tearing, entanglement of a triangular 'threesome' (which Kitayama elaborates upon in Chapter 6 and Part 2 of the book). It almost acts as an emblem of the inexhaustible (for) giving body of the woman. Basak's reference to the Hindu myth of the infant-god Krishna and Putana, the *rakshasa* (demoness), in Chapter 7, brings out the churning ambivalent locus in the mother–son dyad in the Indian cultural context. There Putana in the guise of a beautiful mother tried to kill infant-Krishna by breast-feeding him with her poisoned milk, but in an antithetical development to Putana's scheme, the infant-Krishna sucked her milk as well as her life out of Putana (Kakar, 2005). It appears that the maternal in both Vaidehi and Putana reiterates a similar narrative of maternal ambivalence and betrayal towards their child. For such a reversal of idealised maternal love, they both face patriarchal retribution by embracing termination in their narrative journeys in the larger construction of these mythological tales.

Coming to Ajase's account, he was subsequently gripped with a 'crippling guilt' and suffered from a severe disease which produced such a powerful odour that none could come close to him – except his mother, Idaike. Through this process of caring and healing, and the mother's bountiful giving capacity she could help to create the intra-psychic space in Ajase, alongside the dyadic space as well, for resolution of the mother–son conflict and ambivalence. She paved the way for Ajase's psychic journey from 'persecutory guilt' to 'reparative guilt' (Klein, 1975). Heisaku Kosawa's theoretical contention of the Ajase complex was to establish the quality of matricide and prenatal rancour leading to reparative guilt in the depressive position in the mother–son dyad. Thereby distinguishing it from patricide, incest, and persecutory guilt in the paranoid–schizoid position in the symbolic treatment of the Oedipus complex.

The hegemonic structure of such mytho-symbolic narrations is characteristically determined by their powerful male commentaries. In view of that it is imperative to draw our attention to Idaike's (Vaidehi's) 'forced guilt' in losing her sexually captivating capacity to entice the king – a latent foundational presence in the very development of the Ajase complex itself. In Chapter 4 Kitayama elaborates on this 'forced guilt' in the 'wounded caretaker,' the bountiful maternal-wife. In comparison to the heroic tales of the male characters in almost all mythologies, there seems to be a lack of such heroic narratives of achievements in female characters from ancient stories. Their heroism seemed to lay in their sacrificial absence–presence. They appear only as supportive characters for the heroes and become martyrs to build the heroes. Temporality is a characteristic feature of our 'wounded caretakers' in the larger narrative structure. It is only a very recent phenomenon in the psychoanalytic consciousness that the psychoanalytic theoretical domain has been aroused by emerging women's chronicles. In this aspect, Adrienne Harris' reflection on myths is such a welcoming new wave:

More and more, psychoanalysts are noting both the cultural contexts in which different myths emerge and range of gender-specific kinds of narratives we might tell ... Myths may organize solutions and understanding of common problems of growing and living, but the arrangement is more kaleidoscopic than liner and monolithic.

(Harris, 2009, p. 8)

Basak's attempt to problematise the prohibition of 'Don't Look' by engaging the mother–daughter duo in the submission of it in socio-cultural contexts and psychoanalytic theoretical conjectures (as seen in Chapter 7) adds to the very richness and complexity of the theory itself. Basak explores the reformulation of a prohibition into a saliant cultural power structure by unsealing the gender discourse and sexuality in the prohibition of 'Don't Look.' She examines the male fantasy of its paranoid–schizoid split of the woman between the 'idealised exhaustible giving mother' and the 'animalised gorging woman' (in *The Crane Wife*), augmenting the arguable aspect of the theory, providing an intricate density in the continuing theoretical dialogue between Kitayama and Basak. A compelling aspect of the readiness to simultaneously give and die runs parallel in such accounts of the woman's characterisation. In Chapter 4, Kitayama echoes the 'indigestible survivor's guilt' in the husband having survived at the expense of his wife's life (as portrayed in *The Crane Wife*), perhaps correspondingly resonating with the evolving, caring concern of today's men for the women of their country. This allows the probability of the formulation of another new narrative in future perhaps. In 1965 Winnicott proposed (in *Maturational Processes and the Facilitating Environment*) that mothers needed to withstand their infant's destructive attacks and survive them until the infant matured enough to become sufficiently concerned to assume responsibility for its instinctual destructive impulses. The aspired developmental flow of the infant-experience of *amae*, dependency love (Doi, 2005), would ideally evolve with adulthood to a mutually interdependency love complementing the dyad in a couple. In 1997, Kitayama in *Amae and its Hierarchy of Love*, wrote:

I experience that the person showing 'Amae' is looking up from a lower level and the person being asked for 'Amae' is coming from a higher level just as the Japanese Goddess Amaterasu, which literally means 'shining in the heaven,' shines on us from the heavens.

The very reason why Japanese 'love 愛 (ai)' seldom holds horizontality in its meaning such as equal love or philanthropy in Christianity rests on the hierarchical relationship in meaning and the vertical movement of the sounds of the word '愛.'

(Kitayama, 1997, p. 73)

However, contemporary times resonate an increasingly contrasting and rising voice of women. The earlier identification of women with the mythological maternal characters is undergoing female speculation and psychic re-construction. A structural subversion of changing mytho-symbolic phallocentric narratives into a drive towards emitting a 'female gaze' may be noticeable. A female 'glaring back' at the 'male gaze,' rejecting being their 'object-of-desire' alongside rebuffing the patriarchal seductive myth of desire itself in the larger phallic order of society. They echo a rejection of the sacrificial maternal role constructed from ancient times to be the sole receiving object for all 'destructive attacks' (Winnicott, 1965) from the phallic imagination of society. Kitayama and Basak converse on this in the third part of the book (Chapters 12 and 13) where Katayama talks about the rising female voice in contemporary Japanese culture that is rejecting their maternal role in society, bringing about a significant decline in the Japanese population itself.

An examination of an overruling comparative locale of Japan and India takes us to the imperative embarkment upon its 'shame-based culture' which is rooted in the intricate tapestry of both the countries' socio-cultural reality, its norms and expectations that influence individual/collective imagination, as well as dominate interrelational and collective behaviour. Such endemic autochthonic existence of shame in a culture determines human subjectivity with the internalisation of dreadful disgrace resulting in acute fear of exposure of their unconscious totemistic order of the pledge towards their primordial family and community fortification. Subsequently experiencing a constant internal haunting fear of humiliation. In the Japanese context, the external locus of evaluation places immense emphasis on social conformity and homogeneity. The breaking of which holds severe fear of disgrace and social phobia in Japanese society (Kitayama, Chapter 2). A comparative and engulfing element of shame is ingrained in the Indian system of caste discrimination based on the birth and related occupation of an individual. Crushing systemic inequity and economic marginalisation continues to traumatise generations of the 'low-caste,' most often leading to unconscious internalisation of inferiority and shame among its members. Needless to say, the history of colonisation in India over centuries by a superior 'white' European power has only added further to its incorporation of an aggressive imagination of defilement and vulnerability, all leading to a nation's 'sense of inferiority and disgrace for its natives.' Such 'shame cultures' would more often than not be internally torn between their 'true self' and their 'false self' (Winnicott, 1965) – that Kenichiro Okano (1994) explains as an 'ideal self' and a 'shameful self,' a private self and an adaptive self. Thus, any form of communication in such societies is fraught with compounded meanings, making interrelational dynamics ambiguous, overlapping and complex in nature. Deriving from this, one may now understand why it may be difficult for patients in such societies to overcome their inner resistances and reveal their 'private selves' in the clinical space during therapy (Chapter 1) – the fear of the exposure of their 'hidden debased self' resulting to unfathomable humiliation from it (Rothstein, 1984). The armour of narcissism may often act as a protective shield for such a vulnerable internal mindscape.

The two countries, Japan and India, convey two diametrically opposite mechanisms of cultural resistance to shame. It appears that Japan has embraced 'mysophobia' as a *cultural defen*ce to shame where cleanliness and orderliness reign supreme, often tracing it back to the religious impact of Shintoism in Japan. While, India seems to have embodied 'mysophilia' as its *cultural defiance* against shame, which commands a more nuanced socio-political understanding of its uprising against centuries of 'white' colonial oppression, and its seeking independence and vitality of its own motherland amidst dirt, 'bloody sacrifices,' and dust (Chapter 8) from the dreadful 'order' of the 'white' oppressor. It appears that both cultures have unconsciously imbibed their responses to the quality of shame as one of their constituents for cultural and national identity. As observed in both cultures, in reality the cleansing ritualistic performance of *misogi* obtains dominance as a cultural rite to purify the body and the soul. The sacred river Ganges runs across India and has a symbolic holy presence in every religious and social ritual. The sacramental cleansing runs deep in most crucial cultural ceremonies (like birth, marriage, and death) in both India and Japan. The ancient notion of dirt and purity is equally buried in the mythological narratives as well, where the relevance of animals in those mythological stories not only act as symbolical representations of spiritual vehicles and protectors but also as carriers of the 'animalised' aspect of the human (Chapter 3). The animals indicate the unaccepted, bestialised aspects of the human race. Such mythological transformations of combined quasi-animal and quasi-human *avatars* (incarnations) may be a cultural effort towards accepting the 'anomaly of the human race.' They act like a bridge between the 'unsoiled, pure' idealised godlike human self and its 'dark, tainted' uninvited inner desires.

It may be noticed that often a cultural phenomenon may act like a defensive armour against an examination of the psychic reality of its people. Any psychoanalytic intervention or even cultural interpretation of such phenomenological developments essentially requires an immense amount of time, and due appreciation and understanding of its obscure nuances in the intra-psychic plane of its culture and people. Part 1 of the book concludes with thoughts on transience by Kitayama and Basak. When the cultural ground reality is fraught with intense striving polarities of a 'shame culture,' the concept of transience comes like an almost dreamlike floating ephemeral edifying experience of life at the end of this part. The essence of it is exemplified by Kitayama in his treatment of the 'viewing together' of the 'floating moon,' a 'fleeting goldfish' by the mother–child duo (Chapter 1). They symbolically emphasise the personification of nature as a holding and healing embodiment in Japanese culture. A similar benevolent compassionate quality of nature may be found in the traditional belief and the practice of worshipping nature in

India (perhaps sadly not found so much in the urban space today, but still persists in the collective rituals and community belief systems). Basak's reference to the folk musical form *Bhatiyali* (from Bengal, Bangladesh – the lands of rivers), in Chapter 8, which narrates the life stories of boatmen in water resonates similar setting of a 'wet culture' with 'flooding, muddy rivers' that Kitayama talks about in Chapter 10. It indicates an ambiguous, overlapping, slippery environment. That way it distinguishes the Eastern flowing feminine adaptive cultural phenomenon from the contrasting decisive masculine aspect of the often Western dry cultural climactic conditions.

At another level, Basak in Chapter 8 inspects the quality of transience in deep human losses, as during the pandemic, that embraces mortality in the very life-span of a singular lifetime itself. Transience offers a unique conceptual locale that embraces a simultaneous interplay of life and death in a singular theoretical conjecture. It further searches for intra-psychic correlates of transience and cultural mentalisation through the experience of *amae* (a passive-receptive, dependency, and unconditional love that may switch the roles of giver-and-taker over time and situation) at both the individual and collective level. Interestingly though transience by itself emits ephemerality, yet contradictorily, when adopted in life-practice it acts like an internal anchor to provide resilience to both the individual and the community in order to combat reality catastrophes. Kitayama and Basak conclude their 'viewing together' in Part 1 of the book by reflecting on the finer nuances of transience in culture and life.

Part 2 The triadic tryst

As mentioned in the Introduction of Part 1, the unfolding process embedded in Kitayama's theoretical conjecture of the prohibition of 'Don't Look' continues its unravelling journey with the opening of Part 2 of the book with his chapter on 'Being drawn into a primal scene' (Chapter 9). Both Haisaku Kosawa (in the Ajase complex) and Osamu Kitayama (in the prohibition of 'Don't Look') implied a 'hidden injunction of time' buried in the conceptual development of their theories. Both Kosawa and Kitayama exemplified the symbolism ingrained in their mythological references as well as in the Japanese language, its silences, and its implied hidden meanings (Kitayama, Chapter 1; Basak, Chapter 11). That way it crafts a two-way transmission in the usage of language itself (as may be often noticed in everyday communication in Japan too) – (i) working at the surface level, and (ii) at its hidden subtle implication, giving it an ambiguous duality. As in a dreamlike phenomenon it works in a dual communicative mode – the *manifest* and *latent* work simultaneously in everyday exchange, making communication a complex mechanism (as I too observed when living in Japan). Kitayama's unfolding process of the prohibition of 'Don't Look' was initiated in 'Depth-psychology in shame culture' (Chapter 2) echoed primal prohibitions, while

'Being drawn into a primal scene' which takes us through the tripartite oedipal torrents that are built-in, clandestine, within the prohibition itself.

The gradual illuminating process of the theories prompts a certain psychic maturational time that would enable the reader/beholder with the capacity to contain witnessing calamitous transformations in the breaking of a prohibition which alongside equally breaks down the illusion of an ideal love object, the maternal/parental love object. In this part of the book, Kitayama and Basak directly focus on the primal scene itself in the treatment of their clinical citations, where the child is drawn into its parental sexual engagement by being practically positioned in between its parents in the parental bed itself (Chapters 9 and 11). In Chapter 11, 'Enthralled infancy in a bed of parental tryst,' Basak enquires on the child-rearing practice in India keeping 'co-sleeping' in the parental bed in context – she enquires how it shapes attachments, oedipal design, and sexuality amidst such a culture of a triadic co-habiting (that Kitayama explains as 'the threesome way of thinking'). This intense tripartite bonding may often act as the foundational platform for the Eastern concept of unfathomable filial commitment and community bonding. It reverberates a unified, combined representation in the psychic plane generating security and camaraderie for the child against a contrasting singular lonely psychic survival of the child (as maybe in the case of Western child-rearing customs). This being primary ground for the 'Eastern familial' relational structure, Basak further explores the very distinct developmental course of the child examining how the triadic tryst comprising the mother–child and father in bed – i.e. the 'threesome way of thinking,' – impacts on the evolving sexuality of both the boy-child and the girl-child in her clinical elaborations. Other attachment aspects like intimacy and non-sexual touch of sensual potential equally add to the fertile emotional ground of the growing child that finds resonance in its elaboration in the chapters of Part 2. Along with it, the probable insidious pathogenic potential embedded in this 'dependence dyadic exchange' (in contrast to the interdependence interrelational exchange), that may be initiated during the developmental phase itself gets correspondingly examined by Kitayama and Basak. In Chapter 9, 'Being drawn into a primal scene,' Kitayama takes up the aspect of pathogenicity involved in the primal scene as a result of phantasy and reality getting mixed up in the psychic structure of the child. He reports on Freud's case of 'the Wolf Man' as exemplary of the probable traumatic impact of living in an internal reality that mixes phantasy with reality together, thus creating an impact of dreadful psychic confusion leading to psychic isolation.

Both Kitayama and Basak study the theoretical impact and the clinical implication of the cataclysmic moment of breaking a prohibition, the contradictory passionate temptations inherent in it, along the breakdown of the illusion of its ideal love object. This often acts as a background to understanding the intense emotional and cultural phenomenon of the East, which may often seem unduly 'dramatic' or 'theatrical' in nature. Given the socio-cultural reality of sleeping together with parents in the parental bed as a very 'natural' cultural practice in both Japan and India, it simultaneously indicates a critical study of child-rearing practices in the East and the consequences of breaking the prohibitions around the primal scene. Needless to say, the socio-economic parameters of a country's status may also determine its economic division of rooms among its inhabitants within the domestic space and common living practices as well (as in the case of India). And that way socio-economic and socio-cultural parameters act together in shaping cultural habitats that further nurture certain internal psychic imaginations through rearing practices.

In Part 2 of the book, both Kitayama and Basak explore how the triadic tryst in bed, comprising the mother–child and father co-sleeping together in infancy, may also have a traumatic haunting impact on the growing child's desire and sexuality. The seduction of this traumatic encounter having its impact on the evolving sensual and sexual nuances of dyadic and triadic engagements, its overtly stimulated, interrelated and intimate subjective areas may add further perplexity in its inter-psychic space that is already in bewilderment with the blend of fantasy and reality. Basak draws an interesting contrast to male and female responses to the 'triadic in infancy' (Chapter 11) in elaboration on her clinical cases – while *guilt* in carnal imagination happens to play a dominant impact in determining 'female pathogenicity,' whereas the aspect of *overriding sexual pleasure* and *active proclamation* of it acts as the basis of 'male pathology.' This finds sharp and clear expressions among males and females depending on socio-cultural practices, for example as in the sovereignty of the glorified and ever-desired mother–son dyad in Indian culture. It attempts to bring forth the surreptitious maternal temptations in play in stimulating such cultural provocations that are embedded in the triadic tryst. Needless to say, the internalisation of such maternal insinuating imaginations in women is a reaction to the skewed play of patriarchy within the larger phallic construct of socio-cultural reality. In this context, the maternal gets compounded with the task of being both the creator and the eradicator. It is important to understand the multiplicity of different cultural rearing practices and to appreciate their unique variances, and nuances, along with its different primal and oedipal constellations. And not to necessarily read their clinical contentions as any validation of the pathogenicity of any particular culture. As psychoanalysts such elaborate clinical arguments give us the opportunity to appreciate, value, and include such sharp cultural differences within the larger psychoanalytic discourse and community. Perhaps as part of a growing practice of inclusivity, it is way past our time to start 'listening' and integrating different psychoanalytic voices from the East into the still-existing dominant dogmatic Western psychoanalytic dialect of the world.

Part 3 An interface – listening to Asian female voices

This is the first time in history that the two of the oldest psychoanalytic societies in Asia (and the world I believe), namely the Indian Psychoanalytical Society and the Japan Psychoanalytic Society, established in 1922 and 1955 respectively, have engaged in a joint collaboration of a psychoanalytic dialogue. More so, it is also an interchange between male–female analytic submissions representing intergenerational trajectories. This part of the book reflects a nonchalant interface between Kitayama and Basak. It attempts to echo a conversational and personal flavour into the dialogical exchanges between Kitayama and Basak. Through this open dialogue format between them, it attempts to address some of the concerns raised, and continued, from Part 1 and Part 2 of the book. Also, it is in view of a continuing psychoanalytic dialogue between Japan and India, between Kitayama and Basak, that this part of the book holds special significance for any future developmental prospects in their joint/individual work. Kitayama and Basak jointly critique and appreciate the two specific cultural contexts, their mythological elaborations, clinical experiences and theoretical developments of the prohibition of 'Don't Look' along with the triadic tryst in their approach to deliver unique Eastern cultural practices, and psychoanalytic applications in their definitive clinical styles in Japan and India.

Given the present flux and upheaval of socio-cultural, economic, and political situations across the world, Kitayama emphasises the need for 'listening to Asian female voices,' not only in view of his theories under discussion in the book, but equally of the socio-cultural struggle and arousal of female subjectivity, and their growing voices in Asia. Basak emphasises that such a development is a historical necessity. As a matter of fact, both Kitayama and Basak in their personal narratives of their trajectories echo their maternal gratitude to their respective mothers – perhaps reverberating how the subjective, private inner world shapes one's own objective speculations in life and work.

Kitayama draws attention to the increasing number of 'super-heroines' in contemporary Japanese *manga* (possibly a creative form of modern-day transformative production of mytho-symbolic narratives) with a decline in the cultural appreciation of the mother–son relationship. The alarming rejection of marriage, following motherhood, by the women of Japan has brought about a serious concern about the declining population of Japan. This changing era has brought in a dynamic, assertive female subjectivity both in the clinical space along with the arrival of a growing female psychoanalytic theoretical thinking/writing in our psychoanalytic discourse. Thus, the reading of female passivity and vulnerability uncovers a complex and changing narrative in today's psychoanalytic practice. However, the increasingly rich psychoanalytic dialogue from the East still needs considerable inclusion within the larger global psychoanalytic treatise. So far in the larger psychoanalytic community, the dominance of Western Eurocentric biases in the development of psychoanalysis, and its many foundational axiomatic psychoanalytic concepts, have built substantial chauvinism resulting in the lack of due representation and visibility of non-Western voices in the psychoanalytic community, particularly that of Asian female voices. In that context, this book holds a very unique position citing a changing phenomenon. Perhaps many such psychoanalytic dictums need to revisit their established doctrines for due elaborations, expansions, and inclusion. This part of the book resonates with concerns against the systemic negligence and prejudice that Asian women undergo, not only in their socio-cultural sites but equally in the treatment of psychoanalytic theoretical speculations as well as in psychoanalytic consciousness. They still seem to only attain an 'absence–presence' status with no agency of their own – something that carried forward from the cultural fables to reality to the psychoanalytic realm of our existence and practice. Of course, contemporary times challenge such established hegemonic paradigms. This exchange of views shared by Kitayama and Basak leaves the prospect of a 'dialogue-in-continuum' between them, opening up possibilities for more critical psychoanalytic speculations from the East, being led by female voices, as well as between Kitayama and Basak echoing different eras, different gender perspectives. They both represent two different times and the related concerns that awaken and shape them as different individuals in search of their individual driving passions amidst the greater global psychoanalytic orbit. Equally, they sow the seed of diverse psychoanalytic conceptual arguments creating the vast scope of a probable expansion of the discipline. Through this diverse course, they both speak of the same psychoanalytic quest in their trajectory to continue in the future, which largely amplifies the sense of plurality and inclusivity within the larger global psychoanalytic treatise.

References

Avari, B. (2007). *India – The Ancient Past: A History of the Indian Sub-Continent from c. 7000 BC to AD 1200*. London: Routledge.

Doi, Takeo. (2005). *Understanding Amae: The Japanese Concept of Need-Love*. Leiden: Global Oriental.

Harris. A. (2009). *Gender as Soft Assembly* (p. 8). London: Routledge.

Kakar, S. (2005). Hindu myth and psychoanalytic concepts: The Ganesha complex. In *Asian Culture and Psychotherapy: Implications for East and West* (pp. 76–84). Honolulu: Univ. o Hawai'i Press.

Kapoor, Kapil (2018). *Ajatshatru, The Great King of Magadha*. New Delhi: Rathore Publishers & Distributors.

Keigo, Okonogi. (2022). A history of psychoanalysis in Japan. *Journal of the Japan Psychoanalytic Society*, 4, 3–17.

Klein, M. (1975). *Love, Guilt and Reparation and Other Works 1921–1945*. Los Angeles: The Free Press.

Kitayama, O. (1997). Amae and its Hierarchy of Love. In: *Prohibition of Don't Look* (pp. 68–79). Tokyo: Iwasaki Gakujutsu Shuppansha, 2010.

Kosawa, Heisaku (2022). Two kinds of guilt feelings: The Ajase complex. *Journal of The Japan Psychoanalytic Society*, 4, 18–25.

Okano, Kenichiro (1994). Shame and social phobia: A transcultural viewpoint. *Bulletin of the Menninger Clinic*, 58 (3), 323–338.

Philipi, Donald L. (trans., intro. and notes). (1968). *Kojiki*. Tokyo: Univ. Tokyo Press, 1980.

Rothstein, A. (1984). Fear of humiliation. *JAPA*, 32, 99–116.

Thapar, R. (1990). *A History of India*. London: Penguin Books.

Winnicott, D. W. (1965). *The Maturational Process and the Facilitating Environment*. New York: Int. Univ. Press.

Part I

The prohibition of 'Don't Look' in mythology, culture, and clinical contexts

Chapter 1

Creating bridges

Japanese 'resistance' and approach

Osamu Kitayama

Between 'reliance' and 'non-reliance'

In commemoration of the 50th anniversary of the Japanese Psychoanalytical Association, I translated a set of historical documents of great interest in the history of psychoanalysis in Japan (Kitayama, 2010a). They comprise letters exchanged between Sigmund Freud and pioneering Japanese scholars. This was the first time they had been translated into Japanese.

The Japanese psychoanalysts underwent their training in Europe from 1930 to 1932. The fact that they often mentioned difficulties in studying abroad is very significant. In this chapter, I would like to show that our apparent 'resistance' is due to the conflicts about psychoanalysis that involve 'reliance' and 'non-reliance' in creating bridges.

'Books' and time

Exchanges between Sigmund Freud and Japanese individuals began in 1927 when Kiyoyasu Marui (1886–1953) wrote to Freud with the hope of obtaining permission to publish the latter's books. This is Freud's answer to that letter.

> Of course, your nation is free of many of the prejudices that have caused trouble for psychoanalysis in Europe and America. I would very much like to know what kind of reception analysis will find in Japan – if only I live long enough.
>
> (10 November 1927)

Two years later, in 1929, the psychologist, Yaekichi Yabe (1874–1945) contacted the International Psychoanalytical Association. The following year, Yabe received analytical sessions from Edward Glover in London and attended classes given by Ernest Jones. On the evening of 7 May 1930, while on his way back to Japan, Yabe visited and spoke with Freud. Yabe was also given

DOI: 10.4324/9781003501930-2

permission to translate Freud's books. Yabe, who was certified as an analyst after this, wrote:

> I felt that I had already accumulated considerable understanding as far as books were concerned, and had presumed that things would somehow take form after that time period.
>
> (Yabe, 1931)

There is a report that Ernest Jones advised Yabe 'to keep the group small and of high quality and to send two members to Europe for analysis.' But the organisation grew in size, so they appear not to have followed the IPA's advice. Along with clinical practice, the 'books' Yabe and his group were enthusiastically translating, and 'studying' psychoanalysis in Japan must have been impossible, but the books have taught us much.

A Marui's 'pride'

Around the time that Yabe established the Japan Psychoanalytical Association in Tokyo, Marui, who had not contacted Freud for several years, wrote to Freud to announce that he had completed his own translation of one of Freud's books.

Despite Freud's wishes, the Tokyo Group that included Yabe, which was mostly oriented towards literature and psychology, never achieved integration with the medically oriented Sendai Group led by Marui. This may illustrate the considerable sense of pride and superiority that a professor of medicine at an imperial university felt over psychological scholars, as can be seen in his letter.

> But I dare say that my pride in my life as a scientist, especially as a psychoanalyst, does not allow me to join that society itself.
>
> (2 February 1932)

Kosawa's financial situation and language

The psychiatrist Heisaku Kosawa (1897–1968) was the third person to emerge as a pioneer of Japanese psychoanalysis. He was a member of Professor Marui's class. Kosawa began his stay in Vienna on 26 January 1932, where he visited Freud. The section quoted below is taken from a letter sent immediately before his visit, in which Kosawa asks Freud to read and make comments on a paper of his and mentions linguistic and financial difficulties. Kosawa writes:

> Although I was completely aware that due to my very insufficient knowledge of German I would have great difficulties at the beginning, I

did not want to postpone my journey ... I had to realise that my dream could not be fulfilled because the financial costs by far exceeded my moderate means.

(13 January 1932)

In response, Freud was positive and willing to lower the cost of his psychoanalytic sessions. Freud writes:

I have already agreed to afford you all the support I am able to give and I am very willing to read and to judge your work when it is available in German without you incurring any expenses, of course.

(16 March 1932)

I am still bound by the necessity of earning money, but instead of $25, I would charge you only $10.

(16 March 1932)

Despite Freud's favourable offer to reduce his fees, Kosawa shows 'humble resistance,' claiming financial difficulties again. Instead, Kosawa was analysed by Richard Sterba and received supervision from Paul Federn.

Doi's insight into Amae

The training that these individuals underwent appears to have been very difficult. This, however, could happen to anyone.

Takeo Doi (1920–2009), who made his debut after the Second World War and the defeat of Japan, is another leading figure in Japanese psychoanalysis. Doi underwent psychoanalysis once in Japan and once overseas. I wrote the following passage under the entry for 'Takeo Doi' in *Seishinbunseki Jiten [Dictionary of Psychoanalysis]* (Okonogi, 2002).

[Doi] underwent analysis from Kosawa but decided to break away, objecting to Kosawa's awareness of salvation and analytical methods. Doi went to the US for a second time in 1955 and studied for a year at the San Francisco Psychoanalytic Institute. He received training analysis from Norman Reider but failed midway. After returning to Japan, he began his work of putting his self-analysis and clinical experiences into words.

The terms, such as 'breaking away' from psychoanalysts and the 'failure' of psychoanalysis, that appear in this entry, written under Doi's supervision, have a strong impact. Doi clarified elsewhere how he had interrupted his analysis in San Francisco:

> Because I found myself at a dead end, discontinuing [the analysis] was the only solution.
>
> (Doi, 1958)

I have concluded that behind Doi's repeated interruptions were his disillusionment about undergoing psychoanalysis, and his valuable insight that we now refer to as *amae* or a 'dependence–independence conflict' (Kitayama, 2014).

Several decades ago

For decades they had struggled with psychoanalysis, not only when studying abroad but also when practising it in Japan. When I became a member of the Japan Psychoanalytical Association, many psychiatrists were discussing the management of 'psychotics' and 'borderline cases,' following pioneer works. In a variety of ways, the content of their presentations was about dynamic psychiatry. Close to 90% of the academic presentations in 1994 were given by psychiatrists. In 2015, however, 70% were given by psychologists. As a psychiatrist, I personally thought that an understanding of depth psychology and 'reliable' management was crucial for dealing with serious cases of patients who have fragile 'ego boundaries.'

Particularly during the initial stages of treatment, therapists must handle both the external environment and the internal world. The natural approach is not to choose 'either the inside or the outside,' but to weave both of them together. Even after growing up, a patient is affected directly by his or her external environment and culture. Dynamic psychiatrists assess and manage environmental problems, and sort out and adjust interpersonal relationships that have become entangled in a complicated manner. Once the patient has settled down, the therapist performs repeated sessions in a circular fashion to conduct internal explorations. The Japanese term used here to refer to 'management' is *kanri*. This word, however, carries an authoritarian meaning.

In this context, understanding the conflicts of a patient who wanted to depend on other people but could not, and handling the issue of 'depending on authority' as the manager of therapeutic settings, in particular, were extremely important tasks for psychiatrists like me. The Japanese word for 'dependence' is *izon*, which is an ambiguous term. I thought that, as in English, *izon* should be divided into these three distinct concepts, i.e. dependence, reliance, and alliance. The fact is, the polysemous word *amae* is used and often understood in Japan as *en bloc*, within a hierarchical relationship, in the sense of 'passive dependence.' As a person who prepares the analytical setting, in particular, I find that supplying 'the reliable' is an extremely important task. 'Fear of dependence,' moreover, is sometimes understood as a 'fear of being engulfed,' which is about an individual's fear of becoming dominated or losing his or her sense of self.

Figure 1.1 Fūryū Jūnigatsu – Satsuki (Tangono Sekku) [Elegant Twelve Months – The Fifth Month (Boys' Festival)] (1830–1844) by Kunisada Kōchōrō (Utagawa).
Source: Kumon Institute of Education, Tokyo.

To briefly illustrate a conflictual aspect of this type, I would like to examine two *ukiyo-e* pictures (see Figures 1.1 and 1.2), which were produced about 200 years ago in Japan. The encouraging mother in the first picture is dangling a crab with claws, which may be scaring the clinging boy. In the second one, which we selected from a variety of *ukiyo-e* as one showing the *amae* of a child, the domineering and seductive woman is holding a chestnut in a prickly shell, which may symbolise danger.

Figure 1.2 Yamaubato Kintarō [Yamauba and Kintarō] (1789–1804) by Utamaro Kitagawa.[1]
Source: Kumon Institute of Education, Tokyo.

A case: from dependence toward an alliance

Here, I wish to quote a case that describes the introduction to initial-stage management and a reliable environment, to show you that this is exactly the point at which psychoanalytic work begins.

The patient was a nurse who was working at a surgical hospital: she was an intellectual woman. She was always neatly dressed and well-groomed, but she had an expressionless face. Her major problem was depression. While attending nursing school, she experienced a decline in vigour and motivation. She took a variety of medicines almost on a daily basis, and, after beginning full-time work as a nurse, she was no longer able to hide the fact that she was not well. She was advised to undergo treatment, so she visited my psychotherapy clinic based on a referral from a mutual acquaintance. She was living separately from her parents who managed a variety store, and she had a brother who was five years younger than she was. In terms of her personality, she was a 'good girl' and an honour student, but she told me from the start that she did not want to depend on her parents.

The patient had bought vast amounts of tranquillisers, Chinese herbal medicines, and painkillers, and was taking close to 15 types of drugs, including those prescribed by doctors. The diagnosis of her personality was complicated because of the drugs she took to treat her symptoms, and I personally felt that, based on her behavioural patterns and the state of her symptoms, she had borderline personality disorder and hysteria. Therefore, I understood that, at least for a while, my job was the 'management,' or adjustment of her environment.

In our regular weekly sessions, when drugs became the topic of conversation, she said when she was a young girl her parents had refused to give her any medicine, no matter how much pain she complained of having, because they reportedly were afraid of their daughter becoming dependent on drugs. She also said that she cried often since she was very young. I felt that her mental pain had persisted and had not disappeared. As her parents refused to give her any painkillers, my giving her a prescription for medication was an act that helped establish reliability in our relationship.

I then proposed to the patient, who was simply running away from her 'invading' parents, that she undergo a session with them. I pointed out that she was becoming depressed because she was overstraining herself in a private struggle not to cause her parents any trouble. The patient accepted my proposal. I met her parents and told them that the patient was being taken care of by professionals, and I would contact them if something came up. I also cautioned them not to invade their daughter's personal space, where she could be herself. I told them that, since she needed medication at least for now, they should stop encouraging her to discontinue taking necessary drugs. What struck me was the way the parents worried about their daughter, suspecting that she might be a narcotic addict.

It was around this time that an incident occurred at the ward of the hospital where the patient was working: an injectable solution of a painkiller disappeared from the pharmacy room. She was accused of stealing it, but she justified it by saying that she needed it for abdominal pain. She looked back at the incident and admitted that she had been careless. The people around her became even more distrustful of her, with a co-worker saying that she might be suffering from a serious mental disorder. As her physician in charge, I contacted the hospital where she was working and was told by her superior that she had gotten into the pharmacy room by forcing the door open. As she promised that she would not obtain any drugs on her own, she and I both agreed to her being downgraded to part-time work at the hospital.

Because of these complicated problems with her environment that were entangled in a multi-layered manner, my job for the first six months centred on sorting out and adjusting her 'connections and relationships.' Although the patient was running away from her environment, she gradually became able to create a 'reliable' environment and an 'alliance' with me, and she began to settle down. My comments here cover the period up to about three months after our first meeting. At the sessions, I explained her personality traits to her, as well as the conflict of being a 'masochistic caretaker' (Kitayama, 1991) who wishes to be taken care of by others, but instead takes care of herself, and does not leave things to other people because of guilt about being dependent. I then interpreted the patient's desire to be taken care of by others, advised her not to make light of her abdominal pain, which appeared to be psychogenic, and decided to assign an internist as her physician in charge.

I presented each of these items to her; I explained and interpreted each one for her, obtained her consent, and acted on them. It took us about six months for an 'environment that can be relied upon' to be fully established. Later, she settled down. The importance of the environment had retreated to a mere 'background' factor, as long as problems did not occur. Although it definitely existed, it came to be regarded by both the patient and the people concerned as something to be taken for granted, and it was eventually forgotten.

Thus, the setting was established. Psychotherapy, however, began to be differentiated and it continued, thereafter, for several years. During this period, she no longer felt a need to depend on drugs. Her central theme was that the patient, who had been 'deceived' by being raised like an eldest son, would re-encounter 'father' and 'male' figures, and rely on authorities. If we were to refer to this initial-stage work as 'holding,' it would signify a maternal function. However, I felt that my initial role was to interpose myself between the patient and her family, act as a professional mediator, and give them access to psychoanalytic psychotherapy.

Cultural resistance to psychoanalysis

Naturally, some Japanese psychoanalytic patients we treat, as well as scholars, show their resistance to acceptance when learning about Freudian psycho-analysis. We tend to think, in my opinion, that although we are the same as all human beings, the Japanese people have, at the same time, built a culture that has aspects which show unique thinking and ways of living. The idea that 'I'm the same as you but also different from you' is manifested mainly in the language and ways of raising children. Especially as psychoanalysis regards people's personality and pathology as originating from early infancy and childhood, and seeks verbal clarification about these experiences. Therefore, finding the origin of this resistance in our language and the ideal ways of raising children is psychoanalytic in nature. The script of a person's life that follows a repeating pattern is created during infancy and childhood, together with an important other, or, with one's parents, and is performed repeatedly thereafter while playing opposite different characters.

The meaning of the 'front' and the 'back'

The significance of verbalising, in psychoanalysis, the content of the unconscious that had been suppressed, is catharsis, first and foremost, that can be obtained through expressing it. At the same time, the 'naked' content of the unconscious is not actualised. It is not that the content of the unconscious becomes completely naked and exposed; nor is it that one becomes able to express everything he or she wants to say. To analysts of the Freudian school, there is no true liberation from the animal nature of humans. The closest is to obtain an indirect method of expression such as culture, play, or sublimation.

In Japanese expressions, there is a sophisticated meaning at the front and a dubious meaning at the back. These different use of front and back is also called *tatemae* and *honne* (what you say as opposed to what you really think). Numerous non-verbal exchanges take place in Japanese culture. Verbalisation may bring about effects such as disillusionment and 'throwing a wet blanket on others.' *Amae* and desire for love, in particular, essentially express one's need to be understood without using words, because hopes for a primordial integrated world are liable to be shattered if put into words.

In Japanese, eloquence tends to invite distrust, often being described in a negative light such as chattering or babbling. Thus, although words of love may, on the surface, strongly indicate one's love for the other person, their verbalisation is a mere 'verbal guarantee,' because it does not promise that love will be realised. Therefore, the words of love involve a double consciousness of front affirmation and back negation, they are not used very often in our everyday lives. However, my standpoint is not to remain passively *amaeru* (dependent) waiting to be understood, to express intentionally the behind-the-scenes thoughts that are easily hidden with an ambivalent attitude and behaviour as needed.

Paradoxical appreciation in the Japanese language

Now, I would like to ask everyone including myself whether psychoanalysis changes according to language. This question arises because language is the essential basis of the practice of psychoanalysis. Language in psychoanalysis is expected essentially to convey the content of the mind through the method of free association; therefore, the strict structure of a language can compel a clear organisation of thoughts. This analytical process may occur very naturally, particularly in Western cultures, where logical use of language is idealised.

On the other hand, with regard to the Japanese language, some people conclude that ambiguity is one of its main characteristics. It is also said that Japanese people chiefly communicate ideas while keeping these ideas mainly unspoken. Some people even say that psychoanalysis may be difficult in Japan because logical language is necessary for organising irrational thoughts of the unconscious.

Furthermore, multi-layered ambiguity is said to be a characteristic of not only our language but also of our culture. For example, our art is appreciated for its suggestiveness. As you may know, Japanese poems in traditional forms are very simple and short. Naturally, I think that obscuration or non-verbalisation should be counted as one of the categories of Japanese rhetoric.

I, however, believe that psychoanalysis is possible in Japan too. Psychoanalysis is becoming increasingly popular now in Japan. However, there are many sayings in Japanese that could be translated as 'speech is silver, silence is golden' and 'suggestion is better than revelation' among others. We, the Japanese, do not think that the philosophical term *logos* is the first principle that determines the order of the world. We do not think eloquence necessarily indicates high intelligence.

All of us share and convey many intentions and ideas without verbalising them in words. In my opinion, however, the Japanese concept of ambiguity differs from that of Western cultures. Our ambiguity is not only either undetermined or plurally determined but also 'unfathomable' as I will explain in later chapters. It could be described as a state of 'betwixt and between.' As the English prefix 'ambi-' has the meaning of two sides or both, Western ambiguity is often taken to mean a 'double meaning' due to the intellectual categorisation of meanings. I want to stress that Japanese ambiguity refers mainly to indivisible matter. I think this is very important when you think and practice psychoanalysis in Japanese.

Coexistence of two types of communication

To show you this linguistic state of affairs visually, I would like to cite one of my studies (Kitayama, 1998). I investigated nearly 15,000 copies of *ukiyo-e* and discovered that the number of pictures in which a child was depicted was approximately 500, and of those that of a mother–child relationship was about 370. Through classifying these pictures, I realised that several patterns of the mother–child relationship repeatedly appeared. Based on this classification, I conducted a survey of 350 *ukiyo-e* prints portraying the mother–child relationship. The result was that approximately half of the mothers and children in these pictures have relationships through a certain medium of a bridging object, as illustrated in 'viewing together' (see Figure 1.3).

Furthermore, we have found two types of communication in the 'viewing together' pictures. The first type of communication we discovered between them is a verbal one, and this concerns the linguistic use of symbols. In the area of language acquisition, developmental psychologists have

Figure 1.3 Yōchien: Koitoto [Kindergarten: Carp Streamer] (1905) by Chikanobu Yōsyu.
Source: Kumon Institute of Education, Tokyo.

emphasised the transition from mutually shared experience between a mother and her child to the use of language. From this point of view, Jerome Bruner (1975) stressed the importance of 'joint attention.' The child follows the mother's eyes and looks at what the mother is looking at, and vice versa. As you can imagine in the frightened child in the picture (see Figure 1.1), the united mother and child may be talking about the same object to which they are focusing their attention together. This makes us feel as if we can hear their voices when we look at them. This very fundamental triangular relationship, formed by mother, child and object becomes the foundation to discover, share and use the symbol, which will be repeated countless times throughout life.

The second type of communication is non-verbal, that is, an emotional communication often accompanied by some form of bodily contact. As the classification of 'Parallel' in my study indicates, it is important that the two people are viewing an object side by side, with their shoulders abreast, but not staring at each other. I have found that people tend to feel emotions when they communicate in such a side-by-side position. Yoko Yamada (1987), a Japanese developmental psychologist, termed this kind of human, or mother–child, relationship as an 'abreast relationship.'

This (see Figure 1.4) is Utamaro's work titled *Praying for Rain*. The couple consisting of a mother and her child is staring at a hole in an umbrella, but what is more important is the emotional relationship

Figure 1.4 Fūryū Nanakomachi – Amagoi [Seven Elegant Episodes about Komachi: Praying for Rain] (1790s) by Utamaro Kitagawa.
Source: The British Museum, London.

conveyed by the bodily contact between the two people. The mother and child are painted in the centre, both viewing together the patched hole in the umbrella, which is apparently meaningless. We do not know whether the child is talking or not, and we are not sure what the child is looking at. However, we can see the rich non-verbal communication, which is both psychological and bodily, namely, psychosomatic.

I would like to show you one more example of 'viewing together' in Japanese art outside *ukiyo-e*. Shōen Uemura (1875–1949) (see Figure 1.5) was not only a female painter but also a mother. We see that non-verbal, and maybe verbal, communication in a half-open (oblique) stance becomes the central theme that we appreciate in the picture. In those

Figure 1.5 Boshi [Mother and Child] (1934) by Shōen Uemura.
Source: National Museum of Art, Tokyo.

pictures, we may experience and see the coexistence of both types of mother-infant communication, which may take place halfway between dependence and independence. In this half-open (oblique) stance the infant is interacted with by the mother linguistically, psychologically and somatically or bodily. The *ukiyo-e* pictures show how the stance develops into Japanese cultural entertainment. Below boys are communicating verbally and non-verbally, while viewing the moon (see Figure 1.6).

Living between inside and outside

Fortunately, Sigmund Freud was greatly interested in this sort of ambiguity. He frequently made use of ambiguous words, which were described

Figure 1.6 Fūryū Jūnigatsu Hachigatsu [Elegant Twelve Months: The Eighth Month] (ca. 1760s)
    by Toyomasa Ishikawa.
Source: Kumon Institute of Education, Tokyo.

as 'verbal bridges' (*Wortbrücke*) between the manifest and the latent. In analysing the manifest content of dreams, he pointed out that ambiguous words can contribute to dream formation as well as dream analysis. In the footnote of his report on Dora's dream, he wrote:

> Now, in a line of associations, ambiguous words (or, as we may call them, 'switch words') act like points at a junction. If the points are switched ... then we find ourselves on another set of rails; and along this second track run the thoughts which we are in search of but which still lie concealed behind the dream.

> (Freud, 1905, p. 65n)

Before I start discussing patients' difficulties in understanding ambiguous words, I think I have to mention one distinguished analyst: Donald W. Winnicott. Winnicott (1971), in his papers such as 'Transitional Object,' has also emphasised the bridging area and object, the in-between of a mother and her child, and the external and internal, showing exceptionally poetic use and tolerance of ambiguities in his writings.

We all know that some patients show a marked difficulty in handling ambiguity, in action and thought. Obsessionals, for instance, are characterised by this as they sometimes describe an ambiguous mixture as dirty, ugly, frightening, and so on. If we metaphorise digestive functions in these experiences, the ambiguity is 'hard to swallow,' 'gets stuck in the throat,' or something that 'cannot be stomached.' It is 'indigestible,' 'sickening,' 'nauseating,' and 'repulsive.' These uncomfortable sensations motivate 'sick' people into acts of cleansing, purifying, and washing in order to make the dirty things much clearer.

Some of them 'vomit' the material literally, and 'obsessional vomiting' may be figurative. As the analytic therapy progresses with the exchange and understanding of these expressions, the therapist begins to sense their unconscious urge for dirtying, which is a sadistic impulse, and, as a whole, the patient's ambivalence towards the 'dirty' object. If the therapist interprets this metaphorically, and the patient is able to experience his internal ambivalence, he has then reached the point where he can 'hold it in his stomach' for a while. He may then be able to develop the capacity to digest and appreciate the indivisible ambiguity.

A schizophrenic case

Having been present during this kind of transition in patients whose delusional experiences become, gradually in the course of treatment, able to be expressed metaphorically, I hypothesised the existence of the transitional process and its corresponding period, which could be called the process and period of metaphorisation.

I want to pursue an investigation into the nature of metaphorisation and the possible therapeutic approach to the marked tendency to mix up literal and metaphorical meanings. To show the possible methods of understanding and approaching this state, I want to give you a brief sketch of the treatment of a schizophrenic patient to be discussed later, who said, 'My sweetheart is my sunshine' complaining of sleeplessness due to the dazzling sun.

Let me quote from my paper on metaphorisation (Kitayama, 1987). The patient is a male 25-year-old university graduate, unmarried and unemployed. When he was a student on a preparatory course for a law school, he suddenly developed the idea that all his secrets about an encounter with a girl, whom he met in the same course, were disclosed to everybody. Getting frightened, he left the school and was advised to work part-time in an electrical shop, where the frightening experience of being known to everybody was repeated.

Seven months after the onset of his delusions the parents sent their confused son to me, who said, 'Everyone I meet speaks to me using the words I used. Everybody knows me and reflects what I have done.' Most of his story was paranoid, and there were complaints that suggested auditory hallucination, e.g. 'A pair of pliers in the electrical shop speaks to me.' To assess the possibility of weekly out-patient treatment I interviewed him further, in which the more he talked about his paranoid ideas the more paranoid he became. At one point he burst into tears asking me, 'Please show me the notes you are making about me to show other people behind my back.' Although he looked totally delusional, there were a few positive signs for out-patient treatment. First, when I pointed out that he was relating unrelated events and ideas to himself, he sometimes recovered the 'reality testing' for a while and said, 'Maybe I am thinking about it too much.' Second, when I interviewed his parents, I found them cooperative and on good terms with the owner of the electrical shop, so I could reasonably expect the existence of a 'holding environment.' Third, the psychiatrist before me had prescribed some anti-psychotic drugs and reported that this had helped to some extent, prompting me to continue the previous prescription.

Finally, I was impressed by the fact that he often described his abnormal experiences using similes, metaphors, and allegories, such as 'I was (like) Alice in Wonderland,' 'People reflecting my thoughts, repeating the same scenes,' 'I sometimes feel I am in the theatre where people act.' Whenever he spoke metaphorically without excitement or confusion, I felt as if I were on 'good terms' with him sharing the expressions. From the beginning of therapy, I tried to remain alert to his ability to metaphorise the shared experiences or expressions into his personal pathological experiences and the other way around.

He started complaining of being unable to sleep due to 'the dazzling sun in my heart,' while continuing to ask me to allow him to see his girlfriend. I answered by saying, 'Your girlfriend is your sunshine,' I, who had understood the patient's complaints figuratively, linked the metaphorical and literal meanings of 'the sun.' While using metaphor in this period, the patient occasionally slipped back into the state of experiencing metaphors literally. However, my sharing of the patient's expressions, such as 'I hear the bilingual broadcasting' for his auditory hallucination and 'I need a circuit breaker' to cut it off for his attempts at stopping the endless thinking which he compared to 'eating potato crisps,' served as bridges between us.

Among these, the appearance and usage of 'in-metaphor' (by which I mean metaphor shared only by the patient and therapist), such as 'bilingual broadcasting,' plays an important role in promoting the sense of sharedness or having come to terms in the two-body relationship. In the beginning, he was hearing the bilingual broadcasting almost literally, but with my grasp of the metaphorical reference to his hearing of voices and sounds of two incompatible meanings, i.e. delusional and ordinary, sharing became possible. This is the period in which the patient 'reacts inside a metaphor' while the therapist responds outside as well as inside, or betwixt and between.

The therapy seemed to be progressing on the basis of sharing metaphorical expressions. He started working with his parents in their restaurant but became delusional and felt persecuted as soon as his father was found to have cancer and admitted to a hospital for an operation. He ran away from home and came back three days later and told me he had run away because 'I thought I would be imprisoned as a slave in the restaurant forever.'

The father recovered his health superficially and started working with him as before and the patient's condition also followed his father's recovery to some extent. I wanted to find, from his language, a possible metaphor which could shed some light on the situation that caused or aggravated his psychotic reaction. So, I clarified the frightening situation by saying, 'imprisonment in the restaurant without your father is a sort of life sentence, isn't it?' I used a metaphor of criminality partly because he had been studying to become a lawyer. His wish to continue to study law was also related to the delusional idea that he would be killed, or arrested by the police on a false charge.

He idealised me and in therapy when we were together, saying 'This is a resting place.' Outside of therapy, however, he heard a hallucinatory voice saying, 'Don't go to the doctor.' He kept on talking, like 'eating potato crisps,' about his serious fear of becoming a 'life-long slave' of his mother in the restaurant. At the same time, he spoke about his interest in law. Suddenly, from within his overflowing speech, I noticed him saying 'I was given the sentence of absolute unlimited punishment.' I felt that this expression in literal terms would match the image that I had in mind, in spite of the fact that it was probably an expression of his pathological idiosyncrasy and that I was not sure exactly what he meant by it.

When I asked him what he meant, he explained that 'absolute unlimited punishment' was usually given to political prisoners and that it had been abandoned in most countries on humanitarian grounds. As the prisoners were not told whether or when they would be killed or released, they often became neurotic and sometimes went mad in their confinement. They were kept isolated for an unlimited period and had absolutely no clues as to their fate.

This expression and its variations became a key to a sort of shared insight into himself in various contexts. For instance, it became clear to us both that he had been feeling as if he was being imprisoned in the restaurant, the society and the family. This use of 'as if' may be improper because he had often experienced it as a reality in the delusional state. In addition to that, he must have often felt imprisoned at home since childhood and maybe in his mother's prohibitory holding arms. However, I did not interpret these unverbalised possible facts which he must have experienced literally, as to do so would have provoked him to become more delusional. My interpretive work with him was not to translate metaphor into so-called unconscious facts, but to deal with the latter through the former, neither covering nor uncovering but by weaving a cover.

Whenever he regained a distance from the delusional reality, he became able to use words figuratively. At times I grasped words metaphorically while he had to experience them literally and metaphorically, either at the same time or alternately. It could be said that he was experiencing a 'bridging' process from the psychotic state to the more realistic state.

The therapist interweaves the literally experienced expressions with the metaphorical meanings in his mind. Furthermore, I sometimes interweave the patient's expressions and my words to produce and share compound words such as 'laughing-disease' and 'mind-diarrhoea.' For this interweaving, we need threads from both sides. For example, 'laughing' was the patient's expression and 'disease' was my interpretation.

When the patient said 'My bilingual broadcasting is telling me that you prescribe medicine to stop the [physical] diarrhoea, so that you are not doing your job [as a psychiatrist],' I interwove this with a metaphor refer-ring to him taking medicine to stop the 'mind-diarrhoea.' Thus, the therapist and the patient become two sides of a loom with which they can weave a bridge.

Within this type of communication, which continued for one year, I kept on metaphorising 'imprisonment for an unlimited period without knowing whether or when he might be executed' into the situation between us, where we never knew when he would be released from me and he felt 'imprisoned' in the treat-ment forever. He agreed when I used to add that it was worse than an ordinary life sentence. We started utilising this metaphor to describe the many 'here and now' events and images we shared. I also became aware that this expression referred to the uncertainty, unclearness, and unlimitedness, which had been sur-rounding him since he was born. By sharing this 'in-metaphor' with me, he became able to bridge his absolute imprisonment and our shared reality.

Suddenly, almost a year after the father's illness, his mother, who had been supportive of the patient, was admitted to a hospital due to bloody stools. There was a possibility of cancer. The diagnosis and prognosis were unclear to my patient and his family. She had an operation but her discharge from the hospital was postponed several times.

The anxiety and fear in my patient, uncertain about his mother's situation, increased so much that he identified himself with her and developed faecal incontinence. I pointed out that he was again put in a state of 'absolute unlimited imprisonment.' He smiled, grasping the metaphor, using it to escape from the literal imprisonment within the metaphor. This time he did not have to run away.

Ambiguous metaphors

It is well known by experienced psychiatrists that some schizophrenic patients are good at producing metaphors, although most of them do not achieve shared reality. To identify the 'bridging' metaphors we should find the corresponding link between the patient's literal experience and the 'here and now' of the shared reality. The psychoanalyst, on the other hand, is supposed to be good at bridging the patient's past experience and the experience within the therapy.

It is my contention that the transference interpretations expressed metaphorically in terms of experiences with the mother or father are workable and powerful as therapeutic metaphors as they were or are experienced literally. The metaphorised original events may be experienced with the parents in reality or in fantasy; they may be experienced consciously, unconsciously or undifferentiatedly, but they are certainly experienced literally. As the analytical interpretation in treatment has the structure of metaphor, its effect on re-living the past depends on the intensity of this past experience.

In the case of neurotics, we have to uncover the verbalised material in order to discover the bridging word and the other end of the bridge. As soon as we find the right bridge in the right place we can utilise it. With schizophrenic patients who cannot bridge, we have to work with them to create and use this bridge. I would not like to call this approach a covering method because we neither cover nor uncover but interweave a cover in between, by making terms.

The observation that schizophrenic patients with thought disorders are apt to experience the symbol with what it stands for can be misleading as they sometimes express feelings and thoughts metaphorically (Alexandrowicz, 1962). I think that this is primarily due to the patients' decreased capacity to tolerate or deal with ambiguity. Metaphors are ambiguous by nature, having at least two meanings or no clear meanings.

My experiences with schizophrenic patients suggest that metaphors which stand for experiences of an unclear, uncertain, or ambiguous nature, such as 'bilingual broadcasting' and 'absolute unlimited imprisonment,' are most important among all the unlabelled metaphors. To understand this, it may be useful to consider the fact that they tend to mix up their own internal chaos and external uncertainties, like Tausk's girl who was confused by the unclear expression of 'deceiver' (Freud, 1915, p. 198).[2] These ambiguities are usually hidden and prevented from being seen because of the cultural order of cleanliness but we have to confront and deal with this disclosed ambiguous mixture in the world in time or at times: this is what I call 'the taboo to be broken in time' or the prohibition of 'Don't Look' (Kitayama, 1985).

From this point of view, it appears very natural that the mother should clean and wash the baby to keep away any mess from their environment at the beginning of life because the baby has nowhere to put (or hold) this mess. From the developmental point of view of anality, Sharpe (1950) was farsighted in thinking that metaphors, which dematerialises bodily discharge into a word, evolves alongside the control of the bodily orifices. My clinical experience has shown that patients with 'egorrhoea symptoms' also become able to experience interpersonal ambiguity alongside the playful use of ambiguous expressions which deodorise themselves.

The area for ambiguous metaphor could be considered as the place between absolute chaos and clearly ordered space, where such undetermined things could be put. When we do not know how to articulate an idea or concept effectively, we have to discover and produce a suitable metaphor or analogy, or we can put it aside. In this halfway zone, metaphor stands for ambiguity and the undifferentiatedness of our ideas. Furthermore, if we find symbolic expressions which stand for the ambiguous, this could then point out the place for these ideas to be put. The therapist's perception of, and tolerance to, ambiguous metaphors and facilitation of the patient's ongoing metaphorising of literally lived experiences is essential.

Metaphorisation: the bridging process

By reviewing cases such as this, we can see that the progress of therapy is based on the usage and understanding of metaphorical expressions, if the patient's 'bridging' is at least workable enough to experience the psychosomatic nature of the metaphors. I would now like to explain what I call 'the bridging process,' where the psychological meaning appears from behind the literal and physical meanings.

In more severe cases, patients cannot tolerate the ambiguity of 'grey areas', thus they miss the mid-point, which is very paradoxical. They feel the half-way area can be full of obscure, unclear, unfathomable things, which they cannot come to terms with.

This ambiguous area tends to be suitable for reflecting the delusional and persecutory ideas of paranoid patients. Here, I want to introduce a Japanese example of a paranoid response to ambiguity in the Japanese language. There was a group of patients, who complained of emitting bad body odour, such as anal odours and auxiliary smells; furthermore, they showed a morbid fear of losing the halfway boundary between external and internal, and of eye-to-eye contact and meeting people. They sometimes believed their eyes looked strange, impolite, or too sharp, therefore making others hate them. Some of these patients were frightened of their ambiguous looks, being misunderstood because of the state of 'ego-boundary lost,' which Fujinawa (Kasahara et al., 1984), a Japanese psychopathologist, described playfully as 'egorrhoea.'

Their linguistic difficulty is due to the equation of the indivisible without and the indigestible within and is associated with the lack of ambiguity tolerance. That is why the therapist's interpretation with the proper use of metaphorical expressions may offer these patients an experience of the half-way location between within and without, and facilitate the passage through the 'in between.' Although some linguists compare metaphor to a 'vehicle' of meanings, I prefer the word 'bridge' to illustrate the two distinct ends as the location of meanings and the halfway space in the middle.

I have been making use of many metaphors, sharing the process of meta-phorisation with the reader. When a metaphor starts functioning like a bridge, the two sides will never merge. We can then read this presentation without being literally nauseated. Here, the problem in therapeutic approaches for some psychotics and severe hysterics arises because of their intolerance of ambiguity and tendency to perceive metaphors literally. Intellectual interpretation of transference, which bridges the present therapist-patient relationship and past experiences, does not work for them. However, as I highlighted in a previous paper (Kitayama, 1987), if the patient can handle a metaphor with double meanings, this may indicate the following:

1   A manifestation of creativity and play.
2   Experiencing the halfway location between the inside and the outside.
3   Ambiguity tolerance and appreciation.

Sharpe reasoned that metaphor, which dematerialises bodily discharge into a word, evolves alongside the control of the bodily orifices. My analytical experiences have shown that patients with 'egorrhoea symptoms' would also gain the ability to experience the ambiguity, in a half-open (oblique) stance, alongside the creative use of metaphorical expressions that deodorise them.

Conclusive remarks

The psychoanalyst is supposed to be good at bridging the patient's bodily experience and psychological experience within an analytic therapy. In the case of neurotics, we have to uncover the verbalised material in order to discover the bridging word and the hidden end of the bridge. As soon as we find the right bridge in the right place, we can utilise it. However, with patients who cannot perform the bridging on their own, we have to work with them to create and use this bridge.

The area of ambiguous metaphors is usually 'troubled water,' which could be considered as the indivisible place between the absolute inside and the clearly ordered outside, into which such undetermined things could be placed. When we do not know how to articulate an idea or concept effectively, we have to either find and create a suitable metaphor or analogy, or put it aside. In this halfway space, metaphor becomes a bridge over the river of ambiguity and indivisible ideas. Furthermore, if we find symbolic expressions that stand for the ambiguous, this could then point out the place to put these ideas. The therapist's perception of and tolerance of ambiguous metaphors and his/her facilitation of the patient's ongoing metaphorising of literally lived experiences are essential.

Lastly, let me repeat the conclusive remark in my previous paper (Kitayama, 1987). The Japanese word *hashi* is equivalent to 'bridge' in English. The word '*hashi*' means not only 'bridge' but also, with slight differences in pronunciation, 'edge' and 'chopstick.' If I may make our ambiguous language more enjoyable to English-speaking people, the Japanese 'bridge' means a set of bridging chopsticks between two edges. We need to make use of this instrument because, according to the English adage, 'there's many a slip "twixt cup and lip."'

Notes

1 The frequent appearance of children in these works has a historical background in that the Japanese government banned the publication of blatantly obscene pictures, so *ukiyo-e* dealers created an artistic compromise between pornography and family portrait that exploded the market for these works.
2 I am quoting from Victor Tausk's case in Freud's writings. The schizophrenic girl talked about her boyfriend, whom she called *Augenverdreher*, which literally means 'eye-twister' in English and can have the figurative meaning of 'deceiver' in German (Freud, 1915, p. 198, translator's footnote). She then complained that her eyes were not right, they were literally twisted.

References

Alexandrowicz. D. R. (1962). The meaning of metaphor. *Bulletin of the Menninger Clinic*, 26, 92–101.

Bruner, J. (1975). The capacity for joint visual attention in the infant. *Nature*, 253, 265–266.

Doi, T. (1958). Warewarewa donnafuuni seishinbusekiwo manandekitaka [How did we study psychoanalysis?] [in Japanese]. In O. Kitayama (Ed.), *Japanese Journal of Psycho-Analysis: Selections*, 1, 108–111, 2004.

Freud, S. (1905). Fragment of analysis of a case of hysteria. In *Standard Edition*, Vol. 7. London: Hogarth Press.

Freud, S. (1915). The unconscious. In *Standard Edition*, Vol. 14. London: Hogarth Press.

Kasahara, Y., Fujinawa, A., Matsumoto, M., & Sekiguchi, H. (1984). Seishikyōhu taisyukyōhu [Fear of gaze, fear of body odour]. In Y. Kasahara (Ed.), *Seishinbyō to Shinkeisyō [Psychosis and Neurosis]* (pp. 697–827). Tokyo: Misuzushobō. (Original paper published 1972)

Kitayama, O. (1985). Pre-oedipal 'taboo' in Japanese folk tragedies. *International Review of Psycho-Analysis*, 12 (2), 173–186.

Kitayama, O. (1987). Metaphorization-making terms. *International Journal of Psycho-Analysis*, 68 (4), 499–509.

Kitayama, O. (1991). The wounded caretaker and guilt. *International Review of Psycho-Analysis*, 18 (2), 229–240.

Kitayama, O. (1998). Transience: its beauty and danger. *International Journal of Psycho-Analysis*, 79 (5), 937–950.

Kitayama, O. (2014). Takeo Doi 'wrestled' with Freudian psychoanalysis. *Japanese Contributions to Psychoanalysis*, Vol. 4 (pp. 127–141). Reprinted in *Journal of the Japan Psychoanalytic Society*, 6, 24–27, 2024.

Kitayama, O. (Ed.). (2010a). Freud's correspondence with colleagues in Japan. *Japanese Contributions to Psychoanalysis*. Vol. 3 (pp. 137–160). Reprinted in *Journal of the Japan Psychoanalytic Society*, 4, 59–81, 2022.

Okonogi, K. (Ed.). (2002). *Seishinbunseki Jiten [Dictionary of Psychoanalysis]*. Tokyo: Iwasaki Gakujutsu Syuppansha.

Sharpe, E. F. (1950). An examination of metaphor. In R. Fliess (ed.), *The Psycho-Analytic Reader* (pp. 273–286). London: Hogarth Press. (Original paper published 1940)

Yabe, Y. (1931). Freud Sensei Kaikenki [My meeting with Dr. Freud], In *Freud Seishin Bunsekigaku Zenshū* [*Freud's Collected Works of Psychoanalysis*], Vol. 5. Tokyo: Shunyōdo.

Yamada, Y. (1987). *Kotobanomaeno Kotoba* [*Prelinguistic Language*]. Tokyo: Shinyōsha.

Winnicott, D. W. (1971). *Playing and Reality.* London: Tavistock Publications.

Chapter 2

Depth-psychotherapy in shame culture

Osamu Kitayama

Persona in personality

There is an area not only in psychoanalysis but also in psychology that examines the issue of personality, a term derived from the word persona. This word, *persona*, originally referred to the masks worn by actors in classical plays. So I believe that from the very beginning psychology has been accompanied by the question of how we should deal with these important masks.

In other words, in some respects, people live their lives as if they're on stage, acting in a play, and that is what brings us to the topic at hand. Particularly in psychoanalysis, there is what is called a dramatic point of view, which is especially important in Japan. I say that because among Japanese people there is the idea of the *ura* (back face) and *omote* (front face). They have a strong tendency to thoroughly hide the parts of themselves that hurt others, parts that are ugly, with such feelings as shame and guilt. So there is an element in the people who live in this culture that is showing off, or acting. Therefore, if they are leading their lives like in plays, then the task of the psychoanalytic psychotherapist is to analyse what kinds of hidden lives are being lived, what kinds of theatrical stories are being woven in the form of these dramatic lives, and indeed we learn from many existing dramas. In other words, there is often a great deal to learn from studying stories that are available to the general public.

A dramatic point of view in psychoanalysis

Now let me explain the dramatic point of view in psychoanalysis. Psychoanalysis values elements of drama very much. Psychoanalysis was first conceived and started out by learning from patients with hysteria who seemed to put on 'performances' that were pathological. They were said from the beginning to be dramatic. This is evidenced by a report of a clinical lecture at the University of Paris in France held by Charcot. The patients treated there were referred to as 'actors,' and Professor Charcot, the psychiatrist, was 'far more than an actor' and 'no doubt theatrical' (Gay, 2006). Those who attended the lectures reported that the situation there was just like a theatre. Sigmund

DOI: 10.4324/9781003501930-3

Freud, the founder of psychoanalysis, was there one day in 1885 to witness this. He then wrote in a letter to his future wife Martha, 'My brain is satisfied as if I had spent an evening at a theatre' (Freud, 1980).

So that's how the founders of psychoanalysis perceived this dramatic aspect of clinical practice. Anna O., a patient who was being treated by Joseph Breuer, a famous Austrian physician and also Freud's collaborator at the time, described her daydream-like experiences as 'a private theatre' (Breuer & Freud, 1893–1895/2007). It was indeed a theatre where many terrifying things were happening. This can be said to mark the start of the 'theatre'-like aspects of psychoanalysis. Even after Breuer left the stage, various schools of psychoanalysis continued to consider psychoanalysis to be like the theatre. Freud (1905) certainly did and, more recently, McDougall (1986) likened psychoanalysis to the theatre. This view still holds true today.

We can also see this idea of dramatic psychoanalysis, or psychoanalysis as a play, when it is applied to clinical practice for children. Therapists conduct what's known as 'play therapy,' with which they try to understand children through play. But if we think about it, play can also mean the theatre. So, play, or spiel in German, has two meanings: play as in the activity that's done for fun, and play as in the story that is performed in a theatre. From the beginning, play therapy implied that it was drama therapy. In other words, the drama that's performed in the play was the medium through which therapists tried to understand the children's minds.

A popular theory these days is object relations theory, a concept that also relates to attachment theory. Object relations theory says that there is the self and the object, or the other person, which are established in childhood or during infancy, and the relationship a person has with one person will repeat itself with other people. There's a concept in psychoanalysis called transference, which means that object relations from the past are dramatised – or you could say enacted, put 'on stage' – in the present therapeutic relationship. Past interpersonal relationships and object relations are brought into the therapeutic relationship as if they were a play. That is what psychoanalysis analyses. It's starting to be understood that psychoanalysis is something that examines what is being enacted, using it as a clue to understand the person.

To summarise this dramatic point of view, a person repeats his psychological script from the past while changing the characters in it. The clinician, psychoanalyst, or therapist joins that play, playing and accepting the role opposite the patient, reading that script as it develops, unveiling the patient's script, presenting it as the patient's own story. That is the work we do in psychoanalysis. Why do we do it? Through this psychoanalysis as a drama, the person reads the story he is repeating, and the idea is to turn it into a 'better' story. We can't change the past. We instead try to re-weave the story that has been repeated from the past. This is one of the goals of therapy. When patients come to us, they're already repeating a tragic script and the tragedy is being enacted with changes in the other characters, so we try to re-weave that into a better life story. What really happened in the past cannot be undone. But as the person retells it, thinks it over, looking for the words to describe what happened as he retells it, the lifestyle, or the life story, begins to change.

Shame resistance

Nonetheless, our job of helping patients re-weave their histories into new life stories is not easy. In particular, people in Asia can be strongly influenced by its shame culture. For instance, scandals – whether they involve politicians or celebrities – imply social death; if shameful acts are exposed to the public, the individual is left with no choice but to leave civic life, as if following a pre-formed story, sometimes 'committing suicide.' Seeing that from a young age, it makes me realise how so many people have to enact their lives in a tragic way.

But life is supposed to be lived, not enacted. From a dramatic point of view, though, in life there are elements of creation. Nonetheless, our job of helping patients re-weave their histories into new life stories is not easy. Elements can be recreated just like in a play. It is the 'I' who is playing the main character in the play, and it is also the 'I' who is spinning the story. Then isn't it possible for 'I' to rethink, recreate, and rewrite the repeating pattern that's being played here? That is the suggestion psychoanalysis offers.

We see this way of regarding life as a play in earlier times. In Japan, Hideo Murata had a popular song called '*Jinsei Gekijō*' (Theatre of Life). Overseas, Shakespeare said metaphorically that 'All the world's a stage, and all the men and women merely players.' I believe the British and the Japanese are similar in this respect. In Japanese, even in everyday conversations, we frequently hear dichotomies, such as *omote* (front) and *ura* (back); *kō* (public) and *shi* (private); *honne* (true intentions) and *tatemae* (outward stance). By adopting this dual structure, dramatic elements are inevitably born in between. I have practiced psychoanalysis for 40 years and I believe the reason this dramatic point of view is useful is because the awareness of shame strongly hides even in this dual nature. In Japan, particularly, people tend to hide what is inconvenient to them. They play the ideal self, the wonderful person, while hiding the shameful self. We need to take into account this duality of the self when treating the individual. To apply the metaphor of the play and the dramatic point of view to people who are deeply ashamed of themselves, we can say that they may be playing proper roles in society, while continuing to hide their true selves. They will have to 'exit the stage' if they fail at that. This might be the case in politics, and maybe even in schools, too. We can see that this is a serious issue, one that could even cause some people to take their own lives.

The English paediatrician and psychoanalyst Donald W. Winnicott (1965) talked about the external 'false self' and the internal 'true self.' These are easy concepts for Japanese people to understand. According to his theory, the false self arises from an over-adaptation to one's parents and to the environment during childhood. Every Japanese person might be doing this. If we fail at it, we end up withdrawing. Winnicott says that the false self sacrifices the true self, one's own innate self, as it adapts to external demands and environmental troubles. So, his idea was that people must keep a good balance in life between the true and false selves, the true and social selves. Both are equally important.

To sum up the dramatic point of view, the therapy room is the backstage dressing room of life where the patients reveal themselves. Even in a psychiatry department, the examination room is the backstage dressing room. The hospital is the backstage of life. And the world outside is the stage. Out front, we have to put on our makeup. And taking the perspective that life is a drama, everything then becomes the stage. I have one patient who says, 'Now it's showtime' when she leaves the therapy room.

Behind the double meaning of the Japanese word *ura* is a person's *honne* (true intentions). *Ura* is a very interesting word. It means the back and, at the same time, it can also refer to one's mind, as we can see in words like *ura-hazukashii* (inwardly ashamed) and *ura-sabishii* (inwardly lonely). And the Japanese language indicates that the mind is something in the 'back.' The patient in the therapy room, which is the backstage dressing room, stops his 'performance' and starts to think in the 'back' about the drama he's playing in the world outside. When that goes well, it should be given a term like depth-psychotherapy rather than psychoanalytic psychotherapy as 'psychoanalysis' which often means 'uncovering.' In this hidden dressing room of life, as he considers the way he's been living, he has to go back to his true self and then to the false self too. That's when he will sometimes confess, along with his feelings of shame and guilt, the rebellious feelings toward his parents, aggressive fantasies that can't easily be expressed out in front. There are many of these patients who have two different sides: one in the 'back,' and one in the 'front.' The depth-psychotherapist listens to these patients' secrets and will never disclose them to anyone else. This is very important. We listen to what the patient really feels but what's spoken in the dressing room is kept a secret. We call this confidentiality. And what was discussed backstage is never brought up on the stage. That's the basic rule in depth-psychotherapy.

With that in mind, we must sharpen our ability to understand the life stories of patients. In order to do that, what I would like to share with you is the idea of learning from the stories that have been passed on from long ago. Understanding the various viewpoints of the protagonist is a method proposed by Freud, who came up with what he called the Oedipus complex by studying 'King Oedipus.' So, we have this idea, or suggestion, of learning from these popular tragedies so that we can learn about unfortunate or tragic stories in life.

Learning from Japanese tragedies

Over several decades, I have examined Japanese stories involving the prohibition of 'Don't Look' (Kitayama, 1982, 1985, 2010b). This is because many patients continue to repeat their tragedies. I believe that in some cases, 'uncovering' treatments can be terminated by shameful and tragic consequences. Is there a well-known story that reflects this pre-formed pattern of tragic cases, like *King*

Oedipus by Sophocles which shows our repetitive tragic impulse? Yes, there are very clear links in Japan; for instance, there is a story called *Tsuruno Ongaeshi [The Grateful Crane]*, which has been introduced in English as *The Crane Wife*.

Here's an overview of the most well-known version of the story. An animal-woman – a crane – hides her true identity and marries a human man. She weaves a piece of cloth on a loom and gives it to her husband. He sells it for a high price, making him very rich and much happier, but he begs her to weave more such cloths. The woman agrees but prohibits him from watching her weave the cloth. However, he takes a peek even though he is prohibited from looking. The story suggests that perhaps this violation is in a male's nature as the prohibition is almost always broken as the narrative develops.

So the promise is broken. In picture books, there is a woman weaving cloth behind a sliding door, and that is what the man sees. He sees that she is weaving cloth secretively. What he saw was an injured crane. She was plucking her own feathers from her body to weave them into a cloth. I have collated this scene from many works, some that include this story as a children's story and some as a folk tale. There is a picture that shows the bleeding crane weaving cloth (see Figure 2.1), and I think many of these depict childbirth. My interpretation is that this is a scene of the parturient mother who is in labour, trying to give birth to a baby in her last month of pregnancy.

Figure 2.1 Tsuru Nyōbō [The Crane Wife] (1979) illustration by Suekichi Akaba (story by Sumiko Yagawa), Tokyo: Fukuinkanshoten.

Figure 2.2 Tsuruno Ongaeshi [The Grateful Crane] (1988) illustration by Daihachi Ohta (story by Kyōko Iwasaki), Osaka: Miki House.

This may initially appear to be an absurd interpretation to say it is a woman with her legs open, giving birth. You may think it is not scientific at all. I will discuss this further, but please keep in mind the image of a female about to give birth (see Figure 2.2).

In a picture book published in the US, the same scene is drawn by an American artist (Bodkin & Spirin, 1998). The Westernised husband in that version has a bolder manner. The Japanese husband tends to hide more, peeking in a manner that is reserved.

The story ends with the crane revealing her true self, deeply ashamed of herself, and leaving the man. She flies away. In Japan, this is likened to burnout, or suicide, which occurs often in this country. The escape into illness, cases of missing people, and social withdrawal – we can see how many issues in reality overlap with this scene. This understanding, that it's the mother who, after having given birth so many times, exposes her injury and finally leaves, has a long history. This passive attitude and the fragile characteristic were sometimes considered to be typically maternal; in order to meet our endless external demands, the crane increasingly hurts herself and leaves in the end.

When I talk about this story in other countries, the story of Oedipus often comes up. In the case of Oedipus his mother somehow tried to keep him from looking at the truth, saying 'Yet do not do it. I implore you, do not do it' (Sophocles, 1981). However, in the end she kills herself and he blinds himself.

And if you will please forgive me for my limited knowledge. As a comparison to this story, the story of Jesus Christ is often brought up in some countries. Jesus Christ is also wounded and leaves at the end. Having served the people and worked to save humankind, he leaves. Some might say it is outrageous to compare the crane-wife with Jesus Christ, but in Japan it is the woman who goes away at the end. Perhaps this highlights some differences between the East and the West or between the Japanese and non-Japanese. In our case it is the mother who is hurt. Incidentally in Japanese, the expression 'to have a pain in the abdomen' can mean 'to give birth.'

As far as I know, the mother pelican is considered to symbolise Jesus Christ. According to an ancient legend, the pelican feeds her children with her own blood to nourish them. This self-sacrifice is reminiscent of Christ's self-sacrifice. So in Christian imagery, pictures of a mother bird feeding her young represent Christ and his sacrifice. This sort of imagery can also be seen on the stained-glass in Christian churches.

In Japanese folk tales, it is clearly the woman-figure that is self-sacrificed; it is likely that it is originally a mother bird. In another Japanese myth, the myth of Princess Toyotama, even though the woman giving birth tells the man, 'don't look,' the man peeks and she turns into a dragon. Having revealed her true self, she leaves us because she is so ashamed (see Figure 2.3). Why is the prohibition of 'Don't Look,' imposed? In my opinion, it is expected to serve to avoid our disillusionment in discovering her alienated self.

Figure 2.3 Toyotamahimeno Hontai [True Figure of the Princess Toyotama] in Wakan Ehon Saki-gake [Picture Book of Chinese and Japanese Warriors] (1836) by Hokusai Katsushika.
Source: The Metropolitan Museum of Art, New York.

Izanagi and Izanami

Next is the mythology of Izanagi and Izanami. Going back in time, we can find the story involving the prohibition of 'Don't Look' in this Japanese myth in which the islands of Japan are born. The goddess Izanami dies after giving birth to many islands and deities. Despite her prohibition 'Don't Look,' Izanagi violates it and sees the corpse of the goddess. The first important thing to note is that we see procreation linked to this tale, too. The woman, the goddess, dies particularly after having given birth to fire-deities.

The second thing is that men go against the prohibition and look even though they've been told not to. And then the goddess becomes furious for having been shamed. She chases after the man. She was ashamed of revealing her true self. She was dying. She was abandoned. He was running away from his dying wife. He was chased by ugly women. So, he fled in a great hurry (see Figure 2.4). They continued to pursue him but he managed to escape, ending in a separation from

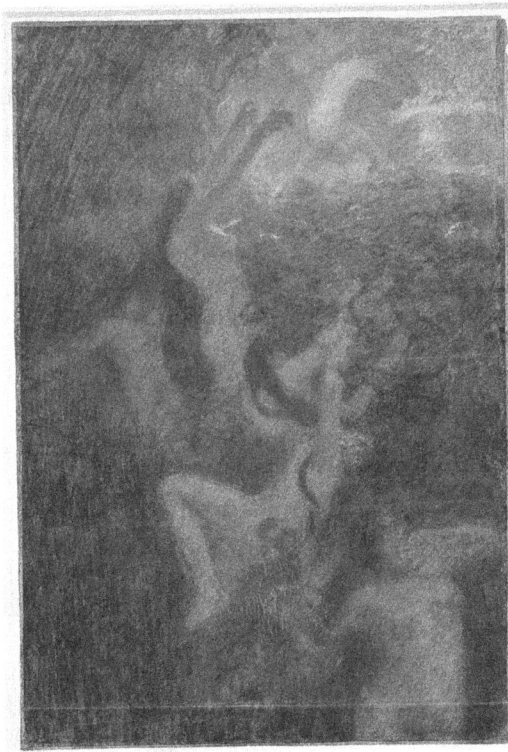

Figure 2.4 Yomotsu Hirasaka [Slope that Leads to the Land of the Dead] (1903) by Shigeru Aoki.
Source: The University Art Museum. Tokyo University of the Arts, Tokyo.

the goddess. So, the unpleasant part of herself was seen. In the end, they were divorced; as they were divided into two worlds.

Clinical case I

In this section, I will introduce two psychotherapy cases. What is going to be important is the negative impulse, such as aggression, towards the mother or the parents. Anger and hatred, or the urge to maybe kill someone, or the feeling of being sorry for the mother, or worrying about having hurt the mother – these are the kinds of negative emotions that I mean. We humans prepare a dressing room backstage where these negative emotions can be expressed, not just the emotions like, 'I love you,' 'I want to be dependent on somebody' (amae), 'My mother was so nice' – though these appear, too. What I would like to show is a process in psychotherapy where we listen to people express their feelings of shame and guilt that accompany those negative feelings.

The first is a case of a 30-year-old woman.[1] Her main complaint was depression. As soon as we began, she said 'I was really dumb, so stupid.' She kept on blaming herself. As I listened to her, I found out about the following episode, which was not mentioned right away. Her therapy went on for a year. She once asked her mother to sew a dress that she needed for a school per-formance. The mother stayed up all night doing it, and the next day she had a heart attack. Anyone may have had a similar experience; something that we spontaneously asked for turned out to be a burden for the other person and, because of that, they became ill.

Since then, the woman has felt anxious about having done a terrible thing to her mother. As a matter of fact, the mother died of heart disease a few years later. It seemed that the patient felt as if her mother had let her daughter know of the illness, which made her worry about it, and then she died because of it. This was not discussed in the beginning. You may see that she feels remorseful about what happened to her mother.

With our understanding that there might be some distress in that area, we began to deal with this episode. The belief that she was responsible grew stronger, and as that belief grew stronger, her depressive feelings in the psy-chotherapy got worse. I think they had to get worse for a short while.

And although she spoke about this episode, she kept saying 'My mother's death has nothing to do with my depression.' However, she gradually started to think that she was not responsible for her mother's death. As she listened to my explanations and as we continued to think about this together, this woman, who felt very responsible at first, was able to reach the point where she could think, 'Maybe I'm not responsible for my mother's death.'

It was difficult for her to think that way in the beginning because she felt she'd been selfish and had done an awful thing to her mother. She thought that it was shameful to think that way and sinful to say such things. In psy-choanalysis, this is called resistance in therapy. My interpretation was:

By having overcome this, having got over the resistance of being ashamed, you're now thinking that you killed your mother and you feel guilty about it. This awareness that you're guilty, or the sense that you're ashamed, is making you even more depressed. But if we think about it carefully, your request to your mother to sew a dress for your performance and your mother's heart attack are not directly related. The reason is, as you've told me, that she'd had heart attacks before. It scares you even now. And while you engage with other people who might replace your mother, you're still afraid that you'll hurt them too.

This was the understanding we developed.

Eventually, she began to recognise that her memories – or distorted memories, perhaps – and fantasies were foolish. She even began to have a terrible thought that in order for her to bring her dead mother back to life, she had to hold an imaginary woman in her arms and have sex with her. She said she felt very foolish about it. So towards the end, there was this image which she felt was the most shameful to her. The possibility that she might have lively sex with a woman was a thought of hers that sounded as if it were a spell to resurrect her dead mother.

That is how her feeling of guilt for having killed her mother was kept unspoken and, in turn, gave birth to sexual dreams and fantasies about her mother. So, she suffered from this anxiety that she might have a penis to act on these sexual dreams and fantasies. She blamed herself, saying again and again that she was stupid and descended into a depressive state.

As a psychoanalytic therapist, I interpreted and understood these things to be psychologically true, and the patient gained insight into them and gradually got better. I remember vividly when she said, 'It's not my fault,' and I said something like, 'You feel that you're responsible,' and then her scream when she cried out, 'It wasn't my fault' – I think that moment was the turning point in the therapy.

Towards the end, she had romantic feelings for the therapist. To her, I was the person who understood her. Also, having talked about sexual things, she developed feelings for me, but that was because she thought that my leaving, or the parting with me, meant she would be disliked and abandoned. She thought I was leaving because she had hurt me, just like what happened between her and her mother. I interpreted:

You're perfectly capable of being on your own but, because you feel that you've hurt your mother, you have been dependent on her while trying not to hurt her. In some respects, I have been like a mother figure to you.

Afterwards, as she gained a deeper understanding, the therapeutic relationship was resolved and our treatment sessions ended. Later on, I heard from a therapist in group work with her that she was doing quite well.

Clinical case 2

The next case is a patient with obsessive-compulsive neurosis who was socially withdrawn (*hikikomori*) out of fear of being cursed. The word *hikikomori* has become quite well-known around the world. This person secluded himself and engaged in prayer rituals in his room. He groaned when he did this, staying in the house. He was afraid of being cursed. Being cursed meant being punished by God for thinking of something terrible. When he came to see me, he was absolutely fatigued and had no energy. When he was hospitalised, however, he got a little better.

When a man withdraws and distances himself from social reality, he feels better. That may be characteristic of these introvert patients, and his fear of being cursed clearly disappeared as if it had been a dream. But right after he was hospitalised, his mother suffered a fracture. This was coincidental, or maybe there was an unconscious motive behind her fracture and falling ill, as a way to call attention to herself in reaction to her son's hospitalisation. Much like the previous patient, this patient also thought there was a causal link between him and his mother's ill health. The patient thought 'Did I hurt her?' 'Did I push her?'

What I stressed to him was, 'Your rituals such as praying and worrying – indeed you're worried now – and your mother's fracture may in fact have not been related.' And I interpreted,

> You've always felt as though you're to blame when you thought you made God angry. If we think about it, it is similar to masturbation and things like that; you feel like you'll hurt someone if you do something that you like, then feel bad about it, or feel like the person's angry at you. But is there in fact a cause-and-effect relationship? Could it not be a fantasy that someone is mad at you?

As we talked about these things, he started to have angry feelings towards his mother image which had made him suffer on the inside. He told me,

> She kept telling me I was bad. She told me that I was hurting her. She showed it to me as if to spite me, while she pretended to be weak. 'You give me so much trouble because you're terribly selfish,' she'd say.

This was when we recalled that his mother had once said in response to her son's selfishness, 'I'm going to kill myself,' and possibly almost hung herself.

While we were beginning to understand how things in the past were being repeated in the present, which is his psychological script, the following event suddenly occurred. He was chosen as chairman of the executive committee for his school festival. Right after he was elected, he began to have diarrhoea. He felt extremely ashamed that he was unable to join the committee due to his diarrhoea, even though he had been appointed to be the chairman. He tried to go, but he got sick and ended up either going to the hospital or staying home.

And then he asked me over the phone to give him medication. As a medical doctor, it was my job to treat him at the hospital. He said he wanted me to treat him somehow, to stop the diarrhoea, so he could go to the festival. He said, 'You're a quack. You won't make me better.' I felt I was being blamed for not understanding him at all, and he began to express his anger at me. I suggested that it was better for him to stay home and rest rather than try to go to the festival. And then his diarrhoea suddenly stopped.

He must have thought then: 'I get diarrhoea when I'm angry at my doctor or my mother.' I'm not sure if the cause-and-effect link is very accurate, but that was the insight he gained.

Through our task of interpreting and understanding, the patient began to think that he had wanted to blaspheme against God, that possibly he had wanted to throw his faeces at the gods, and that when he held it in, it became impure, something that's dirty within. Cultural anthropology also tells us how we fear impurities. Perhaps it can be said that the origin of these dirty things comes from old precepts that used to prohibit our desire to excrete.

That is how he became able to voice what he wanted to say much more easily than before. I remember from our clinical sessions when he said, with great joy, he was able to say 'shit' now. This was a person who couldn't even verbalise that word.

And his obsessive-compulsive prayer rituals stopped. He then didn't have to be afraid. He had the insight that no one would die just because he said the s-word. Towards the end, along with the understanding that parents were vulnerable beings, he started to ponder deeply over what we might call transience: beautiful things eventually fade away, parents and everyone else will also be gone, and that is inevitable. And then he was able to get rid of his obsession with things that were holy as well.

Clinical discussion

Some of the people I have dealt with who suffered from these feelings are people who engage in productive activities. On the outside, they say that they're hurt or they're unable to do what's expected of them. They have difficulties in those areas. Some were people who fantasised about killing someone, and some were unable to hurt others. They could rarely talk about these things to other people. Even as they talked to me, they continued to be distressed, with intense feelings of being ashamed on the outside, and yet inwardly feeling guilty. It seems this somehow originates from experiences the patients had with their parents in childhood. They all recall having been selfish back then.

It's true that parents raise their children in many devoted ways. We can say that about Izanami's prohibition of 'Don't Look.' She was a mother, a goddess, who risked her own life to give birth to this world. Japan was born with the death of its mother. If we think about it like that, it's possible that parents who devotedly care for their children and the mothers who have passed away are affecting the way we think even now.

When I listen to the patients' various episodes in their medical history, the focus can sometimes be the mother, a mother figure, or in some cases a motherly father. Patients often talk about their parents' devotion to them, their love and warmth, and how their parents did this and that for them. The patients say they were unable to deal with those things very well. They couldn't meet their parents' expectations. They ruined them. They damaged the love of their parents. They often can't talk about this since they're still distressed by the shame they felt then, and by the sense of guilt and anger that arises when they try to talk about it.

So, people who suffer from those things come to see us. We believe those patients who have developed symptoms and escaped can still be helped. Therein lies the issue not just of love, or *amae*, but also of anger, aggression, and annoyance that the patients feel toward their parents who loved them, or toward people who gave them affection. When I think about all the brides and mothers in the myths who were wounded and left, I'm inclined to think that we grow by subconsciously killing and hurting a great number of things.

When using these therapies, there is something the patients get scared of, which has to do with confidentiality. They are afraid other people will find out what they said in therapy. That is also a fantasy. The cases of patients I presented here were in the form of stories that I created by putting together a number of different cases. There was no specific individual, but as the patients expressed to me that they were worried about other people finding out about them and their ugly parts, some details have been modified.

Unconscious script

So, our job as psychoanalysts, or depth-psychotherapists is to read the shame-laden patients' 'unconscious script,' which they're unable to tell anyone about, and then to think of how they could 'live' that script. The last patient I discussed said to me, 'Doctor, no matter how much I talk here, not even God can hear me.' Those who perform as actors in the outside world safely return to their true selves, expressing their prohibited inner thoughts and building a new way of life. That is the therapy room or examination room we offer as the backstage dressing room for their theatre.

The misfortunes that occurred in their early childhood can happen to anyone. It can also happen to one's siblings, but each individual may feel differently about the same event. What we always pay attention to is how these vulnerable children feel about the misfortunes that occurred to their parents, to their environment, or to themselves. This has to do with the problem that the weakest person in the family tends to feel, along with shame and guilt, the most responsible for any misfortune. Many children also feel they're the reason why their parents fight. It is our therapeutic theory that patients overcome their shame resistance that they might hurt someone if they express the anger and aggression of their true selves. They confront their hate, and come face-to-face with their own negative feelings without running away from them, but with the accompanying feelings of deeply-seated shame and guilt. This is how the story can finish with a happy ending.

Looking forward to the happy endings

People may have suffered from this sense of shame and guilt, when repeatedly apologising for tragic outcomes. The risk of the mother dying due to complications during childbirth was a serious concern in times when hygiene and scientific knowledge were poor. Until very recently, many mothers died of severe bleeding. I think this was turned into our stories of the prohibition of 'Don't Look.' It's written that Izanami died by burning her genitals after giving birth to the god of fire. My interpretation of this story of the goddess dying of severe burns is that it's a story of severe bleeding.

Why do we impose the prohibition 'Don't Look'? It's to avoid the disillusionment that arises in us. When a woman reveals her true self, the man leaves because he is terrified and unable to look at her. Yohyō (crane-wife's husband), Izanagi, who I will discuss now, and everyone else can't save the woman at the moment of her disillusionment. They are petrified with fear and leave. The women try to avoid the experience of having been shamed. When their true selves – the wounded animal that is behind these beautiful and generous women – become manifest, all the men run away.

Whether the women were ugly or wounded, or they were sick to begin with, or there was danger involved in giving birth, we see a story of men who break the prohibition and intrude, driving out all the motherly women, and leaving them secluded. The motherly women leave, carrying with them their shame, and the men suffer from their awareness of guilt and shame for having hurt the women and finally also leave.

This led me to consider how this story can be turned into a happy ending in a psychotherapeutic sense. I have thought of scenarios in which the men overcome the feeling of being sorry, the sense of guilt, or the awareness of shame, allowing women like Izanami and Tsū (crane-wife) to stay and survive in this world. It is starting to sound like a lesson in morals, but in this way it is possible for us to envision a happy ending.

Note

1 This case is an English woman who was treated in English.

References

Bodkin, O. & Spirin, G. (1998). *The Crane Wife*. San Diego: Gulliver Books.
Breuer, J. & Freud, S. (1893–1895/2007) *Studien über Hysterie*. Frankfurt am Main: S. Fisher Verlag. (Original published 1893–1895)

Freud, S. (1905) Fragment of an analysis of a case of hysteria. In *Standard Edition*, Vol. 7 (pp. 1–122). London: Hogarth Press.

Freud, S. (1980). *Briefe 1873–1939*. Frankfurt am Main: S. Fischer Verlag.

Gay, P. (2006). *Freud: A Life For Our Time*. New York: Norton.

Kitayama, O. (1982). *Higeki no Hasseiron* [*Genesis of Tragedies*]. Tokyo: Kongōshuppan.

Kitayama, O. (1985). Preoedipal 'taboo' in Japanese folk tragedies. *International Review of Psycho-Analysis*, 12, 173–185.

Kitayama, O. (2010b). *Prohibition of Don't Look*. Tokyo: Iwasaki Gakujutsu Shuppansha.

McDougall, J. (1986). *Theaters of the Mind*. New York: Basic Books.

Sophocles (1981). (B. F. Waltling. Trans.) King Oedipus. In *The Theban Plays*. Harmondsworth: Penguin Books. (Original translation published 1957)

Winnicott, D.W. (1965). Ego distortion in terms of true and false self. In *The Maturational Process and the Facilitating Environment: Studies in the Theory of Emotional Development* (pp. 140–152). London: Hogarth Press. (Original paper published 1960)

Chapter 3

Re-weaving the story of the prohibition of 'Don't Look'

Osamu Kitayama

A 'script' for excluding non-humans

By nature, human beings have the tendency to exclude or banish things that they feel are alien to them. Japanese culture, in particular, places value in, and seeks, homogeneity and conformity and attunement, so it can characteristically detect and recognise this sort of exclusion. What I found extremely useful in mulling over these thoughts was a group of stories of intermarriage between humans and non-humans. These are tales, folklore or folk stories about beings that are alien or heterogeneous to humans, such as animals and monsters that transform themselves into humans, and then form marital or sexual relationships with humans. We find numerous stories like this both in Japan and around the world. The fact is that these tales closely reflect our ways of thinking and mindsets. This is why they have a long history and are continued to be told, even today. Moreover, they significantly impact the 'mental scripts' of each member of the group that shares each story. By closely examining these tales that have widely spread, we can gain an understanding of what our default state of mind is, as well as the characteristics of our mythological thinking. Reading these tales analytically therefore creates a cognitive distance from the pre-formed 'scripts' that we share and gives us the opportunity to look at them objectively. In other words, we become able to relativise and scrutinise the 'mental script' that each one of us unconsciously follows. In this chapter, therefore, I would like to look at several typical tales of intermarriage between humans and non-humans and consider the nature of these stories that reflect our ways of living.

Ever since I published my first report on this subject (Kitayama, 1985), I have focused on the prohibitions that appear in these stories. I have used the prohibition of 'Don't Look' as a key phrase, and establish it as a typical representation of prohibitions. It should be noted, however, that, as the violation of such a prohibition is presented in the stories at the same time as the characteristic theme, the action in question may not be absolutely prohibited. The conflict involving this prohibition concerns the question of ethics, so I even consider it appropriate to teach, at school, what I am about to discuss

DOI: 10.4324/9781003501930-4

here, as part of ethics classes. This prohibition is a taboo which is broken when the time comes, and, as such, it is a kind of theme that is closely involved with the growth of each one of us.

The tragedy of marrying a non-human

The Crane Wife or *The Grateful Crane*, which I covered in Chapter 2, are typical tales of intermarriage between humans and non-humans that are still told in contemporary Japan. Other well-known tales include *The Snake Wife* and *The Fish Wife*. Although they do not quite fall into the category of tales of intermarriage between humans and non-humans, I also wish to use, as a reference, the legend of Anchin and Kiyohime, as well as the Izanagi–Izanami myth that appears in the *Kojiki* (compiled in 712 AD by Yasumaro Ō no, 1980), or early chronicles of Japanese myths, legends, and oral traditions.

I have made the outline of each of the representative stories. Let us review it, beginning with *The Snake Wife, or The Blind Serpent Wife* (Dorson, 1962). I must caution you that with folk tales, the fine details of the plot may vary, as the story has been passed down orally. I have already looked at the Izanagi–Izanami myth in the previous chapter, but will investigate it once again.

The Snake Wife

One day, a man who works as a charcoal burner lights a fire in his kiln, and a large snake appears from behind it. To prevent the animal from being incinerated, the man sets it free in the grass outside. That evening, a beautiful woman appears before the man. She asks him to make her his wife, and he marries her.

The woman is a hard worker and helps bring the man out of poverty. The woman soon becomes pregnant. When she is about to give birth, she goes into a room and tells her husband not to look inside until she calls for him. The man keeps his promise. However, when he hears the cry of a newborn baby, he cannot prevent himself from peeping inside the room. He sees a giant snake giving birth and coiling up with the newborn baby as if to surround it. The wife was the snake that the man had rescued previously.

Returning to human form, the woman declares that she can no longer live with the man, since he has seen her as a snake. She disappears, leaving behind a beautiful crystal-like ball and telling the man to have the baby lick it when it cries for milk. The baby licks the milk-secreting ball and grows healthy and strong. However, rumours of the beautiful ball spread and reach a feudal lord, who seizes the ball. Not knowing what to do with his crying baby, the charcoal burner goes to a pond in the mountains, looking for the woman who has now returned to her form as a snake. Hearing her baby cry, the woman appears with a sad expression on her face. She hands out one more beautiful ball to give to the baby. The baby stops crying, and licks it, looking happy and satisfied. The baby grows healthily once again, but this ball, too, is snatched by the lord. Deeply troubled, the man returns to the pond. Hearing the baby cry, the woman reappears. But this time, she is looking down sadly. She tells him, 'The two balls were my eyeballs. I already gave you two, so there are none left.' Realising what he had done, the man laments in sheer sorrow. The woman returns to being a snake and dives vigorously into the pond, saying, 'I will never forgive anyone who makes my precious baby cry.' Suddenly, the water in the pond overflows, washing away the lord's castle.

The legend of Anchin and Kiyohime

A young, handsome Buddhist priest named Anchin who lives in Ōshu Shirakawa (currently Shirakawa City in Fukushima Prefecture, located in northeastern Japan), stays overnight at a certain inn in Masago (currently Tanabe City, Wakayama Prefecture in Western Japan) en route to making a pilgrimage to Kumano along the ancient spiritual roads. Kiyohime, the only daughter of the owner of the inn, falls in love with Anchin at first sight. She sneaks into the room where Anchin is sleeping and begs him to marry her. Cornered, Anchin, who is still in the midst of religious training, reassures her that he will drop by on the way back from the Kumano Grand Shrine, and, having made that promise, leaves the inn. After visiting the Grand Shine, however, Anchin heads home along a different route, not stopping by to see Kiyohime. Since Anchin never returned, no matter how long she waited, she asks a travelling stranger if he had met a young priest returning from a pilgrimage to Kumano, and learns that Anchin had taken a different route to return home. Enraged that Anchin had broken his promise, Kiyohime decides to chase after him. Realising that Kiyohime was pursuing him, Anchin tries to flee by hopping on a ferryboat at the Hidaka River. Kiyohime finds him, jumps into the river, transforms into a huge serpent that breathes red flames, and continues to chase Anchin. The young priest desperately flees into a temple named Dōjōji and hides himself inside the temple bell. Kiyohime, who has turned into a large serpent, coils her body around the bell, continues to breathe out red-hot fire, and burns Anchin to ashes. Later, Kiyohime drowns herself in the Hidaka River.

The Izanagi–Izanami myth

The paternal deity Izanagi and maternal deity Izanami lowered the nuboko, or the heavenly spear, into an open sea that had nothing created yet, and stirred it round and round, causing that area to curdle. When they raised the spear from the ocean, drops of seawater dripped steadily from the spear. These congealed and formed an island. The two gods that descended to this Onogoro Island married, had sexual intercourse, and gave birth to a series of islands. However, when Izanami then gave birth to the fire-deity, it burned her genitals and caused her to die. Nevertheless, saying that he had not yet finished creating the nation of Japan, Izanagi followed Izanami to the land of the dead and begged her to come back. Izanami concealed herself from him and replied, 'I will discuss my desire to return to life with the gods of the land of the dead. Pray do not look upon me until then.' Despite this, Izanagi impatiently turns on the lights, goes in, and sees Izanami's corpse, which is rotten and riddled with maggots. Overwhelmed with fear, he flees. Humiliated and furious from having her corpse exposed, Izanami dispatches ugly females to chase after him, and also goes after him herself. Having fled through the gate to the underworld into the land of the living, Izanagi blocks it with a large rock. Izanami says, 'I will kill 1,000 people of your country per day.' To this, Izanagi replies, 'Then, I will bear 1,500 people each day.' Since then, many people have died each day, but even more people have come to be born. Later, Izanagi says that he had gone to a 'dirty country,' and undergoes *misogi*, a purification ceremony.

Introversion of anger and the pre-formed 'script'

When we look at *The Grateful Crane* described in the previous chapter, *The Snake Wife*, and the Izanagi–Izanami myth, we find that the female protagonists are depicted as hard-working, productive beings. At the same time, we can see that they are sacrificing and injuring their bodies to retain their productivity. In most of these tales with wives as protagonists, the women hide the fact that they are non-human and try to avoid being seen, as such by imposing prohibitions.

In Japanese tales of intermarriage between humans and non-humans, female characters decide to leave their partners after being revealed as non-human. Japanese folklorist Seki (1963, 1966) points out that the common reason for their departure is a feeling of embarrassment and humiliation. On the other hand, in the Izanagi–Izanami myth and the legend of Anchin and Kiyohime, the female protagonists furiously chase after the men who broke their promise. They are seen as non-humans by the very fact that they are driven by rage; they are treated as unattractive beings, and the relationship ultimately breaks up.

I feel that stories such as these reflect the history that women and mothers have experienced. Whereas women sacrifice their bodies, work diligently, and are productive (I call these people 'masochistic caretakers'); men rely on them, and what is more they ultimately betray them. In the Izanagi–Izanami myth and the legend of Anchin and Kiyohime, the female protagonists express anger over their men's betrayals. Women who are enraged like this must have appeared like dreadful monsters, from the perspective of men who have no sense of guilt towards having caused such anger. No matter how angry they get, their anger never hits its mark. I feel a sense of unbearable 'emptiness' in these angry women.

However, as time passes from the days of the *Kojiki*, we arrive at a contemporary folk tale, *The Grateful Crane*. Here, we find that the female protagonist does not express anger towards the man who has betrayed her. She is hurt and leaves him with a sad expression. The storyline now is that the female protagonist, who had been shamed, spontaneously leaves her partner.

In other words, women continued to be angry with men's betrayals and abuse. No matter how many times they show anger, though, the men fail to take heed. This must be a truly unrewarding and terribly frustrating situation. If that's the case, then it would be better if she simply disappeared. Here, the ways of thinking that have evolved through history can be inferred: People who get angry know from experience that, if they get angry, they lose the argument, so they end up simply blaming themselves. The solution we see here is not to turn anger toward the outside but to turn it towards the self. In other words, it is the 'introversion of anger.'

The female protagonist tries to quickly end the story of her life by leaving the scene, thinking that it would be better if she were gone. This combines the mentality of masochism and self-hatred. This is where we can identify the 'script of a tragedy' that has been hard-wired in our minds. There is a possibility that we end up unconsciously playing out this 'mental script,' firmly believing that, if we are seen as being different or heterologous, it would be better if we just leave and disappear.

This may deviate somewhat from the theme of this chapter, but, decades ago, I gave a lecture on tales of intermarriage between humans and non-humans, in Niigata in northern Japan where the story of *The Grateful Crane* is part of local folklore. I remember women in the audience who were listening to my talk saying, one after another, 'This is how women had to live.' They explained that, even though they became angry with, and complained about, the situations they were placed in, nobody listened or responded, so they had no choice but to remain silent.

The Twilight of a Crane is a play based on *The Crane Wife* and *The Grateful Crane*. I will examine this later in this chapter. There are episodes that took place when his play was performed for an audience of women who were working at textile factories. In a scene where a man tries to peek into a room where his wife is weaving fabric on a loom, the audience shouts, 'No, no, don't look!' and many people watching the play were said to have burst into tears. The story echoed a real part of these women's situations. We must remember, however, that this is a tragedy of the weak that occurred not only with women, but also with men, children, and even old people. In this sense, we come to realise that tragedies that have been passed down through generations, such as tales of intermarriage between humans and non-humans, have become the pre-formed 'script' for the weak parties who leave the scene.

The Twilight of a Crane (Yūzuru)

From a series of tales of intermarriage between humans and non-humans, let us investigate, in greater detail, the pre-formed 'script' of a tragedy that continues to repeat. In considering the psychological developments of *The Grateful Crane*'s storyline, we find *The Twilight of a Crane (Yūzuru)* by Junji Kinoshita (1952), a play based on this story, very useful. In the dramatic structure of *The Twilight of a Crane*, playwright Kinoshita brilliantly depicts the psychology of the characters. As a literary resource to see how the mind works, this play, written in precise detail, is extremely helpful.

One day, Yohyō, the male protagonist, discovers a wounded crane that has been shot with an arrow and rescues it. Several days later, a beautiful woman appears before him and asks him to make her his wife. Yohyō agrees and marries this woman, whose name is Tsū. She makes Yohyō promise never to look at her weaving fabric on a loom and weaves a spectacular cloth called *Tsuru No Senba-ori*, or a crane's heavenly woven cloth (made from 1,000 feathers plucked from a crane). Yohyō's friend Unzu takes the woven cloth to town and sells it at a high price. Hearing rumours of Yohyō suddenly becoming wealthy after marrying a beautiful wife, another friend, Sōdo, gangs up with Unzu to plot how to make a fast buck by prompting Yohyō to make his wife weave more cloth. Each time she weaves a piece of fabric, Tsū becomes thinner and more emaciated, and tells Yohyō that she cannot weave any more cloth. Yohyō shows concern, but, incited by the two men, asks his wife to weave more cloth. Tsū reluctantly complies and continues to weave. Sōdo and Unzu, and Yohyō too, break the prohibition and look inside the room. They find a crane weaving cloth from its own plucked feathers. Tsū was the crane whose life Yohyō had saved. Having had her true form revealed, Tsū leaves Yohyō and returns to the sky in a wounded state.

A tragic ending brought about by innocence and greed

In *The Twilight of a Crane*, the male protagonist Yohyō is depicted as being childish and innocent. To make a comparison, however, he is actually the character of the man and the baby appearing in *The Snake Wife* combined into one. In response to Tsū telling him that she cannot weave any more cloth, Yohyō insists that she continue, telling her that they can earn more money, and whines that, if she does not, he will leave her. This is truly a selfish attitude, since he ended up making Tsū pluck so many feathers that she had barely enough left to fly.

Although he appears innocent, Yohyō is actually committing a serious sin. First, he goes as far as breaking his promise to not look at his wife and ends up destroying his marital relationship. This theme is also commonly seen in other tales of intermarriage between humans and non-humans. In *Urashima Taro*, another Japanese folk tale, the male protagonist breaks his promise to Otohime, the princess he had encountered at the Dragon Castle, and opens a forbidden box, leading to a tragic ending, just like Pandora's Box. The underlying theme is therefore the same (Kitayama, 1985).

We can also see that Yohyō is extremely greedy. Blinded by a love of money, he orders Tsū to weave even more cloth. Some say that the way Yohyō is blinded by greed symbolises the history of innocent people who, in the past, were less interested in money, but later transformed themselves into the ringleaders of a wealth-centred society. I think, however, for a very long time, the Japanese have also possessed a sense of greed, or obsession with money and material wealth. However, it may have been treated as a separate entity – as a natural desire hidden behind innocence – and not recognised as an overtly destructive impulse. I believe that, now that our society has become money-centred, aspects such as these have become more obvious, having thrown off their disguise.

In any event, we can see that while Yohyō is superficially innocent, he also possesses the hidden characteristic of being bestially greedy. In *The Snake Wife*, too, a naïve male protagonist hurts a non-human woman. The male protagonists in these stories therefore have something in common. The female protagonist, who is a snake, sacrifices an eyeball to feed her baby. The man, having lost this magic ball, demands another. Since the woman has no choice but to sacrifice her other eyeball, we learn that this man is cruel like a beast. This may also be related to the innocence of a baby screaming and crying to get what it wants without considering his parents' circumstances. The men are also people who are 'insensitive and have no consideration for others' who are unable to understand or sympathise with the female characters' dichotomy of a snake and a crane also being a human being. Considering the causal relationship with the stories' tragic outcomes, we cannot easily forgive the men's cruelty simply because they were innocent and therefore knew nothing about their wives' predicaments.

Non-humans are always excluded

What can be said from these and other Japanese tales of intermarriage between humans and non-humans is the basic rule that non-humans always end up being excluded. We have thus far looked at stories about women as non-humans. There also are stories that treat men as non-humans, although they are fewer in number. One example is a story called *The Monkey's Marriage*.

The Monkey's Marriage

An old man announces that he will give his daughter as a wife to any man who succeeds in drawing and carrying water to his field that has become parched after no rain for many days. Hearing this, a monkey draws water and tries to get the girl. Of the old man's three daughters, the youngest agrees to become the monkey's wife. While returning to her family home, the woman asks the monkey to pick some flowers that are blooming on a tree beside a river. When the monkey climbs the tree and tries to pick a flower, the girl tells him to pick flowers that are farther away from the tree. The monkey tries to go to the further tip of a branch to pick a flower but falls into the river and drowns. The girl returns safely to her family home without having to marry the monkey.

This, too, has a cruel outcome for the animal. The young girl who demands flowers that are blooming on the further tip of a branch is also greedy and apparently has no sense of guilt. And, in the sense that she seems to have planned to kill the monkey from the start, she is by no means innocent. What is important in this story, furthermore, is that contrary to *The Grateful Crane* and *The Snake Wife*, even though a male is the non-human character this time, the non-human is ultimately excluded. The principle of exclusion of non-humans in a cruel way is natural and unwavering, no matter what.

Exclusion of non-humans and the 'mental script'

When we look at it this way, we can see a standard, classic 'script' through tales of intermarriage between humans and non-humans that we have passed down through the ages: human beings, who are homologs and not heterologs, appear naïve and innocent, but are greedy. They are unaware of and feel no empathy towards non-humans who meet a tragic end.

It also seems to have things in common with the mechanism of exclusion that is likely to occur in this highly homogeneous society. Humans who take the position of trying to exclude the other party, i.e. non-humans, are innocent about, and unaware of, how much their partners are hurt. If the non-humans remain quiet and say nothing, the surrounding humans continue to escalate their attacks, egging each other on to demand more and more of non-humans. The non-humans treated in this way decide to disappear, saying 'If only I weren't here.' Humans who are trying to exclude non-humans are not able to foresee this tragic end.

From these facts, we can identify the presence of a 'mental script' that has been ingrained in us. It appears that many of us who continue to narrate these stories are made to unconsciously act out a 'tragic script' that is current in our society. If so, why not make oneself aware of this script, read it, contemplate its meaning once again, re-narrate the tragedy, and re-weave it? These processes are what psychoanalysis proposes.

Overseas tales of intermarriage between humans and non-humans

To recompose these infantile aspects into a mental script in which non-humans survive without being excluded, we must see not only the trees but also the forest; or, in other words, we need to widen our perspective. To do this, let us examine some stories from other countries. There are similar tales of inter-marriage between humans and non-humans in other countries. By getting to know them, and by reading their outcomes, we should become able to further relativise our 'mental script.' Our ways of living are more than just the stories depicted in Japanese folk tales, and are certainly not one, but diverse. If we look at tales of intermarriage between humans and non-humans from other countries, we find numerous stories with a happy ending. One example is *The Frog Prince*, which is included in Grimm's Fairy Tales.

The Frog Prince

One day, in a certain kingdom, a beautiful princess goes out for a walk in the woods, and accidentally drops a golden ball, her plaything, into a spring. A frog appears from the water and tells the princess, 'If I retrieve the golden ball for you, I want you to make me your friend and sit next to each other to eat dinner together, and then sleep in your bed.' The princess agrees to the frog's proposal, but, after the frog fetches the ball, she quickly returns to the castle, leaving the frog behind. The next day, when the princess is having dinner at the castle with her family, the frog appears and demands that the princess keep her promise. On hearing the story from the princess, the king orders her to keep her promise. The princess reluctantly has dinner with the frog, and they go to the bedroom together. The frog demands to join the princess in the bed, but the princess, in tears, refuses. The frog says that if she does not keep her promise, he will tell the king about it. Now angry, the princess tries to slam the frog against the wall. At this instant, the frog's spell is lifted. He becomes a handsome prince once again. Soon, the two become lovers and get engaged.

Strangely, the prince returns to human form, without any detailed explanations, and marries the princess, giving the story a happy ending. The development of a storyline in which the two characters become homogeneous, thanks to 'the miracle of love,' can be seen in *Beauty and the Beast*, a fairy tale which was made famous by Disney, and in other films. It was first published in 1740 as a novel. It has since been passed down, with some modifications, such as shortening the story. A rough outline of the story is that a prince, who had been transformed into a beast by magic, meets a young girl with a beautiful heart named La Belle, which means 'a beautiful woman' in French. In the course of building an emotional bond with her, the beast is eventually restored to human form as a prince, and the two get married.

Both *The Frog Prince* and *Beauty and the Beast* have non-human characters who eventually transform into human beings. Neither leaves the women they love; instead, they marry and live happily ever after. Of course, it is possible to look at the story somewhat differently, for example, that as non-humans, the protagonists were rejected, but were eventually accepted after they had transformed themselves into human form. What was more, *Beauty and the Beast*, as depicted often in films and contemporary stories, shows the process of a non-human changing into a human being through the female protagonist La Belle, who regrets her past behaviour towards the non-human male protagonist, and comes to feel sorry for the beast. La Belle loved the prince not because he had become a human being; she came to love him through her sense of guilt towards the prince who was in the form of a beast. Moreover, neither the frog nor the beast court their partner persistently, but they do not leave on their own initiative, either.

In other words, these stories show the possibility that individuals who may be excluded as non-humans can eventually be loved by their human partners, not by leaving them, but by surviving. The influence of Christianity as well as the historical relationships that the Japanese have with animals and nature may have influenced differences such as this. I am not, by any means, regarding Western ways as being ideal. Still, when considering the story about human life, I think that the more options we have the better it is for a significant outcome.

Non-humans surviving as non-humans

There is also a story whose plot develops in a unique and interesting fashion. It is called *The Duck Wife*, a traditional Inuit story (Ozawa, 1979). Like in *The Grateful Crane*, a female duck takes human form and appears in front of a man. The two marry. However, the wife is revealed to have been a duck and leaves her husband. But the husband chases after his wife who has returned to duck form, and brings her home. This is an astonishing ending for the Japanese. A duck, which is a heterolog, or a non-human, survives and continues to live as a duck. A non-human is not excluded for being non-human.

Moreover, a recent American film, *The Shape of Water* (directed by Guillermo del Toro, 2017), depicts love between a woman who is mute, and a merman who is half-fish and half-human. The merman is not a human being, so it is a heterolog, or a creature of a different species. Since she is mute, on the other hand, the female protagonist can also be seen as a heterolog among human beings. Two non-humans make love while maintaining their heterolog nature. If we think about it this way, we can understand that the development of a story depicted in Japan's tales of intermarriage between humans and non-humans often ends with the couple breaking up. We can also see that what we consider to be our culture is not absolute, but rather, relative. New discoveries concerning these tales have been a tremendous help for me in living my own life. In this sense, it may be extremely important to turn our gaze outside Japan and experience all sorts of other things, such as through literature and movies.

The second person plays a decisive role

We have thus far examined other countries' tales of intermarriage between humans and non-humans. In both Japanese tales and those of other countries, non-human protagonists are not the only characters that play an important role in the development of the story. Rather, another main character, who interacts with the non-human creature that is liable to be excluded, plays a decisive role. In the case of *The Twilight of a Crane*, for example, it corresponds to Yohyō *vis-à-vis* Tsū, and, in *Beauty and the Beast*, it corresponds to La Belle *vis-à-vis* the prince who had been turned into a beast. In *The Twilight of a Crane*, Yohyō forces Tsū to weave new pieces of cloth. He then breaks the promise he made to Tsū, that he would not look at her while she was weaving on her loom, causing her to agonise and leave him. In *Beauty and the Beast*, on the other hand, La Belle regrets her behaviour towards the prince, who is the beast and begins to express love for him. Through these exchanges, the beast returns to his form as a prince, and the two live happily ever after.

If we were to regard Tsū and the beast as the first persons who are the parties concerned, then Yohyō and La Belle correspond to the second persons. Other characters who surround the two key individuals become third persons. The fact is that the role played by these second persons is important in actual interpersonal relationships as well as in the development of these stories.

The third person, known as 'everyone,' cannot be counted on

In *The Twilight of a Crane*, Yohyō, who is the second person, is in a loving relationship with Tsū, and creates a world with 'just the two of them,' or, in other words, an exclusive dyadic relationship. However, after being egged on by Unzu and Sōdo, who are third persons, Yohyō ends up hurting Tsū, and furthermore, breaking the promise he made to her. Yohyō, who is the important second person, is drawn into the intentions of Unzu and Sōdo, who are third persons, and soon becomes like them.

The third persons known as 'everyone,' such as Unzu and Sōdo, are extremely irresponsible beings. This is because, whereas the first and second persons form an important relationship, the third person is a completely irrelevant and unrelated being. The second person whom you, the first person, had become close to, such as your friend or lover, is egged on by a jealous third person, integrates with him/her, and ends up destroying the precious relationship with you, the first person. If this happens, you, the one who should be loved, end up being placed in a helpless situation in which you cannot seek help from anyone. The story of a bride who is killed by the second person who is egged on by the jealous third person can be found in Shakespeare's play *Othello*.

If you wish for a happy ending, it is important to have someone to stand on the non-humans' side to serve as an intermediary and who changes the course of a story by confronting third persons who have no doubts whatsoever about excluding such non-humans, and prompting them to reflect on and change their ways. In this case, however, nobody is more unreliable than the anonymous third persons who surround you and urge you to 'Go ahead and do it.' This situation reminds me of the Colosseum in ancient Rome. A gladiator is in the middle of the circular arena, fighting a ferocious animal. As if to surround them, the people sitting in the spectator seats are cheering and excitedly spurring them on: 'Go, go, go!' They are hoping to see the gladiators and the animals die and are enjoying the spectacle. In other words, these faceless people, who create a particular atmosphere, are beings who eagerly anticipate a tragedy. Even if a gladiator is killed, they feel no sense of loss; many do not even feel guilty for wanting to witness his death. Instead, they simply seek to enjoy the next bout.

In *The Twilight of a Crane*, too, there is a scene where Tsū says that she cannot understand what Unzu and Sōdo are saying; she cannot communicate with them at all. The third person in a close dyadic relationship is someone who will say anything, and the words he or she says frequently make no sense at all and are meaningless.

Thus, when we are being excluded, the third persons who surround us and say anything they want to say, are a creepy presence. Having the potential to become either a silent bystander or a spectator who stirs things up, they appear to be looking forward to witnessing a tragedy. In an emergency, they are likely to speed up the process toward a tragedy, rather than discouraging it.

Getting hold of the important *You*

If a third person called *Everyone* cannot be counted on, then, the role played by a second person becomes important. It depends on the presence of *You* whom you can trust. Whether or not you can find, and get hold of, this important *You* in a group of people, is the key to stopping a tragedy from progressing.

The unfolding of a tragedy is influenced by none other than *You*, who helps you to maintain your loyalty before being engulfed by *Everyone*, the third person, and who should treasure the relationship of trust with you and become your ally. In terms of *The Twilight of a Crane*, even if Unzu and Sōdo jeer, 'She's really a crane!' it is only Yohyō who can acknowledge that even if she is a crane, she is an object of love for him, and that he will stay loyal to her without dissolving into *Everyone*. In other words, whether or not Yohyō can remain this *You*, an important partner for Tsū, is significant.

You and *I* were exchanging words of love and built a world just for the two of us. But soon, *I* can no longer understand what *You*, the second person, says, and *You* end up becoming the same as *Everyone*, a third person. And *I* lose *You* and become isolated, all by myself. As seen, the story ends up becoming a one-person drama or a one-person struggle, featuring only *I*, who has no partner. What is more, if *You* who had built a relationship of trust with *I*, and shared secrets known only to the two of us, becomes engulfed by *Everyone, You* may even reveal, to *Everyone*, the secrets known only to the two of us. To '*I*,' this is terribly frightening.

Am *I* the only one who is being ignored and excluded, and is *Everyone* colluding behind my back? *I* imagine these things and agonise even more. *I* also become unable to sleep at night. The Japanese word for 'collude' is *tsurumu*. Besides indicating 'doing something together,' this term also signifies 'to form a sexual relationship,' indicating that it represents a connection that strong.

As a result of *Your* betrayal, even your secrets may have become exposed and known to *Everyone*. This is as if you are being made to stand on a stage, completely naked. You no longer have a place to hide: there is no backstage dressing room into which you can escape. In other words, your identity as a crane is revealed; you are being looked at, and excluded, by *Everyone* as a non-human or a member of a different species, and are driven into a situation where you have no choice but to leave resolutely without hesitation. Tragedy progresses, and the characters face a disastrous ending.

To prevent this from happening, *I* must get to know the 'mental script' – similar to what has been described here – that I have been hard-wired with and learn its structure and mechanisms. It is also important to get hold of *You*, the second person who will become your ally. This *You* may be your most important friend, or your parents. Mental professionals such as psychoanalysts and psychotherapists also have the potential to become your important *You*. Above all, you might be the *You* for someone else. In this case, you must become aware of the importance of the presence called *You*, and be careful not to carelessly dissolve into *Everyone* and force your partner into isolation.

The true identity of non-humans

To identify the factors that determine the tragedy of the 'mental script' that has been hard-wired in us, I will examine our tales of intermarriage between humans and non-humans in greater detail. In the Izanagi–Izanami myth, it was the maternal deity's decayed corpse that was excluded; in the legend of Anchin and Kiyohime, the female protagonist transforms herself into a monstrous creature that the male protagonist feared. Let us investigate, from a psychological perspective, this story of a character transforming into a monster.

In the legend of Anchin and Kiyohime, we learn that the female protagonist who is ultimately excluded is actually a serpent. In *Ugetsu Monogatari [Tales of the Rain and Moon]*, a collection of bizarre stories written in the 18th century by Akinari Ueda (Aoki, 1981), there is a piece called *Jaseino In [The Lust of the White Serpent]* which is often adopted as a theme for plays and movies.

Here again, the female protagonist who deceives and seduces Toyoo, the male protagonist, is depicted as a dreadful serpent who takes the form of a slutty woman of advancing age.

Thus, this story is about a woman who marries (or seduces) a male protagonist, who is actually a dreadful monster. As I have already pointed out, I believe that the image of a woman, as seen from a man's viewpoint, is being projected here. This means that the man discovers a monster inside himself in the woman who is his partner.

I have also examined this in Chapter 2, but, in the story of Toyotamahime (Princess Toyotama) included in *Kojiki* (Ō no, 1980), Hōri no Mikoto (a God that appears in Japanese mythology) marries Toyotama, who is the paternal grandmother of Emperor Jimmu, said to have been the first emperor of Japan. When Toyotama is about to give birth, she makes Hōri promise not to spy on her during delivery. However, like in many other Japanese folktales, Hōri breaks his promise and peeks at his wife delivering a child. What he discovers is the woman transformed into a thrashing dragon-like monster called Yahirowani (see Figure 2.3).

Folklorist and Japanese literature scholar Shinobu Orikuchi (1975), makes the following interpretation of this Toyotamahime legend: A bride comes from the outside world, such as from a different village. And, in situations where a crisis occurs, such as childbirth, people performed religious rituals, originating in the village to which the wife had belonged. If this is to be further interpreted in terms of depth-psychology, it may be that the form of a monster called Yahirowani is being projected, from those who see it, onto Toyotama's strange behaviour.

In other words, men whose wives and women have come from the outside world with a different culture and customs and are thus heterogenous to them, regard the wives' actions and behaviours as those of a beast and/or an animal. If we think about it this way, the men are likening a presence they cannot understand, or are heterogenous to them, to a monster; so the monster can, in fact, be said to be a human being, just like us. I believe that the men emphasise the heterogeneity of their wives and female partners, who are supposed to be the same human beings as them, likening them to being a monster. In short, the true identity of a monster can be understood to derive from the depth-psychology on the part of human beings who know very little about their partners.

A monster is a projection of desires and guilt feelings on the part of the beholder

Let us examine, even further, the psychology of a person regarding his or her partner as a monster. In the Anchin and Kiyohime legend (e.g. Ury, 1979), Kiyohime appears at Anchin's bedside and tries to seduce him. However, he rejects her, citing his trainee monk status as the reason. This does not necessarily mean that he had no desire to accept Kiyohime, a beautiful woman, and to sleep with her. He is trying to maintain abstinence, telling himself that, since he is still in religious training, such sexual desires are not permitted. Later, betrayed by Anchin, Kiyohime transforms into a dreadful serpent and chases him. The explanation that Kiyohime was actually a snake represents the female protagonist's lustful nature, just like in *The Lust of The White Serpent*. However, the snake's true identity can also be interpreted as a manifestation of lustful desires like that of a snake – or, in other words, beastliness – hidden inside Anchin's mind.

I want to sleep with a beautiful woman. I want to be one with her. These animalistic desires arise in rapid succession. Anchin, who is a monk in training, must shake off these desires. Desire takes the form of a frightening serpent who chases Anchin. Anchin flees so as not to be engulfed by the serpent. This can be interpreted as follows: Anchin denies his own desire – the lust of the white serpent – and 'regards' Kiyohime as a serpent and blames everything on her. In psychoanalysis, this sort of psychological phenomenon of '*minashi*,' or regarding object *A* as a disavowed object *B*, was described as 'projective identification' by Melanie Klein (1946). The legend of Anchin and Kiyohime, I believe, is to be read as a typical story of projective identification. As a result, the passing of blame onto someone else has occurred, as a way of dealing with the feeling that one is in the wrong by regarding the other person as being in the wrong instead.

In *The Twilight of a Crane*, Yohyō demands that the injured Tsū weave more cloth. In *The Snake Wife*, the male protagonist, who is unaware of the true circumstances, demands that his wife/snake give him an eyeball to fill the hungry baby's stomach. In both tales, the characters who make demands appear, at first glance, to be perfectly innocent and naïve. In *The Snake Wife*, in particular, the crying baby personifies the animal instinct called hunger; it has no additional wishes or intentions.

Even though one may be superficially innocent, the responsibility for being greedy and causing a tragic ending does not necessarily lie solely on the side of the non-human crane or snake. It also lies on the side of the male protagonists who are human beings. In other words, we can interpret that Yohyō is addressing his sense of guilt relating to the sacrifices caused by his greedy desires by regarding his wife as evil. We can understand that *minashi*, or 'projective identification,' is occurring here.

Understanding the story and re-weaving its tragedy

We often see, in the real world, people who, although they are undeniably the cause of something, blame it on someone else. There is a person you dislike, and you want to fight with him/her. At times like this, you provoke him/her, make him/her initiate the attack, and say that 'He/she started it.' This often occurs in children's fights.

When war breaks out between countries, moreover, one side often asserts that the other country started it first. The truth is, however, that a country often has reasons to start a war, and that it is nurturing the seeds of war themselves. We find this behind the start of numerous wars.

Therefore, the reason for a creature being regarded as a monster and a non-human, and excluded as being 'dirty,' 'ugly,' 'bad,' and 'scary,' lies not on the side that was considered a monster, but instead, on the side that had regarded it as such. In tales such as these, tragedies occur not because the protagonist is a monster, but because the people surrounding the protagonist projected their mental monster onto the victim, the receptacle, and opportunistically treated him or her as a monster. Unless one can identify this plot and structure, a mechanism will become easily activated in which the weakling is made into the 'hero/heroine of a suicidal tragedy,' with the victim coming to have the 'If only I did not exist' mentality.

If you feel that you are being unfairly excluded, you must scrutinise, to see if there is any mental leeway on your part, whether or not you are unthinkingly taking other people's projections on board, or if people who are insensitive and have no empathy for others are opportunistically viewing you that way. For example, those who loathe worms do not want to admit that they have pictures of such creatures in their mind. Since they project, onto the people around them, the creatures that they loathe, they eliminate us – who have become the receptacle of those projections – by treating us as if we were worms. In the story, Yohyō and his pals peek into the room and shout, 'It's a crane, it's a crane!' This shows that the image of a non-human creature – a crane – was already present in the deep layers of their minds.

At the same time, in re-narrating, and re-living this story called life, it is important to discover *You*, who understands that you are not a monster, or *You* who, even though you are being viewed as a monster, continues to trust *I*, or *You* whom *I* could trust, and to take plenty of time, to maintain the relationship with that second person. I myself hope to become a second person whom my patients trust. Even so, I foolishly fail from time to time. Still, I try again, reconsider, and, as the party involved in this story called 'treatment,' and as a paradoxical 'wise fool,' I continue to stand at a point where opinions and judgements differ. What I need is time; it appears, however, that I cannot count on having an infinite amount of it.

References

Aoki, M. (Ed. & Anno.) (1981). *Ugetsu Monogatari* [*Tales of the Rain and Moon*] (by A. Ueda). Tokyo: Kōdansha.

Dorson, R. D. (1962). The blind serpent wife. In *Folk Legend of Japan* (pp. 118–121). Tokyo: Charles E. Tuttle.

Kinoshita, J. (1952). (T. Kurahashi, Trans.) *Twilight of a Crane*. Tokyo: Miraisha. (Original work *Yūzuru* published 1949)

Kitayama, O. (1985). Preoedipal 'taboo' in Japanese Folk Tragedies. *International Review of Psycho-Analysis*, 12: 173–185.

Klein, M. (1946). Notes on some schizoid mechanisms. *International Journal of Psycho-Analysis*, 27: 99–110.

Ō no, Y. (Ed.). (1980). (D. L. Phillipi, Trans.) *Kojiki* (2nd ed.). Tokyo: University of Tokyo Press. (Original work edited 712)

Orikuchi, S. (1975). Hahagakuni-e tokoyo-e [To mother land, to eternal land]. In *Orikuchi Shinobu Zenshū* [*Complete Works of Orikuchi Shinobu*] Vol. 3 (pp. 3–15). Tokyo: Chūōkōronsha. (Original published 1927)

Ozawa, T. (1979) *Sekainominwa* [*Folktales of the World*]. Tokyo: Chūōkōronsha.

Seki, K. (1963). (R. Adams, Trans.) *Folktales of Japan*. Chicago: University of Chicago Press. (Original published 1957)

Seki, K. (1966) *Mukashibanashi no Rekishi* [*History of Japanese Folktales*]. Tokyo: Shibundō.

Ury, M. (1979). *Tales of Times Now Past*. Berkeley: University of California Press.

Chapter 4

The wounded caretaker and forced guilt[1]

Osamu Kitayama

Idealised sacrifice

The material in my contribution to this volume may reflect Japanese culture, but the cultural phenomenon itself is surely universal. Here I am referring to our tendency to idealise the person who devotes and sacrifices himself/herself to take care of us. Throughout history, a large number of heroes and heroines have given their lives, suffered martyrdom, been immolated, or sacrificed themselves to save us.

We then may feel very deeply that we would not exist without someone else's self-sacrifice. I suppose that the problem of wounded caretakers and their offspring is not specific to a certain culture, just as, if I may draw a parallel on a global level, our being faced with the vulnerability of this benevolent Mother Earth is a worldwide phenomenon.

Injuries of the devoted mother

As we have seen in the previous chapters, a key Japanese myth narrates how our deities and our land were born of a goddess who died after giving birth to them. I explained how the male protagonist, a paternal deity, could not handle the dichotomy between his image of a live, productive mother figure and that of a dying, injured one, an unfathomable mixture which he felt was 'ugly and dirty.' In the end, the hero divorces her and tries to wash the ugliness away by ritualistic cleansing.

Such a painful and disgusting experience in his integrative process of the caregiving and injured figures could very well be one of the elements of what Klein calls the depressive position in her analytical formulation of early developmental stages. This sense of filth seems to give rise to indigestible bad feelings associated with one's survival at the expense of someone else's life. Indeed, a baby may live on his/her mother's body and grow well while badly damaging her body. In the previous chapters, I quoted Japanese myths and folk tragedies to show how difficult it was for each protagonist to accept a

DOI: 10.4324/9781003501930-5

wounded mother figure whose injuries were caused by her inexhaustible devotion in answer to his greedy demands.

In Japanese tales of marriage between humans and non-humans, the most popular plot can be summarised as follows: A young man rescues an injured animal such as a crane, which then disguises herself as a beautiful woman and visits him, offering herself in return for his having rescued her. She is highly productive and benevolent, but she prohibits him from looking at her giving birth, producing cloth, meals, etc. in response to his demand. He, however, breaks the prohibition of 'Don't Look,' secretly peeping in on her and finding an injured animal. The young man gets frightened in awe while she feels humiliated, and they separate.

Winnicott (1971) postulated that the mother should tolerate the baby's attacks and survive his/her destructiveness. According to him, she will survive until the infant is able to be concerned and to take responsibility for his/her own instinctual impulses. His use of a positive term such as 'concern' stresses the spontaneous and reparative aspect of depressive guilt. If we accept that an infant's feeling of guilt stems from the tension between his/her own destructiveness and the mother's capacity to survive, we can then discuss the possibility of forced guilt which can be generated in infants with fragile mothers. The fragile mother may be too vulnerable to survive her infant's greedy needs.

Here I think studying fragile mothers may be of value as it may have universal importance in understanding matricidal guilt feelings. With this in mind, I see the possibility that the sense of 'forced guilt' results from the relativity existing between the infant's destructiveness and the degree of injury to the fragile mother. I will thus discuss how the mother's vulnerability to the infant's destructiveness forms a guilt-inducing background, while the infant cannot be considered just 'guilty.' As you will see, this forced sense of guilt can produce a defensive and adaptive character, a so-called 'masochistic caretaker' who keeps on repairing the injuries of the mother whom he wounds like the heroes of Japanese tragedies.

Masochism and forced guilt

In 1931 Kosawa published a Japanese paper entitled 'Two kinds of guilt feelings – the Ajase complex' that distinguishes between repentant guilt which comes from a matricidal wish and punitive guilt brought on by patricide (Kosawa, 2022). Kosawa points out that in the ancient Buddhist tale of Prince Ajase (the Japanese pronunciation of the Sanskrit Ajatasatru), the deep forgiveness of Ajase's mother evokes a sense of guilt, of penitence in him when, instead of punishing him, she nurses this son who has tried to kill her. Keigo Okonogi (1978, 1979) continuing Kosawa's work, has carefully investigated the text and Kosawa's intuitive idea and concludes that the son's repentant guilt is induced and shared by the devoted mother.

Okonogi (1978) wrote: 'In July 1932, Kosawa visited Sigmund Freud at his home at 19 Berggasse in Vienna and submitted a paper on his original theory of the Ajase complex. However, this paper drew no international interest for more than 40 years' (1978, p. 91).

In the original Buddhist scriptures which used to be distributed almost all over Japan and are still available, Ajase tries to kill not his mother but his father at first. It is this contradiction between the text and Kosawa's interpretation. However, I will not deal with this in any further detail as the main interest of this chapter is in the acute awareness of guilt induced by Kosawa's revealing the idea of matricide.

Although Ajase does not kill his mother, she is so devoted that she is likely to kill herself for her child. The expression 'killing oneself' in everyday Japanese is a metaphor which refers to self-sacrifice, and its literal and metaphorical meanings seem worth analysing. It seems to me that the child's guilt feeling is generated not only by the infantile 'killing' demand but also through the self-sacrificing mother who tends to kill or hurt herself, feeling sorry for the child she so deeply loves. She cannot stop it for 'killing herself' can be pleasurable as well as exhausting. She is usually conscious and even proud of this self-injuring behaviour or self-devaluation and its underlying masochistic fantasy, which she may hide from those whom she takes care of.

Although many an analyst uses the concept of masochism to cover a variety of clinical phenomena, its serious guilt-inducing effect on the person cared for has been understood mostly in terms of a sado-masochistic interaction. Since Freud said: 'Masochism is not the manifestation of a primary instinct, but originates from sadism which has been turned round upon the self' (Freud, 1919, p. 193), many authors have commented that the effect of masochism was to put the other in the wrong; that is to say, masochism is so sadistic that it can generate an unjustified sense of false accusation. Reich (1966) has seen the attempt to justify the 'masochistic provocation' as the wish to express the underlying sadism without guilt and as an attempt to force the other to love the subject.

Brenman (1952) clearly saw the background of the masochist's inexhaustible 'giving' as follows:

> We see first the projection of insatiable demands in the masochist's assumption that all people are as imperiously needy as he ... this 'giving' becomes an aggressive, smothering attempt to control – experienced by the object not as a gift but as an enslavement.
>
> (p. 273)

Berliner (1947) saw it as the presentation of 'an old unpaid bill for affection'; Loewenstein (1957) described the masochism of the seduction of the aggressor and Parkin stressed the 'attempt to recover the lost omnipotence in fantasy' (Parkin, 1980, p. 309).

In spite of slight and subtle differences among innumerable interpretations, most authors seem to agree on the interpretation of the masochist's effect, on others and see it as an attempt to win the other's love or care by inducing in him/her a sense of guilt for not caring. The shift of the accent from masochism as a quest for sadism to masochism as a search for love seems to reflect a shift in our clinical interest from masochistic perversion to moral masochism. Furthermore, as the authors de-emphasise the sexual aspect, I also use the term 'masochism' or 'moral masochism' in a broad sense, meaning the conscious pursuit of suffering and stressing the hazy boundary between pathological masochism and normal pain tolerance.

Guilt-inducing effect of the fragile environment

If we understand that the guilt thus induced by the masochist is 'forced or false guilt,' we then come to realise that it may be induced not only by the masochistic caretaker but also by the non-masochistic caretaker. For instance, Winnicott (1958b) has mentioned 'implanted guilt,' which seems to arise in infants with depressive mothers. That is, the implanted guilt pushes the infant to make forced reparation for the damage that is apparent in the vulnerable and depressive mother. 'This false reparation appears through the patient's identification with the mother and the dominating factor is not the patient's own guilt but the mother's organised defence against depression and unconscious guilt' (Winnicott, 1958a, p. 91).

Freud (1923) also wrote, from the therapeutic point of view, about the difficulty of dealing with the negative therapeutic reaction and 'a borrowed sense of guilt' (Lampl, 1927).

> The battle with the obstacle of an unconscious sense of guilt is not made easy for the analyst ... One has a special opportunity for influencing it when this Ucs. sense of guilt is a 'borrowed' one – when it is the product of an identification with some other person who was once the object of an erotic cathexis.
>
> (Freud, 1923, p. 50)

Theoretically and empirically, we can list external situations arising in the family which may externally induce or force 'false or forced guilt' in a developing infant.

1   Sadistic parental punishment resulting in a cruel superego. Such a cruel superego turns the object of hate around thus bringing about self-accusation.
2   Unwarranted blame for the sudden damage to the caretaker, inducing feelings of self-reproach.
3   Accusation for environmental damage exceeding the infant's reparatory capacity.

4   A fragile environment, generally a fragile mother who is physically and/or psychologically vulnerable.
5   Masochistic mothering which aims at inducing a guilt-ridden concern in the infant. This promotes a 'borrowed guilt feeling' or 'implanted guilt' through mutual identification and introjection.
6   Absence of the father or of a third party to mediate between them and to support and protect both. The mother is then much more vulnerable to the infant's ambivalent feelings towards her, while the infant is even more exposed to the mother's intrusion and control.

Although all the above possibilities may have been touched upon and discussed by analytical authors, it seems to me that in clinical cases of forced guilt, almost all the elements are working together or interchangeably. The masochistic and fragile mother burdened with her own guilt feelings is the most forceful element inducing an acute sense of guilt in the child, especially in a daughter, because of mutual identification.

'The "borrowed" guilt feeling, created by identification with another person who is likewise supposed to feel guilty, may be used in assuagement of one's own guilt feeling' (Fenichel, 1972, p. 166).

Here we come to the point where we have to focus our attention on the masochistic vulnerability of caretaking, which can induce forced guilt in the person who is taken care of.

Masochistic caretaker: a dichotomous concept

To understand the masochistic character not only in terms of sadism, but also in terms of love and care, we have to pay attention to the moral masochist's active attempt at being loved through self-sacrifice, i.e. altruism where the mechanism of projection and identification was found to be crucial.

Anna Freud wrote: 'She had projected her own desire for love and her craving for admiration onto her rival and, having identified herself with the object of her envy, she enjoyed the fulfilment of her desire' (Freud, 1968, p. 127).

In the last footnote of that chapter, she mentions 'another and easy route to the same goal is by way of the various forms of masochism' (Freud, 1968, p. 134). Both clinical experience and everyday encounters reveal the coexistence of masochism and altruism in the same individual. For instance, the method of placing the blame on oneself in the name of love and altruism is a well-known masochistic technique used by religions.

Ramon Ganzarain, in his presentation to the Japanese Psychoanalytic Society in 1987, made the following comparison: Some critics of Christianity comment that when Christ advised his disciples to offer the other cheek when slapped, he was betting on the power of masochism by combining gentleness with pardon, thus attempting to control the world by inducing guilt in others as well as a sense of indebtedness. Mothers seem to be cast in a similar role in all these Japanese legends (Ganzarain, 1988, p. 97).

In the legends to which Ganzarain is referring the maternal heroines have two contradictory aspects, as I showed in the previous chapters. One is a benevolent caregiver who tries to respond to the hero's endless demands; the other is an injured animal who sacrifices her body to meet those demands, and who hides her painful sacrifice with the prohibition of 'Don't Look.' As such masochistic caretaking is culturally transmitted, it seems to form the background for masochistic altruism which we take as our cultural feminine ideal. It is very possible that this social ideal has also been influencing the defensive adaptive functions of Japanese women just as described by many analytic writers in Western culture (Horney, 1973; Brenner, 1959; Blum, 1977).

The dual nature of the heroine, clearly illustrated in each tale, reveals the dichotomy between her outward altruism – she as a giver of love and care – and her inward masochism, the source of her love. To clarify this duality in masochistic caretakers and to grasp their whole attitude towards the self and the object, we need the double concept of altruism/masochism to explain why they sacrifice themselves to take care of others.

Clinical picture

I think that most of the authors who have dealt with masochism have described the condition but more or less failed to grasp the whole picture by highlighting either side of the dichotomy. Obviously, these patients are not sexual perverts but moral masochists, and in my clinical experience, they usually come to us complaining of various symptoms which could belong to an underlying depression. As I suggested, their way of living can be socially adaptive, so to diagnose and treat them effectively we should classify them into three depth-psychological categories.

First, we have what we may call the normal self-devoted caretakers who are able to rest whenever they need to and stop caring about others to look after themselves. They can play the part of caretakers out of love or to contribute to society, sometimes tolerating pain and discomfort almost beyond their limits, but they have, to some extent, integrated both sides of the dichotomy.

Second, we have the clinical group of character neurosis which presents with the features of masochistic caretakers. My experience has led me to divide their characteristics roughly into three dominant aspects: inability to stop taking care of others, inability to look after oneself when possible and even when necessary, and presence of masochistic tendencies or self-destructive habits (Kitayama, 1989). Some of these correspond to the description of 'moral masochism' in the psychoanalytic literature, particularly of the 'depressive-masochistic disorder' by Kernberg (1988). We can assume that their personal wishes and natural needs are suppressed and hidden behind their acculturated and industrialised identities.

In Japanese folk tragedies, the mother snake, in response to the greedy demand of others, gives both her eyeballs to the hero, thus becoming blind, whereas the crane-wife weaves 'two' bolts of cloth from her own feathers which she keeps, plucking beyond all limits. I think if the snake gave only one eyeball or the crane only one bolt of cloth, they could be considered to belong to the normal, social, and adaptive group.

If we can help them to rest and drop their stressful role in the treatment, we may see their real selves gradually emerge and the two sides of the dichotomy – i.e. altruism/masochism become integrated. The case presented below illustrates the integrative process that takes place in brief psychotherapy.

In my experience, there is a third category of patients who would become 'emptied' and possibly psychotic if this dichotomous persona were taken away from them. Only through their lifestyles as masochistic caretakers can these people find their place in society. Thus, we should be very careful in our depth-psychotherapy not to uncover their masochistic trends before making an accurate understanding and giving them an alternative way of being. It may also be essential both to deal with their fear of dependency and to adjust their surroundings since these patients manipulate their environment so that it fosters their paranoid anxiety.

A case of brief psychotherapy

I want to quote here the depth-psychological treatment of a patient of the second category. Although this is a case of short-term psychotherapy it will help us to grasp the whole picture of the dichotomous lives of such patients. I should add that such patients rarely come to us as on the conscious level they do not want to be taken care of.

Case: 50-year-old female. Restaurant owner. Mother of three.

Initial consultation: Chief complaint of insomnia and hating anything and everything. She hates every minute of her life, being surrounded as she is by her foster mother who is 87 and practically bedridden, a husband from whom she is separated, a daughter who only thinks of fooling around with men, and a son who keeps getting into trouble with the police. And yet, her whole life, her *raison d'être*, seems to revolve around doing all she can for others. Her life history tells of her having been separated from her real mother and of her father, who was in the army and became a prisoner of war. Her foster mother, a maternal aunt, was very strict and the patient says that when she was little all she had to say was 'But ...' and she would get badly 'burnt.' It is remarkable that, although she was made to work from the time she was a very young child and her foster mother would tell her 'Get out then' whenever she disobeyed, all the patient wanted was that her foster mother would live. The clinical diagnosis is depressive neurosis. Her attitude towards sessions is one of distance and when asked if she would come every week all she says is 'Well, I can try.'

Second session: 'I keep tidying up after people,' she says, which fits the characteristics of her role of masochistic caretaker as described above. When I point out the self-evident and say 'Actually, you'd like to throw everything out the window,' she answers 'I can't,' and when I say 'You enjoy taking care of others,' she comes back with 'I like eating other people's leftovers.' I suggest that we should focus on the way she is locked up in a life where she keeps tidying up after others and enjoys looking after them while at the same time hating having to live like that, and with this I finish the diagnostic interviews. At this point, although my remarks only pointed out the obvious, I am afraid of having gone too far and too deep on some points, but she follows up with it in the next session.

Third session: She interpreted what I said in the previous session as 'Throw everything away.' Then she adds 'I don't know what to do,' but 'Throwing everything away, that was a discovery.' There she ingratiates herself with, and adapts to me, her therapist, by identifying with me.

Fourth session: 'I am so busy; I'd like to run away. It annoys me so much to have nowhere to escape.' 'I hate it when it's messy. I'm always tidying up.' Since the beginning of her therapy, I have often found myself just listening to the tale of her hardships.

Fifth session: 'I've got to tidy up here, to tidy up there, being a woman I've got to tidy up everywhere. I don't know why they all keep messing up the place,' to which I say 'You like that side of your character that keeps everything neat, don't you?' She responds with 'I am even ashamed to stay in bed when I'm sick.' My interpretation is that she is trying to rid herself of her indigestible guilt.

Sixth session: She reports having gone on a trip before this session, during which she forgot everything, threw everything to the wind, and felt much better. She is getting better at pleasing her therapist and I feel that she is looking after me and my vulnerability, a very pleasant feeling.

Seventh session: 'I understand now. I have been reacting emotionally. But I don't think I could have gone on so long if God hadn't been looking after me.' Thus saying, she complains of not being able to tell whether she takes care of others because she gets emotional and feels sorry for them, or because she really believes that she should. I reply, verbalising what I am sensing in her: 'Deep down, it's your imaginary father who always has been looking after you, isn't it?'

Eighth session: Gradually, her real self begins to emerge. 'I've finally got it. Until now I've just been play-acting, selfish isn't a bad word.' There she says that with the year-end she is busy and since she is feeling well she wants to interrupt the treatment for a while. 'So, you want to be selfish in therapy too,' I answer and change the pace of the treatment from once every other week to on-demand treatment. (Here, what she says and what she does begin to merge in a kind of dramatisation.)

Ninth session: She starts getting relaxed. When she comes after an interval of about a month, she seems careless in her dress. She disconnectedly shows her rejecting side that says no to anything she does not like, and her self-sacrificing side which makes her want to devote herself to someone. She gives the impression of being a little sloppy, somewhat cute, like a child. Her speech too is incoherent, rambling. I interpret her physical symptom of feeling fuzzy as 'You feel bad because things don't fit, don't click together' as I feel I have to take care of the patient instead of her taking care of herself. Naturally, at the back of my mind is the fear that she is getting worse, but I am not acutely worried.

Tenth session: 'I can't think, can't get my ideas together. I don't care anymore, I dilly-dally. But I feel bad not being able to manage.' I actively interpret her complaint that she does not care by putting together and connecting: her wanting to eliminate all that she does not like in her life; her fear of not being accepted if she does; how she defends herself against her anxiety by embracing hardships, etc. (Here we see her going to the pre-Copernican position: to a static self and a universe in movement, to being cared for instead of caring for oneself.)

Eleventh session: She goes back and forth between the present and the past, telling of how she is not afraid anymore of saying what is on her mind but of how she cannot let herself be pampered, and talks of her past relationship with her foster mother who would tell her 'I'm not your mother.' I then understand that the patient has killed her desire to flaunt her selfishness and her discontent, believing it was 'bad,' 'feeling sorry' for her sickly foster mother.

Twelfth session: She has brought her husband along and asks me to explain her illness because nobody understands. I decide to see them together as she is just then about to stop working as an active member of her restaurant and also with the aim of adjusting her environment. So, first, I explain her illness to her husband and the three of us discuss her need to distance herself from her environment. (Looking back, I think that the introduction of this third party helped blunt and disperse her deeply seated need for dependency on the therapist.)

Thirteenth session: From then on, she finally starts to resist therapy: she wants me the therapist to accept her need for dependency and she criticises the treatment saying 'I'm not getting any better.'

Fourteenth session: She says 'I understand what you want to say but I can't change my whole lifestyle.' 'I don't want to be in your care but I'm not going to get better right away, am I?,' utterances which I take to be expressions of anger at the guardian who has failed to care for her properly, rather than resistance due to a negative therapeutic reaction. In other words, I see here in the transference a dramatisation of the caretaker's failure to care for the child, or an expression of trust and love which allows her to express her anger. (What is happening here is not merely a transference but a dramatisation where the patient forms a new relationship.)

Fifteenth session: She brings her daughter along, saying; that 'everybody keeps disturbing [her] whenever [she] tries to relax.' After making sure that we agree that what has to change is not merely her environment but also the patient herself, I explain her illness to her daughter who comes in with her. It seems that through such environmental adjustments the mother feels publicly acknowledged as a patient whom everybody should take care of. It is also worth mentioning that the therapist is put between the mother and the daughter who has been running away from her guilt-inducing environment.

Sixteenth session: From then on the patient begins to show more coherence. Both in and out of therapy, she plays out what she has verbalised and verbalises what she has acted out. She says:

> It feels good being selfish. Until now I kept telling myself, one: put up with it, two: put up with it, there was no three and four, then five: put up with it, but finally I confronted my husband.
>
> I have changed. I used to think that the children were my pawns. I'd try to make them do what I wanted them to, so they rebelled. You know, the crane-wife, sure she sacrifices herself, but I think somehow she is manipulating her partner. So, I have to ask myself how she can balance out her, despair when she cannot manipulate her partner, right? But you know, Cinderella, she has found the prince, but she still can't leave her stepmother and just go, can she?

At the same time, her psychosomatic condition starts improving. (I had brought up 'the crane-wife' as it fit the context, but 'Cinderella' was her own idea.)

Seventeenth session: She continues in a similar vein. Then, the part of her that does not want to get better, in other words, the part of her which says no to everything, confronts the therapist in a very lively way.

> I quite like hearing myself sweetly saying 'Yes, yes.' I've been doing it for 50 years, so changing now is difficult … that's because I am being obstinate. I'm stubborn, aren't I? I seem nice, kind, but if you scratch the surface, there is that demanding me that wants to be coddled.

I respond with 'That's the real you, isn't it?,' to which she answers, laughing, 'Yes, but I hate it. Today, I'll write in my diary that I don't want to get better.' Sensing that this was the crucial point, I at once say 'Are you really hearing yourself sweetly saying "Yes, yes" when you talk like that?' to which she guffaws.

Eighteenth session: For the first time, she tells me of a dream she had when she was in junior high school. In the dream, she helped her foster mother out of a hole she had fallen into, a dream she associates with her wanting her mother to love her while at the same time seeking revenge. Then, she says there was a man too in the hole, whom she left there. In her associations, she tells me how she has never once called her father 'Father.' When I ask her if she was 'still trying to save mother' she says that actually she had another dream in which she did not help her mother out of the hole and that she enjoyed the revenge. Now that she has felt both her true and her forced guilt, she seems quite relieved. She had to abandon her father in the hole, and even her mother in the same hole, to save the good mother, but using the man who is her therapist, she can now join the oedipal triangular relationship which she had never been able to enjoy. (Looking back, I assume that the dream was reminding her of her primal scene where she had been excluded from the family hole. I will discuss the symbolic meanings of the hole in Chapter 9.)

Nineteenth session: As she is now able to distance herself from her mother, I take up the problem of there being nobody, her father being absent, to come between her and her mother. In the second half of the therapy, this affects her transference towards the therapist (me) who tries to rescue her from being her mother's prisoner, and we talk of her 'having no father to teach her how to live.'

Twentieth session: The patient, who used to be a 'heroine of tragedy,' arrives looking really refreshed. We decide to meet two months later to see how she is doing.

Twenty-first and final session: When she enters, I intuitively feel that she means this to be the last session. 'When I enjoy myself, I can take care of grandmother without overdoing it,' she says. When she adds that people tell her that she looks full of life, I reply 'You used to kill yourself but now you allow yourself to live, so of course you are full of life.' I think she was holding back tears, somewhat sad at the separation. This marked the end of about one year of depth-psychotherapy.

Clinical discussion

Such patients originally seek consultation for a variety of reasons. They may come to us with such complaints as insomnia, fatiguability, depressive mood, chronic psychosomatic symptoms, etc. Some may call us about their adolescent children who are delinquent, promiscuous, or just refuse to go to school. When we meet worried and depressed mothers, we easily imagine that their offspring are neurotic or borderline cases, who are trying desperately to escape from their guilt-inducing environment, or 'emptied' depressives, who cannot run away.

The present trend seems to be to treat those unhappy children, who are prisoners of the family, rather than their domineering caretakers, usually one or both parents. Yet, we sometimes have urgently to treat those caretakers since they may become so depressed and desperate that they may attempt suicide, and it is important for us to see the deep underlying depression or emptiness beneath the external adaptation even though they take good care of others and appear to be well.

Fortunately, some psychoanalysts have been trying to explore the psycho-pathology of masochistic-depressive caretakers from a number of angles, a pathology which was illustrated in the case described above and which I shall summarise:

1   Loss of a loved object: it is well-known that the traumatic deprivation of a love object plays an important role in the formation of the self-reproaching mechanism as the narcissistically introjected object becomes persecutory (Freud, 1917). Furthermore, masochistic self-devaluation can be 'a means of perpetuating whatever bond there is to the mother' (Menaker, 1953, p. 209).
2   Rage at failing to maintain omnipotent control over the people they look after.
3   Reversal of sadism or anger on to oneself and identification with the sadistic partner combine to produce a severe and intolerant superego.
4   Female masochism, possibly associated with feelings of inferiority and passive femininity (Deutsch, 1950).
5   Projection of one's own craving to be taken care of onto the object of care, thereby drawing altruistic satisfaction through identification.
6   Vulnerability: need to hide those narcissistic injuries and shameful emptiness to protect and maintain the 'good' external self in the face of imagined accusations from others (see Stolorow, 1975).

If, in addition to these internal mechanisms of the maternal caretaker, she is also vulnerable or fragile physically or environmentally, it becomes very difficult for her daughter (or son) to express her/his aggression directly because of easily induced guilt feelings, which may add to her/his own true guilt feelings. Although there is no generally accepted definition of true guilt, we can define it as the end-product of working-through the depressive position (as seen by Klein and Winnicott); that is to say, the guilt resulting from a gradual awareness of one's 'own' aggression and destructiveness. Yet, the human being normally has the capacity to mend some injuries she/he has inflicted, though not masochistically. If I may again use the digestive functions to metaphorise these experiences as an abrupt and sudden confrontation with a real injury can cause an indigestible experience that the child lacks the ability to easily put into words. The god in the Japanese myth said 'ugly and dirty' after his confrontation with the dying goddess. 'Forced guilt' is mostly induced when the child is blamed for the mother's injuries or hardships which he/she is too innocent to digest; true guilt can be defined as 'digested guilt.' We may then be able to understand that dirt or filth is sometimes seen as a marker of guilt as it symbolises something hard to swallow and retain. In Japan we have the word *kegare*, meaning filth and guilt, which refers to material guilt as a whole (Kitayama, 1988). Because of its materialistic character, we can force it on to each other like filth, which tends to be put in an ambiguous place which is neither within nor without, i.e. the guilt-in-between.

The infant may retain the guilt that was forced on to him/her and force it out onto somebody else, generally his/her own children. This would explain how 'forced guilt' is passed on from generation to generation. Unable to integrate the various elements of his/her personality, the vulnerable caretaker has turned his infantile destructiveness inward into masochism, while trying, in vain, to make reparation through altruistic behaviour. As the real injury in motherhood is the result of the relative interplay between the infant's destructiveness and the mother's vulnerability, we need the objective judgement of a third party in a triangular structure to decide where to lay the blame. This is seen as one of the classical functions of the father, who is needed to preside over the 'family court' to deal with the guilt-in-between and to become part of the holding environment for the mother–infant. The therapist's role is similar to that of the father in that he has to mediate between the aggressively demanding child and the vulnerable, masochistic caretaker that coexists in the patient or the real situation. But, as a therapist, he has to do more than that and help the patient digest his/her guilt and integrate the dichotomous aspects of his/her personality. Only then can he help break the vicious circle of false guilt being forced onto the next generation. I would like to close this discussion with a summary of the psychotherapeutic elements described in the case presented here in the hope that these may be clinically useful.

1   Analysis of the 'caretaker's transference' and its dramatisation in the treatment where the patient becomes the caretaker of the therapist.
2   The patient's feeling and expression of anger in relation to the therapist's possible failure to care for him/her.
3   The patient's dropping her role of caretaker in association with therapeutic regression in a holding environment where she can truly exist and rest.
4   Possible need for the therapist's environmental management of the people whom the patient takes care of and who are supposed to take care of the regressing patient.
5   Vomiting out the indigestible forced guilt and understanding its origin in the treatment.
6   Working-through of one's ambivalent feelings, learning to mend some of the injuries, and to be concerned about one's environment.
7   The patient's development towards positive triangular relationships.

These are surely oversimplified but the resolution of these various elements will lead to the gradual integration of the wounded caretaker's dichotomous personality.

Wounded healer

It is rather interesting that Guggenbühl-Craig (1981), a Jungian psychiatrist, explored the image of the wounded healer, the mythic theme hinted at by Meier (1986), to show how the healer–patient archetype comes into operation when someone becomes sick and meets a doctor. Again, Jesus Christ is referred to as the typical representation of the wounded healer as he was killed to save Man: it seems to me that he, at the same time, left us with the original sin to be digested. Samuels (1985), reviewing the Jungian literature, summarises the idea of an inner healer, saying that a fundamental process in the psychoanalyst may be described 'as activation of the inner healer of the patient which performs a healing function for him' (Samuels, 1985, p. 191). At the beginning of this process, there is a projection onto the doctor of the inner healer of the patient, while the wounds in the doctor 'facilitate empathy with the patient, but the danger is identification' (Samuels, 1985, p. 189). Therefore, we need to be aware of our own vulnerability and wounds.

The Jungian usage of the word 'archetype' testifies to the existence of a powerful shared image of the wounded caretaker which can nourish the helping professions. At the end of this contribution, to suggest the universality of this condition, I want to quote from the life of Florence Nightingale, the famous founder of modern nursing in England, although I have to expect some objections, particularly from her devoted followers. As readers may know, she got sick after her well-known work of self-devotion in the Crimean War and never recovered from her illness. She almost lived the last half of her 53-year life on a couch or in a wheelchair. In spite of her persistent physical complaints, no doctors around her seem to have said that she suffered from any organic disease and could ever succeed in persuading her to take complete rest.

She likened 'the critical advice which had been offered her by so many friends to the vision of a canary pecking at the body of her dead pet owl' (Cope, 1958, p. 36). In her letter to John Sutherland, her doctor friend who kept insisting that she should rest, she said: 'I am so busy that I have no time to die' (quoted by Cope, 1958, p. 37).

As her unconscious underlying motivation is not known enough, I definitely will not describe her as just masochistic in her work; she had many positive features such as 'her astonishing mind ... her penetration, infinite capacity for taking pains, persistence, iron will to work, scrupulous sense of fair play' (Woodham-Smith, 1950, p. 259). On the other hand, one author wrote: 'In private she indulged in bouts of self-depreciation, scorn of others, and guilt for her passion for fame and her destructive use of her allies' (Smith, 1982, p. 22). But the whole lifestyle of productive devotion towards external needs and inability to rest in spite of sickness, may make it possible for us to call her a 'wounded healer,' and the image of a sick nurse is so impressive and painful that people seem to have been moved deeply, even politically, by her self-injuring caregiving.

'If only she would rest: her family, her friend, the whole world in an international chorus implored her to rest' (Woodham-Smith, 1950, p. 261).

Recently, she has been referred to as 'Flossie' by some young nurses who seem to dismiss her as a relic (Christy, 1981, p. 123). This rejection of one of the most influential persons of the 19th century may be because her critics have to get out of the guilt-inducing control of the image of the wounded caretaker which is misleading.

It is my impression too that Nightingale needed nursing and care most of all. Although, because of confidentiality, I did not quote any actual treatment of medical personnel as patients, I think it would be fair to close this chapter by saying that the phenomenon is rather common in caretaking professions.

Note

1 Based on my paper originally published in the *International Review of Psycho-Analysis*, 18(2), 229–240 (1991).

References

Berliner, B. (1947). On some psychodynamics of masochism. *Psychoanalytic Quarterly*, 16, 459–471.

Blum, H. P. (1977). *Female Psychology Contemporary Psychoanalytic Views*. New York: International University Press.

Brenman, M. (1952). On teasing and being teased; and the problem of moral masochism. *Psychoanalytic Study of the Child*, 7, 264–285.

Brenner, C. (1959). The masochistic character: genesis and treatment. *Journal of the American Psychoanalytic Association*, 7, 197–226.

Christy, T. E. (1981). Can we learn from history? In J. C. McCloskey & H. K. Grace (Ed.) *Current Issues in Nursing* (pp. 122–128). Oxford: Blackwell Scientific Publications.

Cope, Z. (1958). *Florence Nightingale and the Doctors*. Philadelphia: Lippincott.

Deutsch, H. (1950). The significance of masochism in the mental life of women. In R. Fliess (Ed.) *The Psychoanalytic Reader* (pp. 195–207), London: Hogarth Press. (Original published 1930)

Fenichel, O. (1972). *The Psychoanalytic Theory of Neurosis*. New York: Norton. (Original published 1945)

Freud, A. (1968). *The Ego and the Mechanisms of Defence*. London: Hogarth Press. (Original published 1937)

Freud, S. (1917). Mourning and melancholia. In *Standard Edition*, Vol. 14. London: Hogarth Press.

Freud, S. (1919). 'A child is being beaten': a contribution to the study of the origin of sexual perversions. In *Standard Edition*, Vol. 17. London: Hogarth Press.

Freud, S. (1923). The ego and the id. In *Standard Edition*, Vol. 19. London: Hogarth Press.

Ganzarain, R. (1988). Various guilts within the Ajase complex. *Japanese Journal of Psychoanalysis*, 32, 93–102.

Guggenbühl-Craig, A. (1981). (K. Higuchi & S. Ankei, Trans.) *Power in the Helping Professions*. Osaka: Sōgensha. (Original published 1971)

Horney, K. (1973). The problem of feminine masochism. In J. B. Miller (Ed.), *Psychoanalysis and Women* (pp. 21–31). Harmondsworth: Penguin. (Original paper published 1935)

Kernberg, O. F. (1988). Clinical dimensions of masochism. In R. A. Glick & D. I. Meyers (Ed.), *Masochism – Current Psycho-Analytic Perspective* (pp. 61–79). Hillsdale: Analytic Press.

Kitayama, O. (1988). *Kokoro no Shōka to Haishutsu [In a Digestive Frame of Mind]*. Osaka: Sōgensha. (New annotated edition published 2018, Tokyo: Sakuhinsha)

Kitayama, O. (1989). Jigyakutekisewayaku nitsuite [A note on the masochistic caretaker]. *Japanese Journal of Psycho-Analysis*, 33, 93–101.

Kosawa, H. (2022). Two kinds of guilt feelings – the Ajase complex. *Journal of the Japan Psychoanalytic Society*, 4, 18–25. (Original published 1931 and reprinted in *Japanese Journal of Psychoanalysis*, 1 (1), 1954. Translation published in the *Japanese Contributions to Psychoanalysis*, Vol. 2, pp. 3–11, 2007)

Lampl, H. (1927). Contributions to case history – a case of borrowed sense of guilt. *International Journal of Psycho-Analysis*, 8, 143–158.

Loewenstein, R. (1957). A contribution to the psychoanalytic theory of masochism. *Journal of the American Psychoanalytic Association*, 5, 197–234.

Meier, C. (1986). (S. Akiyama. Trans.) *Ancient Incubation and Modern Psychotherapy*. Tokyo: Chikumashobō. (Original published 1949)

Menaker, E. (1953). Masochism – A defense reaction of the ego. *Psychoanalytic Quarterly*, 22, 205–220.

Okonogi, K. (1978). The Ajase complex of the Japanese (1) – The depth psychology of the moratorium people. *Japan Echo*, 5, 88–105.

Okonogi, K. (1979). The Ajase complex of the Japanese (2) – The depth psychology of the moratorium people. *Japan Echo*, 6, 104–118.

Parkin, A. (1980). On masochistic enthralment: a contribution to the study of moral masochism. *International Journal of Psycho-Analysis*, 61, 307–314.

Reich, W. (1966). (K. Okonogi, Trans.) *Character Analysis*. Tokyo: Iwasaki Gakujutsu Shuppansha. (Original published 1932)

Samuels, A. (1985). *Jung and the Post-Jungians*. London: Routledge & Kegan Paul.

Smith, F. B. (1982). *Florence Nightingale: reputation and power*. New York: St Martin's Press.

Stolorow, R. D. (1975). The narcissistic function of masochism (and sadism). *International Journal of Psycho-Analysis*, 56, 441–448.

Winnicott, D. W. (1958a). Reparation in respect of mother's organized defence against depression. In *Collected Papers: Through Paediatrics to Psycho-Analysis* (pp. 91–96). New York: Basic Books. (Original published 1948)

Winnicott, D. W. (1958b). The depressive position in normal development. In *Collected Papers: Through Paediatrics to Psycho-Analysis* (pp. 262–277). New York: Basic Books. (Original published 1954–1955)

Winnicott, D. W. (1971). *Playing and Reality*. London: Tavistock Publications.

Woodham-Smith, C. (1950). *Florence Nightingale*. London: Constable.

Chapter 5

Dependence and transience

Beauty or danger

Osamu Kitayama

Polytheism

For many years, Japan has had two scientific organisations concerned with psychoanalysis: the Japan Psychoanalytic Society (JPS) and the Japan Psychoanalytical Association (JPA). The JPS aims to practice psychoanalysis in compliance with the rules set forth by the IPA. With the JPA, on the other hand, the members often practice once-weekly psychotherapy and engage in different types of psychoanalytic or depth-psychological activities. Most Japanese psychoanalysts belong to both organisations. So psychoanalysis in Japan has many aspects, something which Okonogi (1990) described as being 'polytheistic.'

It is true that polytheism can be a defensive shield against a revelation of psychic reality among the people in a certain culture when we try to understand it, but we really have to appreciate it, and maybe even experience it, before analysing anything behind cultural differences. I became interested in studying Japanese folk tales, myths and old paintings as an enjoyable clue to examining how we describe our own fantasies and our past. Discussing the material, I will focus on the theme of the mother–child relationship above all in relation to the concept of transience and its masochistic connotation.

A Japanese anthropologist said: 'There are very few countries apart from Japan where the process of growth and developments of folktales can be traced so well' (Ishida, 1972, p. 145). This point of view has been generally supported by the simple impression that Japan, being an island country and therefore isolated, had naturally avoided the critical invasion of foreign cultures until the Second World War. If we assume that Japanese culture defensively resisted foreign influences, thereby retaining its homogeneity, there would be a possibility that man's primitive experience and fantasies may have been conveyed through generations with little variation. Thus, transience, I believe, is not only a feature of Japanese phenomena but also universal to some extent.

DOI: 10.4324/9781003501930-6

'Disasters strike when you least expect them'

In the setting of psychotherapy sessions in Japan, it is important to maintain the periodicity and regularity of circular time. Forty years ago (Kitayama, 1979), I wrote, 'A therapist must carefully comply with the regularity of circular time.' The most important factor in once-weekly psychotherapy, which is the most popular type in Japan, is 'the sense of rhythm' (Okada, 2017), which comes about from the regularity of the sessions. Maintaining it, however, is a challenge. For instance, natural disasters and abnormal weather events become irregular factors, in which the management of the sessions plays a crucially important role. Whether or not to cancel a psychotherapy session that has been held regularly until then, on a day with a typhoon, or heavy rain or snow, for example, and whether or not to charge a cancellation fee, carry an important meaning.

To cite my own domestic experience in relation to the concept of natural transience, it was in January 1995 that a big earthquake struck Kobe, the most beautiful port city in Japan. As a result, more than 5,000 people died and many historical buildings such as temples and shrines were destroyed. This disaster affected almost all of the Japanese people to varying degrees and naturally produced many associations in our patients in analytical therapy. It was a week after the earthquake that one of my male patients, who used to suffer from depression following a narcissistic injury, related to the enormous destruction and typically said to me: 'Everything that is born must die. Nothing remains unchanged. Things come and things go. So everything is transient, yet life is worth living.' I think that this 'insightful' sense of the impermanence of things is a very common reaction to an irreversible loss in the middle of the acute transition to a new beginning.

Therefore, it is not unusual for a psychotherapist with a private practice to worry about his or her patients making their way through typhoon weather while keeping an eye on the weather forecast. On the day of a major storm, a therapist may continue to wait endlessly for the arrival of his or her client whom he or she cannot contact, while, on the other hand, patients may finally manage to arrive at the office after spending half the day braving the storm. Here again, the psychology is to try to protect the 'regularity' that is precious, because this is a session held once a week. The anxiety that is mutually experienced is usually of an unexpected nature: a vision may suddenly appear, such as the psychotherapist thinking that the patient may be dead, or the patient fearing that he or she might be abandoned by the therapist.

The joy and the thrilling emotions felt when the two finally are able to meet in the midst of a storm also bring about new developments in the flow of the sessions. What frequently occurs is that Mother Nature enters my relationship with the patient with whom I meet only at a limited frequency, shakes up the situation, and, as a result, we exchange dialogue inside the therapy room, against the backdrop of an atypically violent nature. And, while perceiving the fear and anxiety of having something quiet and gentle suddenly and violently showing its fangs, or seeing a person one loves suddenly pass away, we metaphorically and symbolically discuss the duality and unpredictability of nature, as well as the transience of existence (Kitayama, 1998).

Japan is a country prone to natural disasters. It is often said that 'Disasters strike when you least expect them,' and I have discussed this danger of carelessness or unpredictability by quoting the prohibition of 'Don't Look.' As shown before, one Japanese myth contains a passage in which a male protagonist thoughtlessly looks at a forbidden object, becomes confused by the duality of the richness and vulnerability of Mother Nature, and finds himself unable to look squarely at the injured love object. This prohibition is a 'taboo to be broken in time.' The maternal deity represents our mothers and Mother Nature, so injury to her symbolically represents the destruction of nature. I interpret these tragedies as depicting the anxieties of the survivors who, despite depending on nature and becoming one with her, cannot give her full control.

A recent history of studies of Japanese mythology

Most of the Japanese people who were born before the Second World War have complicated feelings towards their own myths nowadays because the military government tried to force people to believe that our mythological stories were true stories. It is narrated in the *Kojiki*, the oldest official record of Japanese myths, that our emperor is the descendant of the gods and goddesses. If that myth were real, the Japanese emperor would be a living god. This belief was strongly administered by the government and shrines, so as to establish the absolute centrality and power of the emperor in religious and political systems of the Japanese society and mind, particularly in order to win the war.

The Japanese word *kami* means god or goddess in Japan. In order to encourage the people effectively to fight against the Allied Forces for the sake of *kami*, the fascist government involved almost all academic scholars and teachers in this compulsory education for the people, who were taught to believe that the emperor was a living *kami*. Around the same time it was said that divine winds, called *kamikaze* in Japanese, would destroy American battleships as in 1274 and 1281 when two *kamikaze* typhoons sank the Mongol invasion fleets. The Japanese word *kaze* means wind in English. Some may remember that Japanese aeroplane pilots called *kamikaze* attacked Allied ships in suicidal dives near the end of the war. *Kamikaze* fighters, who were believed to be flying on divine winds, were famous for their frightening way of sacrificing themselves for the sake of the nation and the emperor without caring about their own lives.

When Japan was defeated in August 1945 most of us suddenly became disillusioned with the omnipotent power of our own myth as well as the emperor. We then realised the negative power of the Japanese myth and therefore our parents felt that they should not read it or teach it to their children anymore. As I was born in 1946 immediately after the war, I was surrounded as a little child by their ambivalent feelings about our myth and other cultural traditions, which were often criticised together with the idea of the emperor. We were interested in and curious about the people's inconsistent and selfish way of dealing with myths, but most of us did not feel like reading them, mainly because those ideas of Japanese original culture appeared weak and unattractive to us. We liked the seemingly logical and rational way of thinking of the West rather than the apparently irrational logic of mythology. Hearing about what happened during the war, we could not understand logically that *kamikaze* pilots killed themselves for the sake of the nation, and I could not accept that Japan was famous for its self-destructive tendencies, including *harakiri*, a form of suicide in Japan, although I somehow could understand them emotionally and partly appreciate their idealised beauty of transience.

I encountered psychoanalysis, which was, and still is, struggling to integrate rational thoughts and irrational fantasies successfully. To me, studying psychoanalysis and thinking psychoanalytically was an attempt to integrate modern Japan with the old Japan, which appeared rather contradictory. That was one of the reasons why I was attracted to psychoanalysis, to find a way of dealing with the acute dichotomy. Then I decided to investigate Japanese myths, folk tales and old pictures, and I had some of my works on this subject published. Although now, few people in Japan read mythological works, I can enjoy reading them and discussing them for several reasons. First, I gain precious insights into human thinking, as our cultural heritage reflects people's mentality and vice versa. Second, the myths and pictures that we share have many clinical implications.

Transition and transience

As I mentioned in Chapter 1, I have studied a huge collection of *ukiyo-e*, or literally 'pictures of the floating world,' as material that illustrates the traditional lives of middle-class people in Japan.

Studying them, I have noticed the frequent appearance of a mother and child viewing the same objects, such as a moon, a goldfish, a boat floating on the water, and a fireworks festival (see Figure 5.1). I named the figure of two people looking at the same object as 'viewing together' and found that more than one-third of the mothers and children in these pictures shared such relationships. This ratio is quite high in comparison with Western pictures, as the tentative result of my incomplete study of artistic pictures in the West is that the percentage of the appearance of 'viewing together' is about 5%.

I would like to summarise a few characteristics of 'viewing together' and the objects that the mother and the child view together in those *ukiyo-e* pictures.

(1) Side-by-side: the two people viewing the object are usually side-by-side, with their shoulders abreast, sometimes hand-in-hand.

Figure 5.1 *Ryōgoku Hanabino Zu [Firework Show at Ryōgoku]* (1880) by Kiyochika Kobayashi. Source: Tokyo Metropolitan Library, Tokyo.

(2) Joint attentive position: scholars who study this in terms of 'joint attention' (Bruner, 1975) from the point of view of developmental psychology have found that the acquisition and usage of symbols are promoted through this cultural sharing. In other words, in these positions mothers and children speak and contemplate together, forming a proto-symbolic triangle, a pre-oedipal triangle, composed of a mother, a child and a shared object. There are father figures too for boys but mainly mother figures to join them as the father is supposed to be stabilising the situation, not intruding. This position is very popular in Japanese art like this couple viewing the moon together (see Figure 5.2).

(3) Transience: these objects do not only connect the two sides but also put a distance between them. The distance looks as if it is gradually widening. Furthermore, objects often appear that can be described as 'floating away' or 'transient.' Examples are a swaying toy fish, a hazy moon, a face reflected on the water, soap bubbles and a snow rabbit. Fireflies (see Figure 5.3) lighting and delighting will die soon. Cherry blossoms (see Figure 5.4) will fly away soon. A paper windmill will soon stop turning. A swaying toy fish (see Figure 1.3) will also stop in a moment. A snow rabbit will melt and bubbles will vanish. This process is not only fort/da, but also da/fort, that is presence/absence. You may have been reminded of Winnicott's discussion of transitional objects. He wrote: 'Its fate is to be gradually allowed to be decathected, so that in the course of

Figure 5.2 Tsuki wo Miru Boshi [Mother and Child viewing the Moon] (1801) by Hokusai
Katsushika.
Source: ColBase – https://colbase.nich.go.jp/.

years it becomes not so much forgotten as relegated to limbo … It is not forgotten and it is not mourned. It loses meaning …' (Winnicott, 1975/1953, p.
233). He, I think, was describing feelings of transience as well as transitional
movement, but Western writers including Winnicott may have difficulty in differentiating them, particularly when they use similar words.

What I refer to here as 'transition' and 'transience' are different concepts in
everyday language in Japan, since *hakanai* (adj.) or *hakanasa* (n.), which we
usually consider to be equivalent to 'transient' or 'transience' means not only
transition but also emotions and sentiment relating to 'mutuality; transiency;
evanescence; emptiness; frailty' (*New Japanese English Dictionary*, 3rd ed., Katsumata, 1954, p. 371), while *ikō* means 'transition.' We have another Japanese
word *mujō*, referring to 'impermanence, transience, and mutability,' which is

> Originally a Buddhist term expressing the doctrine that everything that is
> born must die and that nothing remains unchanged. Japanese have tra-
> ditionally been keenly aware of the impermanence of things, and the
> sense of *mujō* has been a major theme in literature.
> (Kōdansha International, 1995, p. 276)

Figure 5.3 Hotaru Gari [Catching Fireflies] (ca. 1793) by Chōki Eishōsai.
Source: The Metropolitan Museum of Art, New York.

More specially, the cherry blossom season is short and the petals fall after about a week. This transience of life expressing *mujō* in the material world is even celebrated and cherished.

If I may simplify matters, the transitional object is transitional in space and transient in time. Writing this chapter, I want to differentiate them clearly, for transition is a phenomenological description of movement while transience is mainly an emotional state, although they usually go together. I think that if it is mourned, the transitional object becomes emotionally transient rather than just transitional. In my opinion, a transition can be just joyful but it is often accompanied by a sense of transience or transiency that is more or less a painful sentiment, sometimes even involving an artistic sense of beauty as well as senses of sadness, emptiness and depression.

Owned by Kumon Institute of Education

Figure 5.4 Hanami [Cherry Blossom Viewing] (1818–1844) by Eisen Keisai.
Source: Kumon Institute of Education, Tokyo.

Transient figures

Furthermore, these prints are not realistic reflections of objective relationships but are associated with imaginations and fantasies. I think that *ukiyo-e* artists were trying to illustrate the experience of transience, maybe so as to remind us of how these experiences softened the nature of the transition from our intimate relationships, by representing the floating objects as symbolic experiences with the object to be missed. Children and mothers in *ukiyo-e* look happy, excited and safe, maybe in an idealised way, but we know the potentially pathological consequences of traumatic disillusionment or sudden confrontation with critical discontinuities.

When we clinically handle a weak, fragile ego, it is important to 'create a cover.' It is also important for a depth-psychotherapist to not invade or violate, and similarly to not force a patient to see what he or she cannot see. I have understood this 'cover' to correspond, in psychoanalysis, to a 'wall of repression'; according to developmental theory, a capacity to 'cover' or 'retain' oneself is established between the pre-oedipal stage when an individual is dependent on the mother, and the oedipal stage when he or she heads toward independence, with a 'dividing line' (Abraham, 1973) found in the boundary between the two.

This is why we feel that, in situations where internal content is being leaked and exposed, a 'wall of defence' must be fortified. In Japanese, 'things that are beyond description,' and 'things that are ugly (*minikui*, a Japanese term meaning "ugly," also means "hard to see")' which come to be exposed as the protective wall breaks, should be experienced altogether, along with the 'ugly' mix-up causing mental nausea or 'unfathomable' disgust. Let us use these perspectives to simplify the differences between depth-psychotherapy and psychoanalysis performed in Japan. To generalise my and other scholars' thoughts, 'once-a-week' sessions leave many things to 'the course of nature,' and do not actively break the prohibition of 'Don't Look.' A dependable sense of circular time carries an important meaning here, and its natural periodicity or 'ebb and flow' may function either to regulate regression or to support the ego. The natural forces of Japan, including heat and cold, day and night, and the four seasons, are richly represented here. Something unpredictable, however, must take place in the course of nature as pointed out by M. Muraoka (2017) in her works on the psychotherapeutic turning points.

Psychoanalysis sessions, on the other hand, are held frequently, more than once a week. This means that, in the event of natural disasters and other incidents, the parties do not have to push themselves to keep to the agreed schedule. Sessions can be relatively easily cancelled if emergency situations arise. If the parties wait for time to pass, then, in the course of time, their relationship immediately – or if they spend as many as a few years – becomes a world reserved just for the two of them. The prohibition of 'Don't Look' comes to be broken 'in the course of time,' and the world of the unconscious comes into the picture, and, behind the scenes are, according to Freud's metaphors, 'foreign territory' (Freud, 1933), that is the unconscious that cannot be thought of easily.

Case 1: 'Ms Wall'

Here, I would like to describe a case of a once-weekly patient. The patient's family name was Kabe (pronounced ka-bé), which literally means a 'wall' in Japanese. Ms Kabe was aged 34 on initial examination. She repeatedly over-ate, then vomited; she had a slender figure, was narcissistic, and unmarried. Her therapy continued for 20 years, mostly with once-weekly sessions, from start to finish. Her father, who was strict with her, had passed away several years previously. She took care of her mother, and, saying that she could not depend on her mother, she operated a store, so she could only manage to come to my office late at night on a weekday, once a week.

Her complaints other than over-eating and vomiting (bulimia) were her low self-esteem and chronic lack of confidence. She was a lonesome type and generally did not do well in relationships with other people. She did not get along well with her store staff. Another problem was that she was almost delusively and compulsively concerned about her looks, her build, and age spots on her face, which she hated, blaming herself for them.

Her complaints other than bulimia remained mostly unchanged. Not depending on other people, she was cut off from the experiences and feelings associated with losing objects and people. There were, however, things that slowly began to change. A leading example was the issue of value. In the beginning, she regarded therapy as 'worthless and having no value.' She wanted to quit treatment immediately and suspended it twice during the first half of the entire treatment period. After several months, however, the patient returned to my office, saying that there was nowhere else for her to go.

I had sensed that something was slowly and quietly changing and felt that the matter-of-fact pace of treatment, held just once a week, suited the patient who insisted that she did not want to depend on other people. There were incidents that sometimes made me feel like shaking this hard and stubborn patient. Still, it appeared that I was just responding to her single-minded devotion, to coming to therapy with sincerity. This pattern was repeated rhythmically; then, after about ten years had elapsed, the patient began to verbally acknowledge the value of this therapy, although faintly, saying, 'This is the only place where I can talk about these things.' Around the 13th year, I felt as if her dependence was now being directed at me, so I shifted from the face-to-face therapy method to the once-weekly free association method, using the couch.

However, changes in our relationship that were not visible to the eye were not a major deal for her, at least on the conscious level. As something that was absolutely unchangeable, her method of over-eating and vomiting was superbly controlled. In other words, her eating and vomiting had stayed within a set scope, with her weight and slender figure remaining unchanged. Every night, she continued her ritualistic act of over-eating, vomiting into the toilet, and flushing down the vomit, which was carefully kept within limits. She listened to my interpretations, such as 'You want to depend on your father and on me (the therapist) and be pampered (i.e. *amae*),' and 'You are thinking about what would happen if your mother passed away,' but seemed to forget them during the course of the week between sessions. I felt that words were useless and that they would not seep into her.

There was a 'wall' that remained, hard and stiff, even if I had scratched it or beaten myself against it. Within the steady rhythm of our once-weekly sessions, which came around each week, the space inside the therapy room also resembled a world in which time had stopped. Once, she became distressed about a conflict with her neighbour over a boundary line; other times, a weasel had sneaked into her attic and caused a commotion. In the end, however, these incursions past her boundary line were blocked by her strongly defensive actions. I, too, felt like a weasel that had been exterminated.

Soon, moments began to accumulate during which the patient felt that no visible results could be obtained and that no changes were occurring despite talking about everything. A sense that the sessions were being uselessly repeated began to occur in her as well. She, too, hit a 'wall,' and began talking once again about how the therapy had been a waste of time, despite having come to treatment for as many as 15 years. At the same time, her body and the passing of time, i.e. 'ebb and flow,' began to assert themselves. Until now, she had maintained a youthful figure by controlling her eating and vomiting. After reaching middle age, however, she was slowly getting out of shape due to the forces of nature, which was something even I began to notice.

At the same time, she said that, now that she had reached her 50s, there was nothing good in her life, so only dying was left. In other words, she began to realise the fact that life was finite. I felt that, together with the circular time that was being repeated, the experience in which this circular time was mixed together with irreversible linear time, was truly a breakthrough. In looking back, these were signs that her sense of omnipotence started crumbling.

It was around this time that a major earthquake and tsunami struck Japan, mostly in the northeastern part of the country. The scenes of the tsunami hitting the coastline, which she had watched from afar on television, had a major impact on her. If I were to reassemble her experiences, which she had described in fragments, I believe that this major earthquake disaster became for her a horrific scene that represented the destruction of her boundary which, until then, had remained rock-solid and unperturbed.

In her description of this event, made in an unsettling atmosphere, she reported witnessing scenes of houses being swept away by the waves, and people and objects being engulfed in water; her mind overlapped them with the fact that she was eating, vomiting, and flushing the vomit down the toilet. Even after this, I, too, recalled the same images several times, with the scenes I had just watched on TV being overlapped with numerous images of the patient vomiting into the toilet bowl and flushing down the vomit, as well as throwing my own understandings and interpretations into the toilet, while still alive.

I felt that, once the earth and the people's minds become filled to the verge of overflowing, they forcibly eject what has piled up inside. Although I hesitate to report this comparison to you, the dreadful scenes of the *tsunami* overlapped inside my dark therapy room, and, in my imagination, everything – people, houses, dogs, and even pastries – got mixed up, still living and functioning well, and were swept away by the waves.

The patient then began saying that she had to separate the earthquake disaster from her personal problems, and learned that the things that she was distressed about were 'trivial matters.' In terms of her actions and behaviours, her daily bulimia disappeared, except for a single episode. However, her recognition that the age spots on her face were a trivial matter lasted only for several weeks. Her feeling of emptiness did not change, even with the elapse of time; even though her symptoms disappeared, her self-esteem remained at a low level.

My words stopped reaching her again; our conversations became like something thrown into the water. The sessions continued merely to 'eat the words, vomit them up, and flush them away.' I felt that, even though her actual act of eating and vomiting disappeared, nothing had changed. So, approximately one year after the major earthquake, we began discussing the possibility of discontinuing treatment. It was then that something that may be referred to as 'synchronicity' (an important Jungian concept) occurred once again: her mother suffered a fracture and was hospitalised; she developed pneumonia as a complication and hovered between life and death.

The patient was deeply shaken, and her mind started hovering. At the same time, moving forward from her understanding, which I had mentioned just now, that her symptoms were 'trivial,' she began talking, this time, with a sigh and a sense of helplessness, about 'What things are important?'

I took up the word '*arigatai*,' a Japanese term that carries both a realistic understanding of 'the improbability of actual existence,' and the psychological meaning of 'thankfulness.' This term became the keyword for her treatment. She then finally admitted her sense of dependence: that she and I could not separate right away. She regarded a member of her staff, whom she used to look down on, as an ordinary, straightforward person, and began uncomplicatedly feeling her dependence on other people, and now felt thankful for being looked after and protected by the people around her.

She was ashamed of the destructive associations that overlapped her eating–vomiting with the scenes of the *tsunami* and did not mention them again. I believe, however, that she turned her attention to the fact that she had flushed down many things through eating and vomiting, and saw the results of her own unexplainable destructions. The 'nauseating' scenes, mixed up with her own vomit and the huge *tsunami* that was surging ever nearer, progressed in slow motion. It was a scene beyond anybody's imagination, not seen anywhere in real life, either in fiction or in news.

We sat side by side on a couch – on 'high ground,' so to speak – and witnessed the scene, 'slowly,' numerous times, without saying a word. I felt, at a later date, that what had disappeared into the water was Izanagi's beloved Izanami, whom he had abandoned.

The impact brought about by the earthquake disaster made us tremble with fear. Prior to this, however, she, too, was experiencing the 'wall,' which she had protected strongly until then, beginning to collapse spontaneously. Together with the passage of nature, inner nature synchronised with outer nature, bringing about the recognition that it is a tragedy to end one's life without gaining anything, and that being alive was '*arigatai*,' or something that was in itself improbable and which she must be thankful for. I stood beside her and supported her ego in acquiring the difficult-to-gain recognition that all things in life are transient.

The treatment terminated two years after this earthquake. The patient, who has mellowed compared to before, made up her mind at one time but oscillated until the planned termination date. After a series of hesitations and indecisive moments, she decided to 'try quitting' for now, also to gain confidence. I felt that, in many ways, this was a sort of a 'natural cure' that had followed 'the course of nature.' The patient has not contacted me since then.

'Holding the situation in time'

We all know that the depth of psychoanalytic work does not follow the formula of Work = Power × Time. However, I was able to treat unexpected developments analytically through my prior depth-psychological understanding of my own culture or 'Japaneseness' that helped me to anticipate and prepare for the deep work to happen despite our once-a-week sessions. Generally speaking, the Japanese experience of *kawaii* (cute) or *kakkoii* (smart) is often accompanied by a 'fear of filth' just as formlessness and ugliness are associated with decomposition or deformity, which was described in the Japanese myth (Figure 2.4). There is a tendency to emphasise purification and cleansing in awe of unfathomable impurity, that is *kegare*, which means sinful dirtiness in Japanese culture. Therefore, I think that the clinical process of losing form in 'earthy' formlessness or disintegration is often a case of passing through, or drowning in, an ugly – *minikui* = difficult to see – world full of deformed substances. The consequences would also be to encounter 'transience' or 'emptiness.' So, in analytic practice this 'impure experience' is going through the impure (excluded from the pure) that also plays an important role.

Although we may find the clinical ideas of 'unintegration' and 'formlessness' for the ugly or unfathomable experiences in Winnicott's writings, I would like to stress earthy textuality in these transformative experiences. Furthermore, I remember that Winnicott (1975/1954–1955), in his paper on the 'depressive position,' emphasised 'holding the situation in time.' Continuously holding things is a maternal function; on the other hand, there is an irrevocable cutting of continuous time which, I feel, is paternal in nature. Therefore, it can be said that the patient had lived in a 'depressive position' with Mother Nature, who regularly brings about blessings as well as with 'Father Time,' who suddenly severs his 'connections' with her, and that she started living her life, living an Oedipus complex.

We can make several interpretations from a developmental point of view, as the psychopathology of the heroes in those tragic tales reflects 'Sudden transition from the pleasure principle to the reality principle' (Freud); illusion to disillusionment (Winnicott); the paranoid-schizoid position to the depressive position (Klein) (Kitayama, 1985, p. 184). Having mentioned analytical interpretations of the prohibition of 'Don't Look' and its tragic consequences, I must stress the historical fact that it was not unusual in the old days for the mother to be seriously injured, very sick, or even die at the time of delivery, so the legend of the injured or dying mother reflects the external reality of ancient times.

The readers identifying with the male protagonist may feel endlessly indebted to nature, as he never has the chance to repay his debt to the wounded crane wife who flies away in the end. The term 'debt,' I think, is more useful as it explains the mechanism of endless repaying accompanied by masochistic identification. By breaking the prohibition, the hero undergoes irreversible disillusionment with the omnipotent fantasy. This prohibition is expected to operate as a defensive signal against the tragic separation. This is, however, such a fragile form of taboo that the hero cannot help breaking it in time. These tragedies can reflect the danger in the development of infants, particularly at the time when they undergo the painful disillusionment from the wish-fulfilling fantasy with the mother and then experience ambivalence towards her. I believe this needs to occur very gradually and at an appropriate stage. If the relationship is too prohibitory and the disillusionment is sudden, the consequences are disastrous.

I have therefore concluded that the unacceptable animal, as an original appearance of the mother figure, appears to represent the psychic pain or trauma resulting from a maternal failure in the disillusioning process as well as an insufficient capacity to perceive and introject the mother as a whole object. I wrote,

> Japanese folk tales, differing from Western fairy tales which end happily, reveal a tragic failure in the integrative process; they keep only a good part or a good product, casting away its animalised producers, some of them having been injured.
>
> (Kitayama, 1985, p. 180)

I have also suggested that the 'animalisation' involved in symbol-formation in folk tales is derived from a kind of dissimilation as a primitive defence mechanism. My interpretation may be related to Freeman's idea of the contribution of a prolongation of the pre-oedipal and early oedipal stages to mythopoeic creativity (Freeman, 1981).

Identification with the injured object

The unavoidable confrontation with the injured or dead mother can be so traumatic that the person who sees this immaturely may become a devoted caretaker to compensate for the limitless sense of debt for the mother's devotion. From my clinical experiences in Japan, I can say that most of the neurotic patients, for whom I have to handle intense shame and debt, are often socially well-adapted and sometimes very successful. They work very hard in spite of the hidden self-destructive problems such as serious suicidal attempts. In psychiatry, those people I call 'masochistic caretakers' are given a variety of diagnoses, such as depression, paranoia, masochistic personality disorder, and so on. In neurosis, the private self and the part that wants to be taken care of seem hidden; however, by finding a safe place of its own in a consistent relationship with an analytic therapist, this true self often drops its adaptation of remaining private and hidden and emerges little by little. We then may find that the patient has been suffering from a serious sense of debt and obligation for debt repayment as a consequence of traumatic confrontation with the fragility of the 'good' mother. When analysing this conflict, which may find expression in the patient's transference and repeated acting out through masochistic or suicidal behaviour, we may discover a conscious or unconscious pathological accumulation of debt or guilt towards the benevolent mother with whom the patient usually identifies.

As the real injury in motherhood is the result of the relative interplay between the infant's destructiveness and the mother's vulnerability, we need the objective judgement of a third party in a triangular structure to decide where to apportion responsibility. The analytic therapist's role is similar to that of the father in that he has to mediate between the aggressively demanding child and the vulnerable, masochistic caretaker who is in conflict in the mind of the patient.

Case 2: empty or chaotic?

Face-to-face psychotherapy is more common in Japan because of the low frequency of the sessions, usually once a week, and because most patients are severe cases. The second case, a woman working as a secretary, was 30 at the time of the initial consultation. Our relationship lasted eight years until 20 years ago when she discontinued her therapy.

In the beginning, showing hardly any resistance, she easily gave me her medical and life histories. She had long been suicidal and had attempted suicide several times but she had no history of psychiatric consultation. Although she had been asked to marry, she had been replaced by another woman, and as that wedding drew near she had to have a hysterectomy because of a malignant tumour. On top of all this, while she was in the hospital, a cat that she saw as an avatar of herself had died through her mother's carelessness, and she began to complain of insomnia. She also had occasional visual and auditory hallucinations of which she did not complain.

While hospitalised in gynaecology, she was referred to the psychiatric outpatient clinic, where we met. What was most impressive about her was her very humble attitude that made everybody comfortable, and the smiles that she had for just about everybody. She said that she was just faint from lack of sleep and that she had pains all over, but never did she let any pain show on her face. She also showed strong paranoid anxiety and was convinced that the drugs she was given were placebos as our relationship began with my medication. She got worried about what was on the other side of the curtain of the consultation room, suddenly stood up and opened everything. She absolutely refused to be hospitalised, and therefore I offered to see her at my office in private practice so as to; talk more quietly. She accepted with a smile.

A few months had passed when I found out that she always carried a knife around: she intended to commit suicide if and when she had to be taken care of by others and caused any trouble to them. Before long, her condition worsened: she swallowed a large dose of sleeping pills and was admitted to a psychiatric hospital. But she 'played the role of a well-behaved prisoner' for a while and left on the grounds that she just could not share the lavatory or the public bath with other patients. At about that time, while observing this woman who would not lean on anyone, the image that came to my mind could be expressed by 'do not live with the shame of a prisoner.' This sort of expression used to be very popular among Japanese soldiers and *samurai* who were supposed to kill themselves when they were deeply humiliated. Promising, at least in words, that she would not die, she began to come to my clinic again, and saying, laughingly, 'Well, I could die any time,' she went back to work to make a living.

Because of the severe nature of the patient's psychopathology, the treatment branched out into many directions, particularly during the first two years of the therapy, during which her management involved all sorts of things: medication, physical tests, communication with the department of gynaecology, her admission to and release from a psychiatric hospital, interviews with her family, etc.

She said that she did not want to be understood, to be seen through, to depend on anyone. Moreover, she expressed her dissatisfaction with me, saying 'I have told you so much and I am not getting any better. You are not doing anything for me.' Also, our conversations were superficial, and the interpretations that I sometimes presented were made rather ineffectual. She was very defensive and kept saying 'Doctor, you only say things I already know,' or 'I wish you wouldn't humiliate me by pretending to understand.' At such times, I had the feeling that she shallowly skimmed over the meanings of the words in my interpretations.

On the other hand, her social adaptation was astonishing: she was smiling, talkative, looked really healthy and could work as a talented secretary. I could describe her as masochistic but she was too ashamed of this pathological side to reveal it to me. Her self-injuring habits such as tearing off her fingernails became clear only later. She often felt itchy and scratched herself until she was bleeding all over, but she hid this until she began to feel a little safer with me – almost three years later. She also had a fear of melting when she took a bath, which was also well hidden and could only be glimpsed. I understood that she was ashamed of her psychosis too and felt that there was no substantial content, completely emptied or chaotic, hidden behind her mask of shame.

For all these reasons, I concluded this was not an interpretive therapy in which unconscious fantasies are analysed and dealt with mainly verbally. The main focus was on supportive management with psychoanalytic understanding not on uncovering material. The treatment with her continued for about six years. In the middle phase of treatment, I pointed out that she was like the 'crane wife' who tried not to disturb others, hiding her injured self. She accepted this completely, but she did not want to change her masochistic way of life.

In particular, to show you her transference and my countertransference, I want to pick up just one episode from the middle part of her long therapy in which she started settling down into the therapy very gradually. She then became openly aggressive to some extent towards me, and for several months she threw such words as 'goof,' 'stupid,' and 'incompetent' at the therapist who was 'unsuccessful' according to her. Yet, at the same time, her aggressiveness did not turn into suicidal behaviour, and as long as it was verbalised or played out, the therapist felt he did not have to worry. She seemed to come to lash out at the therapist, to test him, and she seemed to enjoy it when the therapist failed as a 'caretaker.' I thought that she was regressing.

One day, three years after first seeing her, she was sitting in my chair when I walked in. Having lost my chair, I was a little amused and felt that she had taken over the job from me and would take care of me, and for the time being I quietly sat on the bed of the consultation room. It was a beautiful day and the afternoon sun was gently coming in. I then got irritated at having lost my chair, because of the anger that I had been tolerating for a long time, sometimes masochistically. Unexpectedly, I became sleepy, having the feeling that I had been freed of my role of caretaker, being taken care of by her. Then she said: 'This is your chair, isn't it? When I sit here, it is as if you are holding me in your arms.' Remembering something she had told me, I was not sleepy anymore and interpreted that she had taken back the place that had been taken away from her when her little brother was born.

Her 'sitting in the therapist's chair to rest' went on for about five sessions. She had told me earlier that her brother was three years younger than her and that she had never liked him. She probably felt that she had been thrown out of her mother's arms at her brother's birth, just like the poor cat that had died. Moreover, she told me later that her mother had put mustard on her nipples to wean her. So we can imagine how she as a baby was humiliated deeply by the damaged breast, which she had to introject, identifying herself with it.

There is another story to tell you. I had a Benjamin tree in my consultation room. Seen from a distance it looked like one tree, but actually there were two trees entwined together. Looking at it, she said: 'Is this two trees? They are twisted together, very much like me.' And then one day, she bought one Benjamin to keep at her home.

One year later, she wrote me a letter after a consultation during which she said she was surprised she hadn't killed anybody. In the letter, she wrote 'As I don't water the Benjamin tree, I see it lose its leaves one by one and die in front of me.' I now think that the 'umbilical cord,' or the emotional tie, which is expressed symbolically as the two intertwined trunks of the Benjamin tree was broken by her. She repeatedly showed this symbolism of her ties being broken. For instance, she came to my clinic wearing a half navy blue and half red sweater vertically split by colours. I associated this with a cross-section of an umbilical tie of blood with the mother as I will discuss in later chapters.

When, in the seventh year of the treatment, she became able to sleep sometimes without much medication and got better symptomatically, I felt like introducing her into analytic therapy with deeper work and more frequency and stopping pharmacotherapy. But she refused it and decided to discontinue the treatment because she was, I felt, still ashamed of her injured self and psychotic part, and her need for dependency. She again cut the tie abruptly and did not allow me to get in touch with her internal chaos and confusion.

Transference and shame

Some patients become frightened of therapists because of the exposing nature of analytic therapy, and they put up a prohibition of 'Don't Look,' which may make treatment almost impossible. The shame anxiety, however, may not become real as long as their shameful inner experiences are respected. In other words, shame anxiety is not only a manifestation of fear of rejection but is also accompanied by a strong wish for acceptance and love. As I see it, a depth psychotherapist should not try to penetrate the strong shame resistance or persuade such a patient to reveal secrets. If he or she does so, the patient will disappear just like the heroine in the folk tales.

Almost none of the Japanese gods or goddesses, i.e. *kami*, used to accept the revelations of bodily disorders. However, *Ubugami* (the guardian god of childbirth) is willing to come into an isolated place for parturition, in spite of people's fear or disgust, to protect a mother and her newborn baby. A therapist in Japan is generally expected not to get disgusted and embarrassed by the revelation of a patient's secret inside and is sometimes idealised like *Ubugami* for the defence against the anxiety of disclosure and humiliation. Therefore, before touching upon their secret contents, we should handle, in a course of therapy, the shame complex, which is composed of the expectation of acceptance, fear of intrusion and rejection, the anal impulse of retention and dirtying, which may be projected on to the therapist etc. To do this we have to know about the nature of their fantasy concerning the therapist's receptivity towards the patient's disclosure, which can be painful. Analysis of transference will reveal that a patient is shamed because he or she has been shamed by the love object internally or externally.

Both of the cases that I have quoted were socially adapted and successful. They worked very hard in spite of the serious self-destructive problems. In the second case, from the beginning I noticed her psychotic fear and thought that there would be serious emptiness or psychotic confusion behind the apparently superficial adaptation. In other words, there was no substantial content behind her mask of shame. I still think that she would have fallen apart if we had taken away her masochistic caretaker persona from her. You might imagine that there was a true self behind her smile and shame but this could be just imaginary. She could not rest for fear of going to pieces if she slept. As I found her to be ashamed of her own psychosis too, the immediate objective for us in therapy had to be to find her a place where she could rest. I thought at the end of the therapy she had somehow found her own hiding place again. If shame anxiety is a product of the defensive functioning of a non-psychotic part, it may serve as a protective shield for the psychotic part in the same personality.

At times I interpreted her murderous fury towards the mother mainly in terms of oral sadism, referring to her suicidal behaviour and sadistic acting out. I also pointed out her playing out of the fantasy of identification with the dead or damaged mother for whom she had felt responsible and guilty, while she treated my words in a rather sadistic manner with her 'cool' smile. You can see the therapist becoming partially involved with the masochistic identification with the seriously damaged patient. Identifying her masochism with an idealised way of life in Japan, I myself as a doctor felt responsible for her damage, and now I think that I was unconsciously ashamed of my 'forced' failure. I now admit that my own feelings of shame as well as anger made me sleepy and produced a limit in my analytic capacity, although I think that the therapist succeeded in the supportive psychotherapy for her latent psychosis, while surviving her destructiveness and holding the situation. Surely, she was then confronted by her own dependency need while I carried out the infant role, one of the inhabitants of her mind, in her transitional theatre of the mind (McDougall, 1986).

Usually with neurotic problems, it was necessary to wait for her patient's omnipotent wish to be fused with the mother, and her attempt at mitigating the superego that prohibits this. But even in this neurotic case, the patient needed a long-term process of finding a chance to reveal herself and to talk about her private contents.

Emotional transience

As for Japanese legends, there are some versions with happy endings, too, although I have been focusing on the tragedies of a primal type because of our clinical interest in their tragic process. *The Snake Wife* loses her two eyeballs, which secrete milk to feed her baby. In the tale of *The Crane Wife*, the hero demands cloth from her twice without knowing he is damaging her body. She is sometimes illustrated as pecking at her own feathers from her chest to weave cloth. Although the secret is usually hidden from readers too, in the pictures (see Figures 2.1 and 2.2) taken from children's books, she is weaving cloth, figuratively giving birth to baby cranes between her wings. Furthermore, she may be angry because of narcissistic 'injury,' being intruded and shamed, just like Izanami, who got angry when the prohibition was broken in the myth. But she, a crane wife, is too ashamed passively to express it. These tales show us how difficult it is for us to see a wounded mother figure whose injuries are caused by the mother's inexhaustible devotion. So, I conclude that the secret hidden by the prohibition of 'Don't Look' is the fact that our goddesses have been dead because of our abuse over a long period of time. I hope that this discovery leads to the experience of 'give up' and 'let it go,' accompanied by a sense of guilt and gratitude and, maybe after a transitory pause, to a transition to a new beginning.

The Japanese word *arigatou*, which is almost equivalent to 'thank you' in English, literally means 'difficult to exist,' so it is extremely important to appreciate the transience of things. In Japan there is a concept of *mono no aware*, which is a literary and aesthetic ideal in Japan and which, at its core, refers to 'a deep, empathetic appreciation of the ephemeral beauty manifest in nature and human life, and it is therefore usually tinged with a hint of sadness; under certain circumstances it can be accompanied by admiration, awe, or even joy' (Reischauer et al., 1993, p. 1002).

It is said that most of the works in Western art have been produced to achieve eternal value because of the fear of transience, but I have found some pictures in Western art that do contain transience in their themes. However, it seems to me that the sense of transience described by Western people is being experienced individually. Even Freud could not accept a poet's emotional appeal concerning 'transience' in his well-known essay 'On transience.' He wrote, 'I did dispute the pessimistic poet's view that the transience of what is beautiful involves any loss in its worth. On the contrary, an increase!' (Freud, 1916, p. 305).

I understand why Freud did not accept the concept of emotional transience. Probably he perceived the seductive call of the dead and understood the danger of poetic sentimentality that he might have appreciated. On the other hand, I believe the sense of transience is consensually validated in Japanese culture. The *ukiyo-e* pictures also show how the sophisticated sense of transience develops into our cultural entertainment. In everyday life, the concept is symbolised by cultural objects, such as cherry blossoms, which are often associated with the two-way transition between life and mortality, or between this world and the other world.

Before we end this section, I want to touch briefly upon the transience of sexuality described in those *ukiyo-e* pictures. You may have noticed that some of the pictures are pornographic, and you may have felt that the interactions between the main characters in tales are sexual in spite of the overall desexualisation of children. The positive sense of transience is vital in determining adult sexual activities too, for many sexual experiences are transitory if we include the whole process from start to finish of anything sexual. With the help of *ukiyo-e* artists, and, of course, with the knowledge of psychoanalysis too, we can understand that a mother-infant relationship and an adult interaction become interchangeable as an artistic motif because of the common nature of sensuality, although I have concluded that the neutral (neither idealised nor pessimistic) sense of transience should be a result of maturation as it naturally develops in time.

Ebb and flow

Why is once-a-week treatment the most common type in Japan? In a word, it may be because the dependence-inducing settings, which psychoanalysis provides, put us in a dilemma. Moreover, we tend to regard things that are natural and spontaneous as the best, and feel that, just like the tea ceremony, flower arrangement, and English conversation lessons, a once-a-week session is most natural for us. We do not prefer unnaturally frequent encounters. However, even though we may want many things to take their own, natural course, and live our lives naturally and spontaneously, we cannot live entirely in this way. Like this patient, we try to erect a 'wall' by constructing a levee against nature, and we may resist the unstoppable 'ebb and flow.' Still, our sense of omnipotence is eventually crushed as physical ageing progresses, as well as the fact of being subject to external events like *tsunamis* and loss of objects.

The Japanese people hear a song in the cries of a bell cricket and perceive a meaning in it, so we are said to co-exist with nature. During the hours outside the treatment room, many of our patients not only meet outside people and things but also encounter nature. They engage in dialogue with the environment and become involved with it. A harmonious symbiosis with nature, though, may only be a one-sided understanding: we are destroying it and at the same time, abandoning it. Since the dawn of history, we have been in a situation where we want to depend on other things – Izanami who is the symbol of Mother Nature, the Earth, and now, this psychoanalysis – but cannot; we want to depend on them but cannot; and, to quote from Takeo Doi, we want to *amaeru* but cannot.

The Japanese normally call each other by our family names. My family name, Kitayama, means 'a mountain in the north' in Japanese. Many other people have family names that signify nature, such as Matsuki, which means 'a pine tree,' and Fujiyama, which means 'a wisteria mountain.' Nature is our family, so to speak, and synchronisation tends to occur between ourselves and nature.

I feel that the fact that human beings want to live naturally but cannot creates, in us, the task and challenge of solving the irrationality and contradictions that come from a dependence on nature. The flickering on and off of transient objects that accompany these items is rhythmical: they are not only 'Fort–Da,' but also 'Da–Fort,' or not only 'ebb and flow,' but also 'flow and ebb' (see Figure 5.5).

Figure 5.5 Kanagawaoki Nami Ura [The Great Waves off Kanagawa] (date unknown, originally 1830–1832) by Hokusai Katsushika.
Source: (personal collection).

References

Abraham, K. (1973). (D. Bryan & A. Strachey, Trans.) A short study of the development of the libido, viewed in the light of mental disorders. In *Selected Papers of Karl Abraham* (pp. 418–501). London: Hogarth Press. (Original published 1924)

Bruner, J. (1975). The capacity for joint visual attention in the infant. *Nature*, 253, 265–266.

Freeman, D. (1981). Mythological portrayal of developmental processes and major intrapsychic restructurizations. *Psychoanalytic Study of Society*, 9, 326–340.

Freud, S. (1916). On transience. In *Standard Edition*, Vol. 14. London: Hogarth Press.

Freud, S. (1933). New Introductory Lectures on Psycho-Analysis. In *Standard Edition*, Vol. 22. London: Hogarth Press.

Ishida, E. (1972). *Momotarō no Haha* [*Mother of Momotarō*]. Tokyo: Kōdansha.

Katsumata, S. (Ed.) (1954). *New Japanese-English Dictionary* (3rd ed.). Tokyo: Kenkyūsha.

Kitayama, O. (1979). Psychotherapy and time factor: part 2 [in Japanese]. *Japanese Journal of Psycho-Analysis*, 23(2), 78–84.

Kitayama, O. (1985). Pre-oedipal taboo in Japanese folk tragedies. *International Review of Psycho-Analysis*, 12, 173–186.

Kitayama, O. (1998). Transience: its beauty and danger. *International Journal of Psycho-Analysis*, 79 (5), 937–950.

Kōdansha International (1995). *Japan: Profile of a Nation*. Tokyo: Kōdansha.

McDougall, J. (1986). *Theatres of the Mind*. London: Free Association Books.

Muraoka, M. (2017). Therapeutic process and turning points [in Japanese]. In A. Takano (Ed.) *Syūikkai Seishinryōhō Josetsu* [*Introduction to Weekly Psychotherapy*] (pp. 120–130). Osaka: Sōgensha.

Okada, A. (2017). On the Rhythm of Weekly Psychotherapy [in Japanese]. In: A. Takano (Ed.) *Syūikkai Seishinryōhō Josetsu* [*Introduction to Weekly Psychotherapy*] (pp. 45–60). Osaka: Sōgensha.

Okonogi, O. (1990). Problems of free association and frequency in psychoanalytic therapy in Japan [in Japanese]. *Japanese Journal of Psycho-Analysis*, 33(5), 387–396.

Reischauer, E. O.*et al.* (ed.) (1993). *Japan: An Illustrated Dictionary.* Tokyo: Kōdansha.

Winnicott, D. (1975). Transitional objects and transitional phenomena. In: *Collected Papers: Through Paediatrics to Psycho-Analysis* (pp. 229–242). New York: Basic Books. (Original published 1953)

Winnicott, D.W. (1975). Depressive position in normal development. In: *Collected Papers: Through Paediatrics to Psycho-Analysis* (pp. 262–277). New York: Basic Books. (Original published 1954–1955).

Chapter 6

Various narratives centring on 'under the bridge'

Osamu Kitayama

A complex of sin and hatred/disgust

Concerning the prohibition of 'Don't Look' theory, the discussion of which began with my Japanese articles, about an issue I became aware of while an adolescent that still remains in my mind. It pertains to a question I have pondered ever since I was small: Why was it that only a woman, who was looked at by a man, had to leave, and why did the man, who broke the prohibition and looked at the woman, survive?

In the Izanagi–Izanami myth, the maternal deity gives birth to a fire deity, which kills her. Before she dies, she prohibits the paternal deity from looking at her dying body. To interpret this in a contemporary and scientific fashion, since the maternal deity dies as a result of sexual intercourse and childbirth, the man, too, is responsible for her death. The paternal deity who broke the prohibition became disgusted and fled, abandoning his wife who felt ashamed of having been seen. Here, he became stricken by a mixture of guilt and hatred/disgust, and we can interpret that it inevitably turned into filth and impurity, and remained inside him.

In the myth, the now-dead maternal deity is banished, and the paternal deity ends up ruling the Land of the Living. To wash away the filth that is accompanied by a sense of ugliness and defilement, he performs a purification ritual. Here, we can understand the duality and contradiction of life and death, of a mother who was vibrant, strong and bore children, later rotting away and dying, being dirty and ugly, being something that cannot be directly confronted. With the added difficulty of being unable to assume responsibility for the woman's death, moreover, this mixture spreads an image of being a filthy object that remains inside the mind. *Misogi* is a ritual that is performed to cleanse, purify, and release such filth. Seen through contemporary eyes, we can read this myth as an ancient record of mysophobia, or fear of filth, on the part of the Japanese people. The story also indicates the psychological mechanism by which banishment and discrimination occur.

DOI: 10.4324/9781003501930-7

Kegare: *An unfathomable thing*

My understanding of *kegare* (uncleanness/impurity) is greatly helped by the thoughts and writings of Japanese researchers in the field of ethnology and anthropology. However, as I wrote in my book, *Kokorono Shōkato Haishutsu [In a Digestive Frame of Mind]* (Kitayama, 1988), as a physician who handles mysophobia and compulsive behaviour in clinical situations, I find close to no studies that examine and explain *kegare* from the perspective of the offenders' hatred/disgust and exclusion impulses of wanting to make the situation even more dirty and impure (*kegashitai*). I would have to say that this is the attitude of Susanoo, a deity in Japanese mythology with contradictory characteristics of both good and bad, who declared that his 'intentions were pure and clear' (*Kojiki*), and denied the violent nature of his disorderly conduct and sins directed at beloved individuals. It is also the same as the difficulty found in discussing bullying from the viewpoint of the offender's desire to bully. In psychoanalysis, these types of desires and impulses are generally called 'anal sadism.' As I will show you hereunder, however, this is not their only meaning.

Moreover, in the scene in the myth in which the male character breaks the prohibition, the story goes that, when he peeked in, he saw a woman's decaying body. Since the woman becomes enraged with having been humiliated, there is also a possibility that she was, in fact, still alive. Were this true, the man who abandoned her would have committed the sin of 'leaving her to die,' an expression that triggers an intense sense of guilt in the Japanese people. Thus, moved by mysophobia, the paternal deity banished inhabitants of the Land of the Dead as a filthy land where ugly females lived, and then cleansed himself. In this way, the myth of the birth of a country depicts the excitement of sex and love, and the danger that accompanies the birth of a child, which can cause the mother's death, as a series of processes, and describes how they are all then bundled together and banished. In this context, the ambiguity of the Japanese language, *minikui* (醜い) which means ugly, and *minikui* (見にくい) which means 'hard to look at,' are clearly of great interest. The truth is the inability to see something can lead to *itoshii*, or something beloved, and *amae* (Kitayama, 2010c). The word *itoshii* (愛しい) includes the painful feelings experienced when an object is too adorable even to look at, but so sweet that you cannot ignore it and feel compelled to do something for it. I therefore believe that the male protagonist broke the prohibition in search of the women he loved, and felt the urge to peek inside.

Here, different elements are mixed in, including hatred, disgust, curiosity, shame, sin, contempt, and lust. Excessive concentration of meaning has occurred because of overdetermination and condensation in this complex. The problem is that, because of this, a negative mass that has become unfathomable and makes us uneasy is being forced only on women, who feel ashamed, and the projection of this state is unlikely to be accepted by their male partners. For example, there are places in Japan called parturition huts where this feeling of unfathomable uneasiness that accompanies reproduction, as well as the difficulty in handling ambivalence, took shape and became a custom.

There is a place known as the Ōhara Parturition Hut, located in the suburbs of Fukuchiyama City in Kyoto Prefecture. Today, it has become something like a sacred tourist destination. In places like this, partly because it is deeply involved with death and sex as well as life, it is easy to imagine the circumstances in which a pregnant woman who had lost her life in a gruesome fashion due to *kegare*, especially to haemorrhaging, was subjected to extreme hatred/disgust and awe. Moreover, it is possible that not a few birthing centres were set up close to rivers or the sea, like this one in Ōhara, Kyoto, based on the assumption that water was needed to perform purification and *misogi*, or a cleansing ritual. Historically, the cycle of natural water flow that purifies filthy discharges must have been inevitably associated, at these watersides, with the circulation of blood and food inside the womb that nourishes the foetus.

'We picked up (this child) from underneath a bridge,' an expression that was frequently used by child-rearing parents until several decades ago, describes discrimination within a family, and may be an extended form of this association with watersides. As far as I can remember, 'underneath a bridge' was a place where people who are today called the homeless had to live. I believe we used this metaphor to show despise for reproductive behaviours and to emphasise that those children are 'lowborn.'

In Japanese ethnology, uncleanness concerning death, called 'black uncleanness,' is differentiated from uncleanness concerning child delivery and menstrual bleeding, called 'red uncleanness.' However, at parturition huts, where pregnant women's deaths were inevitably witnessed, these two types of uncleanness became intertwined due to people's unsophisticated views of uncleanness. Here, a mother and her child encountered the possibility of both life and death. This was why they were quarantined inside the birthing centre, in response to this taboo, and the child thus born was probably considered a 'lowborn.' Needless to say, quarantining may have been practised not only because of uncleanness but also to allow postpartum women to rest and receive God's blessing and protection.

Mysophobic mythological thinking still exists today but does not surface in our ordinary lives, thanks to our scientific ways of thinking. However, as it became clear with the psychology of bullying and discrimination seen during the nationwide state of emergency caused by the COVID-19 pandemic, there is no telling when such thinking will be triggered, and towards whom (Kitayama & Ogimoto, 2021). What we should be aware of in advance is the mental structure that triggers release and exclusion due to physiological aversion when we inadvertently allow the everyday dichotomy of life and uncleanness to enter and become mixed into our thought processes. What is always needed in situations like these, faced with the mythological thinking that causes mass hysteria, are time and psychological understanding to allow both sides, including the victims, to calm down.

The trauma of the primal scene

From the analysis of the stories thus far, I believe that the readers can guess how I have come to have an interest in the primal scene, or a child's experience of witnessing his or her parents engaged in sexual intercourse. Since the myth of the birth of Japan, which begins with sexual intercourse between the maternal and paternal deities, is the starting point of the prohibition of 'Don't look,' which is the central theme of this book, I am sure that the readers can understand, here, that this myth is also a story about the primal scene.

For example, the story that opens the Japanese creation myth, which features a heavenly spear, may also incorporate an image that derives from the primal scene. Being depicted are Izanagi and Izanami lowering the spear into the ground, stirring it round and round, causing it to curdle. On pulling it out of the water, drops of seawater that fall from the spear tip aggregate to form an island. This scene may also be described as 'erotic.' It was on Onogoro Island that our nation was later created through the deities' memorable sexual intercourse. The description itself of an island being created by stirring this swamp-like land with a spear may speak of the image and excitement of copulation and conception. Although this is my personal association, if the spear is a penis, the swamp represents a womb.

An infant's primal scene experience of seeing and hearing this while sharing their parents' bed can also be interpreted at times as a major spectacle. A close look at the continuity of mythology and clinical practice in Japan shows its pathogenicity and traumatic nature to be not as universal as those shown in Freud's case report on the Wolf Man (Freud, 1918). Freud, too, faced the recurrence and aggravation of the Wolf Man's pathology, and could not escape thinking about the limitations of psychoanalysis. The development and limitations of discussions on Freud's primal scene were pointed out by researchers such as H. Blum (1974) and D. Knafo and K. Feiner (1996).

If we bear in mind that *shunga* pictures, which were culturally shared among the people in Japan, were also called 'comic pictures,' and are generally regarded as depicting 'acts of love' and accepted as such, then not all primal scene experiences are necessarily traumatic. The outcomes will also vary according to the frequency of sightings, the child's age, and the personalities of the child and his/her parents. It should be noted, however, as I will show this in my case report, that in not a few cases, the primal scene experience becomes something 'unfathomable,' or which confuses the child. Psychoanalysts may think that most of the primal scene experiences are violent and traumatic. What is important with this trauma, I believe, is that it is unfathomable and over-stimulating and that during that time, the child is abandoned and ignored by the parents. What is clear from my clinical experience with patients who report it with fear and anxiety, and from my self-analysis, is the need to consider its influence on biased thinking and on the discriminatory mindset in various aspects of everyday life, such as the tendency to duplicate the self, and to 'pretend not to see,' transcending mere artistic beautification and/or excitement.

In this connection, Hiroyuki Myouki (2024) discusses the significance of the practice of a family sleeping side by side with the child in between the parents or together, forming the Chinese character 川 or 'river,' to calm it and put it to sleep, and points out that, if the child wakes up in fear in the middle of the night, he/she feels safe in having his/her parents close by, and that this sense of security helps the child to go back to sleep. Myouki focuses on this function and finds that the following clinical issue arises: if a child witnesses its parents engaged in sexual intercourse, which is 'unfathomable' to him/her, to prevent this from becoming a violent trauma, it is necessary to 'translate' it, using a child's language, and consider ways to help the child go back to sleep. Moreover, in discussing the culture or practice of a family sleeping alongside each other, we should not only state its pathology, but also emphasise the possibility that it may foster '*amae*' among the Japanese people, or a sense of solidarity and security, as shown by the Japanese word 連む or *tsurumu* (coupling or mating together). On the other hand, pathogenicity and trauma in the past are combined with other raw and graphic elements such as images of child delivery and the mother dying from blood loss. There is also the possibility that, because of other diverse and varied determinant factors, an even uglier, dirtier and scarier image has been created.

Connections of the sound '*chi*'

If the coupling of two individuals occurs in the culture or the practice of a family sleeping alongside each other, the remaining family member is liable to be excluded and banished to 'outside the mosquito net' that protects family members, sleeping side by side, from mosquitos in warm weather. Being placed outside it metaphorically signifies that one is left out of the group. Conversely, regarding the polysemy and stratification of the sound '*chi*' that occurs 'inside the mosquito net,' I will point out one more cultural fact associated with the Japanese language.

The Japanese language uses two written forms. We use Chinese *kanji*, or ideographic characters, to clearly highlight the meaning of a word. We also use *kana* which are phonetic characters that can cause semantic associations/correlations to occur in the background. We are therefore living in a bilingual fashion within the Japanese language. The huge numbers of homonyms that are created as a result enrich phonetic associations and wordplay, making it easier for polysemic exchanges and communications that go along with this to occur. I believe that the associations and correlations at the level of these *kana* characters ultimately support the awareness of inner-circle connections; here, we are avoiding rigorous clarifications that could be made through third-party censorship and disclosures. In the sentences I write here, the word 水 (water, pronounced *mizu*) is used in terms and phrases such as 水に流す (literally meaning 'to flush away with water' to signify 'forget and let bygones be bygones') and 水子 (a stillborn or aborted child) also conveys the meaning of the homonym 見ず (*mizu*, meaning to 'not see'). In psychoanalysis, which emphasises verbalisation for reasons of third-party style clarification, the most distinct characteristic of the Japanese language is that we analysts are immersed in semantic associations/correlations not only at the *kanji* level but also at the phonetic *kana* level.

Let me use, for example, the sound '*chi*,' written as 'チ.' Here, we must pay attention not only to sexual connections in the narrow sense, such as 膣 (pronounced *chi-tsu*, meaning 'vagina') and *chin-chin* (colloquially meaning 'penis') but also to the fact that the Japanese people experience diverse connections of the sound チ (*chi*). We can say 'multiple decision-making' in one word, but its constituent factors will contain a series of words that include the sound '*chi*' which are items of interest (or value, or *kachi* in Japanese) for psychoanalysis, such as 血 (pronounced *chi*, meaning 'blood'), 乳 (pronounced *chi-chi*, meaning 'breast' or 'milk'), and 父 (pronounced *chi-chi*, meaning 'father'), but also 口 (pronounced *kuchi*, meaning 'mouth'), 知 (pronounced *chi*, meaning 'knowledge' and 'intellect'), 痴 (pronounced *chi*, meaning 'foolish' or 'crazy'), and even ウンチ (pronounced *un-chi*, meaning 'poop'). Moreover, scholars of mythology such as Takeo Matsumura (1958) discovered the vital and mystical power from Japanese words and names such as *orochi* (a mythical serpent), *ikazuchi* (a mythological god of thunder), and *inochi* (life). However, people who are isolated from the Japanese language's polysemy and stratification at the rich sound level do not understand its gravity because they are not enjoying it. To help you learn about the richness of its semantic associations, therefore, I will quote passages from various historical dictionaries.

> *Chi* (spirit): The meaning of *chi*, spirit, seems to have changed to 'blood,' based on the idea that a spirit (*chi*) flows inside the human body. (*Dictionary of Classical Japanese* by S. Matsuoka, 1963)
>
> *Chi-chi* (father): As a word to praise the supernatural that has power, *chi* (spirit) appears twice (*Daigenkai* by F. Ohtsuki, 1932) and (*Japan Etymology Dictionary* by T. Maeda, 2005)
>
> *Chi-chi* (breast, milk): *Chi* (blood) changes and creates *chi-chi* (father) (*Daigenkai* by F. Ohtsuki, 1932) and (*Japan Etymological Dictionary* by T. Maeda, 2005)
>
> *Chitsu* (vagina): From 'breast milk [=*chi-chi*],' the word expanded to signify *chibusa* (breast), *mune* (breast or chest), *futokoro* (bosom), *kakushi-dokoro* (hiding place), and *inbu* (genitals or private parts) – *be-be, bo-bo, he-he, chinchi, chinko, chinpo, ma-ma, no-no, so-so* (*Japan Etymological Dictionary*, J. Yamanaka, 1976)

Chinko and *chinpo* refer to the penis. At this sound level in the Japanese language, *chi* may become a penis, father, and/or breast. I personally feel that, if you want to confirm the vibrancy of the sound *chi*, simply add *chi* to '*kata*' (template) to create the word *katachi* (form), and you breathe life into a static and inorganic form. The sensation of *tsunagari* (connection and bond) and *tsujiru* (to communicate) that is created here is sensory rather than logical like Tsū, the heroin's name in *The Twilight of a Crane*. At the same time, people who are alienated from this rich polysemy and stratification are liable to be placed 'outside the mosquito net,' and fail to understand the meaning. We, however, perceive the play on words that dance around, or the workings of *kotodama*, or the spiritual power of language. Although these networks are now being covered up by an adult sense of shame, a group of *chi* sounds having a fishy, half-rotten odour, stand in a row behind the words, along with the *chi* sound, such as *chu* and *chū* which signify 'kissing,' *chome-chome* which are written as blank spaces to mainly imply sexual intercourse, and *ecchi* (lewd and sexy) that put all these together. And, while placing these multifarious combinations of meaning at the back, we are able to continue pure and clear discussions at the *kanji* level. This, too, is proof that I am placing something clear in the front and the rest in the back, thinking even here in Japanese fashion, not in English.

As a clinical problem, a patient may become drawn into the *tsunagari* (connection and bond) in the back (in other words, behind-the-scenes recombination and communication), become drowned or entangled, be kept as a prisoner, become bound, or feel suffocated. On the other hand, he or she may experience difficulties, such as becoming banished to 'outside the mosquito net' and not being able to connect, or having connections cut off (*chigireru*, or tear off; *buchigireru*, or get violently ripped apart), or be despised by tutting (*tsk*). The patient may even feel that he or she is not talking in their mother tongue, cannot communicate, and cannot make their words and feelings reach other people. What the mother may actually say, such as 'I don't know any child who does things like you do,' 'You are not my child,' and 'I don't remember giving birth to you,' as well as 'I must have picked you up from underneath a bridge' and '(You are) an unwanted child,' may turn into fear and the threat of having the 'connection of the *chi* sound' cut and thereby being banished. They may also extend to social threats such as bullying and discrimination, and being ostracised in the adult world and labelled as a 'noncitizen.' I also wish to emphasise that this expression, 'I must have picked you up from underneath a bridge,' which I will quote in my case report below, comes up extensively in the analytic treatment of adult patients as an element that comprises the accumulation of 'small traumas.'

It may also be a good idea to know that, in addition to *chi*, which is a sound having a 'fishy, half-rotten' nuance, if the *hiragana*-based association of the *yu* sound is used, as in *yurushi* (forgiveness), *yu* (hot water), *yurumi* (looseness and laxation), *yukkuri* (slow), and *yoyū* (leeway), then *chiyu* (cure, healing) appears, like magic. The Japanese people's love of hot baths and hot springs pairs up with their fear of filth and contamination. When people soak in a hot bath, they often utter 'Ah, *gokuraku, gokuraku*' (this is heaven!). This must be because they feel that their sins and impurities are being washed away with the water, freeing them from the past and from unwanted experiences. In the face of the magic and ambiguity of this type that is so characteristic of Japanese culture, many scholars and intellectuals are simply struck dumb.

The onomatopoeia of amphibian experiences

The wet, damp magic of the Japanese language may be implied by the sound *yu*. Indeed, in Japanese culture, child-rearing families sleep crammed together (雑魚寝, which literally means 'sleeping like small fish') or side by side to form the Chinese character 川 (river). On the other hand, water is often used in rituals such as purification, exorcism, and cleansing, showing that water-based sensations stand out in connection with problems related to uncleanness and filth. Moreover, watery onomatopoeia focusing on voiced sounds and consonants that depict relationships and attitudes, such as *beta-beta* (sticky), *guzu-guzu* (slow and dilly-dallying), *zubu-zubu* (drenched and deeply immersed), and *zuru-zuru* (slithery and dragging on), often appear in the fields of underground, or 'back' culture. This is in contrast to mainstream, or 'front' culture that looks for clear or unvoiced sounds and sharply enunciated consonants such as *sara-sara* (clear and smooth) and *sukkiri* (clean and clear) that are created by 'washing clean' with water.

A leading symbol that is used in Japan's psychoanalytic theory of the liquid states that accompany sexual relationships, is honey, which was applied to the mother's body in the Ajase story. This is another of my personal associations, that in sexual relationships I believe we metaphorically become animals that reside at the waterside and in swamps. Like in the tales of marriages between humans and non-humans, we can turn into a crane, a snake, a frog, a snail, a mermaid, or even another human being, or become involved with non-humans.

And, as was pointed out by Norinaga Motoori (1730–1801; a Japanese classical scholar) in his book, *A Study of the Three Modes of Pronouncing Chinese Characters* (Motoori, 1970), Japanese language speakers prefer clear sounds to a greater extent than speakers of Western languages. Voiced sounds are liable to be disliked and avoided in contemporary choral music, for example. I will emphasise this once again, but awareness of uncleanness in clinical situations is often accompanied by wet, voiced sounds such as *gucha-gucha* (messy and chaotic), *doro-doro* (thick and muddy), *guzu-guzu* (slow and dilly-dallying), and *zubo-zubo* (the sound of piercing of soft substances). These may be said to be the sound of a marsh that brings mucus to mind. They can also be said to be the sounds of actions that are a focus of psychoanalysis, such as oral or lip activities, excretion, urination, and sex. In particular, since the vagina becomes wet during sexual intercourse, love scenes in Japanese dramas were commonly called 'wet scenes.' The world of sexual love is therefore wet. This means that, when this type of onomatopoeia occurs, it also causes a 'wet' experience at watersides and underneath bridges. A mother's remarks that she had picked up her child from underneath a bridge demonstrates not only the psychology of intra-family contempt: it also contains truth about water. In other words, just as a baby was picked out of a river in the Momotarō legend, and, in psychoanalysis, just as was discussed by Otto Rank (2013) in *The Trauma of Birth*, we are conceived inside the mother's womb, grow up immersed in water, and are swept into this world on a river-like gush of liquid. Indeed, this is believed to be a universal memory of human beings concerning birth.

Therefore, it would be perfectly natural for many birthing centres to be located by watersides, as a place for people to undergo the amphibious experience of 'crossing or migrating' from an aquatic existence inside the uterus to terrestrial life outside the uterus. It was also inevitable that, although it was a place to pray for safe childbirth, it also became a place that was greatly feared because of the risk of death. The place where life was mixed with death was regarded as impure; a sense of contamination and filth came about that ordinary people had no choice but to wash away with water, so it subsequently attracted a taboo.

I created this figure (see Figure 6.1), based on the taboo theory set forth by anthropologist Mary Douglas (1966), the concept of 'betwixt and between' advocated by Victor Turner (1977), and diagrams drawn up by Edmund Leach (1976), among others. Figure 6.1 makes it possible for us to illustratively understand the areas that are mapped onto each other as being 'unfathomable' or 'cannot be understood' that are not incorporated into logic or order, or areas where amphibious experiences are considered a taboo. Two books that I read in my youth and which particularly struck me are the *Kojiki* in Japanese and *Purity and Danger*, an English book by Mary Douglas. The book's Japanese title is *Oaito Kinki*, which literally means 'filth and prohibition/taboo.' This Japanese

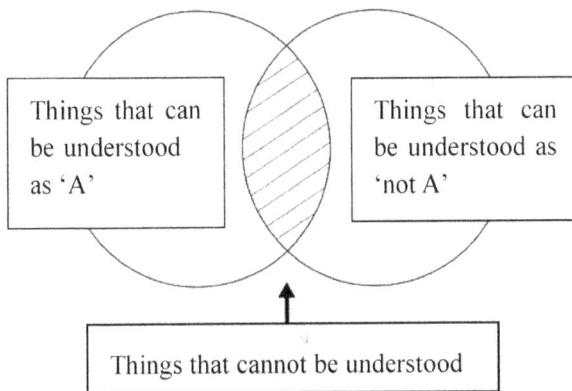

Figure 6.1 The unfathomable. The overlapping area indicates an unfathomable (and therefore a taboo) area

title is both extremely unique and accurate meaning-wise. Filth and prohibition taboos occur in this 'betwixt and between' area, or, in other words, the field of 'Things that cannot be understood.' The figure should help you imagine how the mind is activated when facing an agonising conflict of 'this or that' becoming dissolved and 'washed away with water' to forgive and forget. In the umbilical cord, moreover, the umbilical artery and the umbilical vein are clearly differentiated. After birth, however, a mix-up between the 'entry' of nutrients and the 'exit' of wastes becomes directly connected to the mix-up between life and death, so I am sure you will agree that, under the circumstances, this must be strenuously avoided.

Muddy River *underneath a bridge*

The Ajase story, which often comes up in Japanese psychoanalysis in this field, is part of the Buddhist scriptures. It is based on the story of Ajase, who ruled the prosperous Kingdom of Magadha in ancient India. Out of hatred for his father, who was then the king, Ajase imprisoned him and ascended the throne. The father was given very little to eat, making his wife – Ajase's mother – so concerned for him that she covered her body with honey and secretly visited her husband in prison to feed him. Ajase was deeply disturbed by learning about this. Heisaku Kosawa and Keigo Okonogi used this story as the basis for developing a concept regarding parent–child relationships in Japan and called it the Ajase complex (Okonogi, 2001). The story noted the possibility of trauma on the part of the son who suddenly became disillusioned after learning that his mother, with whom he was united as one, had 'coupled' with her husband. This can be said to be a tragedy that occurred because of the strong relationship that a child has had with the mother, who was a 'second person' to him/her. The duality of the mother's body that a child licks is also being licked by the father who does this as the object of sexual love, appears to have caused disillusionment and disgust/hatred on the part of the child.[1]

   To put this understanding in a more modern-day context, I will use a novel by a contemporary Japanese writer and make some visual interpretations. As a story depicting the prohibition of 'Don't Look' immediately after the Second World War, I would like to choose *Muddy River*, a novel written in 1977 by Teru Miyamoto (2014). [2] It was also made into a movie of the same name in 1981. Directed by Kohei Oguri, it is a heart-stirring masterpiece. In it, actress Mariko Kaga plays the role of the mother of a friend of a boy, the leading character. At the movie's climax, the boy goes to his friend's houseboat, attends a rather violent and cruel play burning small crabs, then peeks inside one of the rooms on the boat and confronts the friend's mother, a prostitute, engaging in sex with a tattooed client. From a window, he sees her eye-to-eye. This brings to mind Harunobu Suzuki's *shunga*, which I cover in Chapter 9 (Figure 9.5), where the mother is looking her child in the eye.

Likewise, various relationships which had been 'pregenital' break down at this instant. The movie ends with the prostitute's boat leaving the shore, gliding along a 'muddy river.' This is believed to be the typical ending of a story of the growth related to the prohibition of 'Don't Look.' Elements which the boy had wished to somehow separate until then, such as sexual love and pregenital love, life and death, and sex and violence, became mixed together and brought an end to his days of innocence as a child. This is my personal association, but as the boat moves away from the shore, the boy chases after it, calling and shouting, but fails to catch up. This scene reminds me of the famous haiku by Matsuo Basho, 'Exciting to see / but soon after, comes sadness / the cormorant boats.' On watching this scene, the audience will learn what the *doro-doro* (thick and muddy) things are in the *Muddy River*. In the primal scene, adults and children, and human beings and animals come together, cause ripples, and lovingly get mixed in, like mud. What the title *Muddy River* symbolises must be the inevitable merging of waters in a story where life and death are woven together by sex.

Towards the end of the novel, a huge carp (*koi*, in Japanese, which also means love and romance) appears, chasing after the departing boat. Wanting to tell the people on the boat about this, the boy then shouts from a bridge. The carp does not appear in the movie. However, in the final pages of the novel, I, as the reader, imagine myself as a carp (*koi* = love) swimming in the 'muddy river.' Being of the same generation as the author Teru Miyamoto, I feel deeply that this depicts the energy of the love and 'life = sex' of the people who lived and swam in the postwar days of confusion. As I stated in my discussion in 2024 with Yuko Tanaka, a scholar of the Edo period, I feel that sex during that era was proof that the people in those days lived vividly and at close quarters with death. In other words, this was the libido itself.

Let me cite one more movie. In the Japanese film *The Ballad of Narayama* (1983), directed by Shohei Imamura, a woman appears having sex with her husband while comforting her child. In contrast to the image of a mother who responds to the biological demands of sex between a man and a woman, as well as childbirth, their elderly mother is abandoned and dies on *ubasute-yama*, which is literally a mountain to which old people, once past their usefulness, are carried and then abandoned. Here again, there is the taboo of 'Don't Look:' the snow begins to fall where the elderly woman is left to die. The son says, 'She is indeed fortunate; it snowed heavily here' (*The Ballad of Narayama*, 1964, a book written by Shichiro Fukazawa, on which the film is based). This is a moment of good luck where the snow covers the old woman's dying body and hides it from view. I can thus see that many artists of my generation tackled the prohibition of 'Don't Look,' and truly feel the significance of the Japanese people having left intact the word *sei* as a homonym, implying both sex and life.

A case report: 'I was picked up from underneath a bridge'

From my clinical experience also, I find that many of today's middle-aged and older Japanese people were told by their parents, when they were small, that they had been picked up from under a bridge. As the cultural background to this, I must cite the fact that, as mentioned previously, people's reproductive activities are often described using metaphors related to water.

The male depressed patient I report about herein started psychoanalytic treatment in his 40s. In the sessions, he began talking about the fact that he grew up being told by his biological mother, who was compulsive-depressive, that he was 'a child who had been picked up from under a bridge.' I assumed that the term 'under a bridge,' which he had used while lying on the couch, was a place where homeless people gathered. The fact that his biological mother referred to her own child's birth in this way implied, according to my understanding as a therapist, that she regarded the patient as a child who had been born as the result of sexual intercourse, which she felt was 'lowly and vulgar.' To the patient, who must have been her own biological child, it signified 'a child who was not related by blood,' and, at the same time, he felt that the image covered him in mud and labelled him as an outcast or an untouchable, according to the traditional caste system of Japan, and a 'lowborn.' On top of this, his father was a pleasure-seeking wastrel. The family lived mostly on the mother's income, and because of this, the mother constantly looked down on her husband.

The patient, an only child, did well at school. After growing up, he became an individual with a strong sense of duty, believing that he must study and work diligently. He worked as a local government employee in the field of social welfare. True to his motto of being sincere and living decently and respectably, he married a woman from the same respectable workplace. The couple had no children. Immediately after having been promoted to a senior position, he lost his motivation. He became even more depressed after he found himself unable to manage his group successfully, and visited my office.

The patient was what I call a 'masochistic caretaker.' Although he was worn out due to over-adaptation, he concluded that there was no need to take a leave of absence, since he was managing to do the necessary minimum at work. At one of our free association sessions, which began at a rate of twice a week, he said that his key problem was his poor self-image. He always lamented what his mother used to say, that he had been born 'under a bridge,' and that she would 'renounce their blood ties.' The patient also had a minor limb physical disability, and, to hide it, he was following a way of life in which his 'front' – an over-adapted self – drastically deviated from his 'back' – an awkward and clumsy self.

Soon, he began talking bashfully about a place where he could remain his true self, in his own way: a sofa placed in the corner of a room. He always enjoyed lying there, on his days off, immobile and not thinking about anything. In contrast, his wife, although busy at work, was an extremely outgoing and sociable type, and enjoyed her life while keeping her distance from him. Deep down, the patient was both jealous of his wife and angry at her. Theirs was an 'arranged marriage,' and he had stopped having sex with her several years previously. He explained that his interest in, and desire for, sex had faded. Even though he made an appearance at his wife's social groups, he could not take part in their activities or conversations. Simply going along with the group exhausted him, and he was unable to enjoy their company. He felt that doing nothing on the sofa showed him to be 'dead' and 'empty,' and he was increasingly being 'cornered.' Paradoxically, he liked the corner of the room and found solace there.

For the first three years of his treatment with me, his condition remained completely unchanged. The patient used to state that things were becoming neither better nor worse and that he had nothing to live for. He felt a growing sense of emptiness. He could not feel that the treatment was working, no matter how much he talked during therapy, so, when leaving my office after the end of the sessions, he frequently heard voices inside his head that denigrated me, such as 'This will never work,' 'I can't believe you're a professional therapist,' and 'If things go on like this, my only recourse will be to die.' They were mostly statements that recalled his mother's words and attitudes. The fact that he was unable to do his job sufficiently well was also being criticised by his mother inside his mind, and, since he was also unable to do well in therapy, his mood deteriorated even further. At the same time, his marital relationship went from bad to worse, and the patient began to feel that he could not seek help from his wife, who ignored him.

In his treatment also, his mind was revealed to be seething with ugly and dirty emotions such as grudges and rage towards people close to him. This was absolutely not something he had wanted. The sessions became a litany of things that he detested recalling, as well as unpleasant memories. He felt that he should not have taken on such treatment in the first place, and, while expressing his dissatisfaction, at the same time, he did not know what he should do. He became miserable, and complained to me that 'everything has become *gucha-gucha*' (messy and mixed up). This was toward the end of the third year of treatment.

Seeing his wife cheerfully leaving the house to see her friends, he recalled having phantasised about his mother having extramarital sexual relationships and abandoning her son (the patient) and her husband. He came to phantasise that his wife also had a lover. He felt that he was once again being abandoned, demoted to the state of being 'below a bridge.' He also felt that becoming jealous was entirely pathetic and shameful, which further intensified his self-abasement. He felt that no matter how hard he tried to crawl back up, he was pushed back down, an endless number of times, to 'below the bridge,' and agonised about this. I interpreted his relationship with his mother, but his condition did not improve. The patient lamented that, just as his family used to despise him for being clumsy and awkward, the therapist merely watched him from a bridge: he was a helpless child who was looked down upon by adults and lived his life at the lowest level, crawling on the ground.

The patient said that, when the year-end and the New Year came, everyone seemed to have an especially fun time, so he felt miserable and confined to the corner of a room. He then momentarily recalled how he waited patiently for his parents to have sex on the other side of a folding screen. He told me that, when he was a young boy, he curled up in his *futon* mattress and waited nervously and anxiously, becoming excited as well, for his parents to simply finish the act. He said that this 'was a filthy past that I should be ashamed of,' adding that, even if everyone around him were *tsurumu* (coupling or mating together), he alone was thrown 'outside the mosquito net,' and was powerless. I understood that, even on my couch, he was reliving the experiences of his painful past. However, the patient said that I was a pleasure-seeking wastrel, like his father, and someone 'far away and unapproachable,' and added that, were he to acknowledge his jealousy, it would make him even more miserable.

With his condition deteriorating even further, he increasingly began wishing to die. He considered taking a leave of absence or retiring from work, grumbled about this and that, and began to waver. I considered the possibility of medication as well as of further increasing the frequency of the twice-weekly sessions and conveyed these ideas to him. After this discussion prior to the summer break, he began to rely on the possibility of interventions on my part as support. Because of the summer break, however, he had trouble making an appointment at the medical institution that he wanted to visit. I therefore added two special sessions, at the start and the end of the summer break. However, I felt as if the established therapeutic structure was breaking down. At the special sessions, moreover, the patient started telling me that, instead of keeping still like before, he had fallen into a state of *gucha-gucha* (being messy and mixed up), *dara-dara* (dragging on), *guzu-guzu* (being slow and dilly-dallying), and *goro-goro* (relaxing lazily). He conveyed to me that he could never reveal this state to anyone at home, but, on the couch in the therapy room, he expressed his experience of being in a raw and garish *gucha-gucha* (messy and mixed up) state, using the onomatopoeia of voiced sounds. He pleaded with me to do something about his distress that was filled with humiliation. Although I myself was able to understand it, I could merely listen and do nothing; I felt powerless and that it was futile, but this was exactly what the patient was feeling.

He regarded many things as annoying; he was also aware that he himself was an annoying person. His *gucha-gucha* state lasted for more than six months. Things were agonising and unbearable; inside his mind, he could hear voices that criticised him; the sound of people banging on the door was heard, as if they were berating him. He complained that he had never dreamed that he would become such an 'annoying' person, and said repeatedly that he wished he had not undertaken therapy from me. In response, I continued to feel that all this was inevitable, and that nothing could be done. From this point, the unchanging *gucha-gucha* state dragged on (*dara-dara*), and gradually a somewhat positive/affirmative state was added to the mix, of acknowledging that he was living his life in *doro-kusaku* fashion (literally meaning 'smelling muddy' and metaphorically 'in a drab but steadfast way'), one step at a time. This by no means meant that he had recovered from a state of regression. Instead, he followed a path of consistently coming to the office on time, paying the fees as agreed, and adapting to this mishmash, rather than resisting it. To do this, the following occurred haphazardly, so I will list the contents of the mishmash in random order. As the course progressed, he found himself no longer requiring medication or increased sessions.

Interestingly enough, although resting immobile on his couch at home made him miserable and was not permitted because of 'tainted sorrow,' a sensation began to be mixed in that the couch in the therapy room was a place where he was allowed to belong. This showed that the states expressed with voiced sounds, such as *gucha-gucha, zuru-zuru* (slithery and dragging on), and *uda-uda* (going on and on; idling away) also implied that they were *yuru-yuru* (loose and relaxed), *yuttari* (roomy and comfortable), and *yurumu* (loosened and slackened). In other words, the *yu* sound continued to be mixed into voiced sounds.

Another thing was that he regarded me as a 'person above the clouds,' and expected me to pull him up from 'underneath a bridge.' However, the notion gradually came to his mind that I was just an ordinary person who had no special power. Optimism and pessimism therefore became mixed together, making things even muddier. He felt that not having any hope was painful, but began to think that it didn't matter whether there was hope or not. In other words, he was saying that anything is okay, that he doesn't care, and that most things are meaningless. He no longer cares about most of his previous worries; it doesn't matter if he gets better or worse with treatment; and it no longer matters if he is 'on a bridge' or 'underneath a bridge.'

My understanding was that, with this sort of process, the 'internal saboteur' (Fairbairn, 1944), who attacks the dependent patient, was being heard as his mother's voice. In the course of his fighting it, however, it gradually weakened. Just as we were about to win that battle, a voice was heard, warning the patient not to trust what the therapist says. He then said that he hated returning to his family home in the countryside and seeing his parents; he also confessed that putting on airs was painful to him. Seeing him murmur and mumble inside the consultation room, I felt that he was being *guzu-guzu* (slow and dilly-dallying) and *dara-dara* (dragging on). I came to understand that this shameful experience showed that he was dependent on me or that he was being *beta-beta amaeru*-ing (clinging to me, seeking emotional support and pampering). Whenever he did not feel that he was a dirty, soiled being, his mental and physical disorders no longer mattered. To him, I alternated between becoming his ally and his enemy.

The therapeutic setting that I initially established became slightly more flexible as a result of my considering the possibility of medication and offering special sessions. As far as the significance of this change was concerned, however, the patient remarked, 'I don't know if it was good or bad,' and 'It's betwixt and between.' I personally felt it important that, to the patient who felt that he 'was not eligible to be here,' the sessions have become 'a place to belong to, for a fee.' I also felt that, despite their limitations, the sessions had become something more realistic that he could safely grasp, rather than 'unconditional love from above the clouds.'

Based on this understanding, therefore, I believe I was able to hold and be with his *gucha-gucha* (messy and chaotic) and sloppy experiences. Before long, the patient lost special interest in all sorts of things. The most important issue, after starting the fifth year of treatment, was why his mother had threatened to 'renounce their blood ties,' such as referring to the patient as having been 'picked up from under a bridge.' Although the patient became accustomed to many things and calmed down considerably, the only thing he was unable to forgive was his mother's remarks. A major question remained as to why she had described her child in such a scornful manner. He could not fully agree with the explanation that his mother denied having borne the patient: a miserable, pitiful child who had no choice but to roll over on a *futon* mattress since he was unable to move smoothly due to impaired limbs.

I therefore conveyed to him my understanding of the mother's remarks of having been picked him up 'from under a bridge,' that it implied her 'forced guilt.' That is, since the mother had regarded sexual intercourse as something lowly and despicable, the meaning of 'an unrelated, lowly and despicable child' may have been imposed on her.

In response, the patient uttered 'Ah ...' Recalling the anger he had felt towards his mother at the time, he began describing a dream, almost as if he were surprised at himself, that he had experienced when only an infant. 'In the wilderness, there is a monster that eats humans. Seeing it, I'm thinking, "Mother is being eaten by the monster, but I'm too scared to help her." I froze there, crying.' He then made an interpretation himself, while crying, 'I think the monster that is eating my mother is me.' To this, I made the interpretation, 'Isn't this the actual scene of your parents having sex which you saw, or imagined?' I also added, 'Isn't this why you've always felt sorry for having devoured your mother, together with your father, and then abandoning them?' He replied, 'That's why Mother always told me that I was useless and no good, since I did something bad.'

These exchanges fully convinced the patient about his strong sense of self-hatred that he harbours towards sexual desire and masturbation, which he perceives as 'dirty, like mud.' I felt at that point that we had overcome a major challenge and climax in our analytical treatment. Since then, his over-sized mother image became weaker, instead of stronger. He recalled seeing his father, who was a carefree, pleasure-seeking wastrel, agonising and struggling, and said, 'So, everyone ultimately gets stuck in the mud and struggles,' showing that he had acquired a polysemic view of the world. His feelings of depression lightened, enabling him to live a little easier.

Nazumu, or 'becoming familiarised with' mud

In my clinical analytical practice, I often handle things that are regarded as taboo, such as these. In the treatment of this particular patient, various experiences unfolded, filled with liquid-type sensations described using the onomatopoeia of voiced sounds such as *gucha-gucha* (messy and chaotic), *dara-dara* (dragging on), and *goro-goro* (relaxing lazily). In Japanese culture, which prefers clean and unvoiced sounds, this sort of wet, crude and muddy phenomenon is therapeutically precious and psychoanalytically important. Handling it is, by no means cheerful or entertaining; it absolutely cannot be dealt with easily.

It also is a process which, even if being viewed by the surrounding people as ugly, or is subjected to discriminatory projections, proves to be meaningless and does not matter at all. I believe this occurs frequently in my practice, as represented by the following exclamation by another patient, who was going through this process and who discovered its meaningless: 'Looking at Rorschach inkblots again, I can tell that they are all *gucha-gucha* (messy and chaotic), and have, in fact, almost no meaning, right?'

In clinical situations, there are times when two different poles get mixed together and make the circumstances appear as if 'either is okay.' To me, if the *gucha* (mild messiness and sloppiness) of voiced sounds and consonants is repeated rhythmically to form a state of *gucha-gucha* (a full-blown mix-up), then, gradually, a sense of play and meaninglessness develops inside music. If *buka* is repeated as *buka-buka*, and if *don* is repeated as *don-don*, and if *gū* becomes *gū-gū*, if *bū* becomes *bū-bū*, if *doro* (mud) becomes *doro-doro* (thick and muddy), and if we chant 'London Bridge is falling down, falling down' many times like that Mother Goose song, we feel that seriousness and misery become meaningless.

Let us here consider how an everyday Japanese word, *doro* (mud) becomes *doro-doro* (thick and muddy). Expressions that use the word *doro* (mud) in Japanese, such as *doro o haku* (to spit out mud, or confess to a crime), *doro wo kaburu* (coating oneself with mud, or taking the blame, or doing the dirty work), and *doro wo nuru* (applying mud to someone's face, meaning to dishonour or disgrace someone), have no positive meaning. If we learn that they signify 'admitting one's crime and confessing to wrongdoing,' or 'taking sole responsibility for something,' and 'embarrassing someone,' then the word *doro* (mud) may signify a sense of guilt. Here again, we can understand the psychological process that brings about a way of liquefying one's sense of guilt and conflict, washing them away with water, and disposing of them. In my previous case example, for example, the surroundings were filled with *doro* (mud) and were *doro-doro* (thick and muddy).

The work of psychoanalysis is to deal with the issue of a sense of guilt such as this by facing it directly. In our clinical practice, the analyst and analysand sometimes force this issue on each other, and, as a result, the therapeutic relationship likely becomes 'bogged down.' Within parent–child relationships, too, parents may impose a sense of guilt onto their children and vice versa, ending up with mutual mudslinging. The mindset of a therapist in this situation causes a feeling to develop of becoming *doro-doro*, or thick and muddy, or 'handling 泥 (*doro*) mud.' Indeed, the Japanese word 泥む (*nazumu*), written with one Chinese character and one *hiragana* character, can be read as '*doro-mu*.' It can also be written as 滞む which can be read as *nazumu*, whose meaning ranges from 'to stagnate, to care deeply for, and cling to,' to a newer meaning, *najimu*, or 'to become accustomed to.' I therefore looked up the word *nazumu* in Nihon Kokugodaijiten [Dictionary of the Japanese Language] *(2nd ed.)* (2001), and found the following information. Here is an excerpt.

1   People, horses, boats, etc., try to move forward but have a difficult time doing so.
2   Things are beginning to proceed not as smoothly as expected.
3   Things a person is trying to do fail to go well, and he/she becomes distressed and troubled.
4   Fuss over; cling to, or obsess over.
5   Care deeply and wholeheartedly about someone. Become infatuated with someone. Fall in love.
6   Become used to; become familiarised with.

The above dictionary explains the word's historical continuity as follows.

During the early modern period in Japan (from the early 17th century to the mid-19th century), the meaning of (5), 'to be deeply infatuated with someone,' arose from the meaning of (4), of 'to cling to.' Based on the closeness in meaning, as well as the similarity in sound to *najimu*, the meaning of (6) came about in mid-19th century.

As you can see, the history of the Japanese language has developments that may be described as 'therapeutic.' Accepting mud and coping with it are certainly not just about getting dirty, since if you are fully immersed in mud, you become *najimu*, or accustomed to problems such as distress and worries. It may help to understand if some people try to position these thoughts and analyses of mine that are based in the Japanese language within psychoanalytic theories such as Bion's 'containment.' The origin, however, goes back to my explanations that I wrote about in the Japanese translated edition of *The Meanings of Fear*, a book on behavioural therapy by Stanley Rachman (1979). And, unlike English, the word *nareru* in Japanese can be written two ways, i.e. 馴れる and 慣れる. While the former implies an animal becoming domesticated and attached to people, the latter, which means 'getting accustomed to problems,' contains a verb that is used only with humans. This fact, and where it leads, illustrates the clinical potential of the Japanese language. It appears to me, moreover, that this potential is a development that integrates the current dichotomy and resultant conflict between psychoanalysis and behavioural therapy (Kitayama, 2024).

I therefore feel that the changes that occurred in the patient cannot be ascribed simply to therapeutic regression. Rather, the act of *nazumu*, in which a person becomes able to hold, or contain, *gucha-gucha* (messy and chaotic) experiences through having them held or contained, should be regarded as nothing special (such as regression and insights), but as 'becoming normal.'

A 'wet' clinical practice in the context of the culture of parents sleeping with their child in between, like the Chinese character 川, for river

Before ending this chapter, I would like you to recall the *ukiyo-e* again that depict an image of a mother and her child viewing something together. The woodblock print (see Figure 1.4), created by Kitagawa Utamaro, depicts a mother and her child looking at a hole in an umbrella praying for rain, while '*tsurumu*,' or coupling 'behind the scenes.' In other words, a mother and her child who, despite appearing open to the outside world, are connected behind the scenes and are in fact closed to the outside. These ways of a mother and her child are positions that evoke nostalgia in many Japanese people. The attitude portrayed here, of a mother and her child not looking at each other face to face, but 'looking at the same object together,' or 'viewing together,' or a 'joint-attentive position,' has taken the form of 'coupling, or *tsurumu*, on the emotional level,' similar to when a mother sleeps with her child in the context of the previously mentioned 'wet' culture of a family sleeping together, side by side. The fact that duplication of the 'front' and 'back' is being conveyed through the mother can therefore be shown by illustrations such as this. If these showed the typical example of 'love that is being coupled, or *tsurumu*, behind the scenes,' that is fostered within the 'wet' culture, then I would like to express my deep admiration to the artists who make honest depictions and records such as these.

As an analytical therapist, I, too, stay beside the patient who is lying on a couch, and, while sharing his *gucha-gucha* (messy and chaotic) and *doro-doro* (thick and muddy) experiences, I realise a 'horizontal dyadic relationship.' And, like in the *Praying for Rain* picture, if the patient and I can see a hole in the umbrella, and if I can put into words the wet and sentimental mindset of 'waiting for rain,' I feel that things will somehow work out using verbal therapy.

There is question I would like to ask readers in English-speaking countries: The word 'wet' signifies many things in Japan, as it does in English – such as in 'wet nurse' and a 'wet dream' – are there many other common examples?

Notes

1 Ajase's disgust toward his mother's betrayal is clearly depicted in a Japanese film *Syaka [Buddha]* (1961) directed by K.Misumi.
2 Teru Miyamoto's *Muddy River* won the Osamu Dazai Prize in 1977, while *River of Fireflies* was awarded the 78th Akutagawa Prize the following year.

References

Blum, H. P. (1974). The borderline childhood of the wolfman. *Journal of the American Psychoanalytic Association*, 22 (4), 721–740.

Douglas, M. (1966). *Purity and Danger: An Analysis of the Concepts of Pollution and Taboo*. London: Routledge and Kegan Paul.

Fairbairn, W. R. D. (1944). Endopsychic structure considered in terms of object-relationships. *International Journal of Psycho-Analysis*, 25, 70–93.

Freud, S. (1918). From the history of an infantile neurosis. In *Standard Edition*, Vol. 17. London: Hogarth Press.

Fukazawa, S. (1964). *Narayamabushikō [The Ballad of Narayama]*. Tokyo: Shinchōsha. (Original published 1957)

Kitayama, O. (1988). *Kokorono Shōkato Haishutsu [In a Digestive Frame of Mind]*. Osaka: Sōgensha. (New annotated edition published 2018, Tokyo: Sakuhinsha)

Kitayama, O. (2010c). Amae and its hierarchy of love. In *Prohibition of Don't Look* (pp. 68–79). Tokyo: Iwasaki Gakujutsu Shuppansha. (Original published 1997)

Kitayama, O. (2024). Introductory essay [in Japanese]. In O. Kitayama, & K. Ogimoto (eds.). *'Kawanoji'-bunkano Shinsōshinrigaku: oyakonosoineto 'mirunanokinshi' [Depth Psychology of 'River' Culture: Co-Sleeping between Parents and Children and the Prohibition of 'Don't Look']* (pp. 80–99). Tokyo: Iwanamishoten.

Kitayama, O. & Ogimoto, K. (2021). COVID-19 and Japanese mind: beyond mythical thinking [in Japanese]. *Japanese Journal of Psychotherapy*, 47, 150–155.

Knafo, D. & Feiner, K. (1996). The primal scene: Variations on a theme. *Journal of the American Psychoanalytic Association*, 44 (2), 549–569.

Leach, E. (1976). *Culture and Communication: The Logic by Which Symbols are Connected. An Introduction to the Use of Structuralist Analysis in Social Anthropology*. Cambridge: Cambridge University Press.

Maeda, T. (Ed.) (2005). *Nihon Gogendaijiten [Japan Etymology Dictionary]*. Tokyo: Shōgakkan.

Matsumura, T. (1958). *Nihonshinwano Kenkyu [Sudies of Japanese Myths]* Vol. 4. Tokyo: Baifūkan.

Matsuoka, S. (1963). *Nihon Kogodaijiten [Dictionary of Classical Japanese]* Tokyo: Tōkōshoin. (Original published 1929)

Myouki, H. (2024). Relationships between parents seen from the 'river' or co-sleeping culture [in Japanese]. In O. Kitayama, & K. Ogimoto (Eds.), *'Kawanoji'-bunkano Shinsōshinrigaku: oyakonosoineto 'mirunanokinshi' [Depth Psychology of 'River' Culture: Co-Sleeping between Parents and Children and the Prohibition of 'Don't Look']* (pp. 63–79). Tokyo: Iwanamishoten.

Miyamoto, T. (2014). (R. MaCarthy, Trans.) Muddy River [Doronokawa]. In *Rivers*. Kumamoto: Kurodahan Press. (Original published 1978)

Motoori, N. (1970). Kanji Sanonkou [A study of the three modes of pronouncing Chinese characters]. In S. Ō no & T. Ohkubo (Eds.), *Motoori Norinaga Zenshū [Complete Works of Motoori Norinaga]* Vol. 5 (pp. 375–433). Tokyo: Chikumashobō. (Original published 1785)

Nihon Kokugodaijiten [Dictionary of the Japanese Language] (2nd ed.) (2001). Tokyo: Shōgakkan.

Ohtsuki, F. (Ed.) (1932). *Daigenkai [Great Japanese Dictionary]*. Tokyo: Fuzanbō.

Okonogi, O. (Ed.) (2001). *Ajase Complex* [in Japanese]. Ohsaka: Sōgensha.

Rachman, S. (1979). (O. Kitayama, Trans.) *Kyōfuno Imi [The Meanings of Fear]*. Tokyo: Seishinshobō. (Original work published 1974)

Rank, O. (2013). (J. Hosozawa*et al.*, Trans.) *Shusseigaisyō [The Trauma of Birth]*. Tokyo: Misuzushobō. (Original work published 1924)

Turner V. (1977). *The Forest of Symbols: Aspects of Ndembu ritual*. London: Cornell University Press. (Original work published 1967)

Yamanaka, J. (Ed.) (1976). *Nihon Gogenjiten [Japan Etymological Dictionary]*. Tokyo: Azekurashobō.

Chapter 7

Cultural invocation of maternal-fusion in males – India and Japan

Jhuma Basak

Introduction

The post-Freudian era brought about a significant shift in the cultural positioning of the Oedipus complex that opened up a vast new psychoanalytic discourse from the East with their own theoretical conjectures on primal and oedipal developments. Girindrasekhar Bose (the 'father of psychoanalysis' in India), as early as 1949 stated that the 'Oedipus complex offered the child two possibilities of satisfaction, an active and a passive one' (Bose, 1949, p. 225) – opening up the locus of a psychoanalytic argument on bisexuality in Indian society and its related employment around the Oedipus complex in different cultural contexts, explaining its varied impact in object relations as well as in the intersubjective development of sexualities. Decades later, in view of the application of the Oedipus complex in the East, the eminent psychoanalyst from India, Sudhir Kakar said 'The Oedipus complex, in one variation or another, may well be universal, but it is not equally hegemonic across cultures' (Kakar, 2005, p. 84). And to arrive at this conjecture Kakar explored deeper into the maternal-feminine embedded in the dominant Hindu cultural myths and fantasies in the conceptualisation of the *Devi* imago, 'One of the more dominant narratives of this culture is that of *Devi*, the great goddess ...' (p. 78). Thus, the all-encompassing phallic goddess-mother Durga with her ten hands and weapons – a community imagination that becomes the compelling magical artistry of every Indian Hindu household and male fancy. The male imagining of a divine strength that equally nurtures and protects him found its manifestation in the mythological creation of a warrior goddess in *Maa Durga* (a combined semblance of the protective, phallic mother and the bountiful, (for)giving mother with ten hands), making her a ruling cultural icon and providing a religious identity for the whole community. This, thus, created grounds for opening up an entire hegemonic discourse on the patriarchal, masculine artifice that determined the maternal-feminine ruling of the Indian culturo-religious and national imagination of the woman.

DOI: 10.4324/9781003501930-8

Invoking the mother–son dyad in the East

Over time Freud's Oedipus complex has gained much critical acclaim for its traditional reinforcement of gender norms and somewhat conventional views of women. The primal mother–son dyad in the East stands distinct from the Western oedipal triad that Freud encountered, as a probable hegemonic proclamation of Christianity in the West (Tseng, Choo Chang, & Nishizono, 2005), where the father (and the Church, as a phallic order) acted as the pivotal point of all declaration at that time. Post-Freudian feminist psychoanalytic findings brought forth the enigma of the semiotics of the pre-oedipal, which is more like the prosody of language than the denotative meaning of words (in the phallic order, Lacan in Minsky, 1996) as experienced in the oedipal phase. Within this potent primal semiotics lies buried a web of desire for both the mother and the child. In the Indian context, a cultural provocation and reaffirmation of the mother–son symbolic duo never quite reaches its absolute satisfaction – it survives as a lingering nuance in the background mirroring a seductive communal cultural characteristic. It appears to remain like a floating continuum of an enveloping umbrella alongside all cultural mutations across generations.

In the Indian context, it maybe observed that the emotional bonding of the mother–son dyad is far more intense than the husband–wife duo. The unique passion inherent in the irreplaceable maternal figure acts as the locus for the mother–son duo. Such intense investment in the valuation of the boy-child of the family is due to its socio-cultural predetermination that echoes patriarchal dominance, and its reaffirmation which is prevalent in Confucian societal philosophy (Slote, 1992) pertaining to filial piety and ancestral worship (something performed by only the male heir of the family). The female child in the Indian family is meant to be 'given away' to another family in marriage, making the daughter's filial piety duplicitous and essentially non-committal to her family of origin (subsequently her inheritance rights are also weighed with equal dubiousness by her family of origin). In this sense, the daughter of the family gets socio-culturally planted in the familial periphery that resonates a breach of trust to begin with. Needless to say, this is a unique socio-cultural patriarchal construct of the phallic order that ensures female serfdom from birth. In this way, the mother–son dyad attains a culturally glorified, sanctified status – a cultural counter-fantasy constructed out of a phallic order of society. The son feels loved and secure through the mother's active participation in this dyadic bonding, thus he does not see the father as the rival as such. The mother turns to the son for male presence and comfort that she may not be receiving from her absent husband, thereby filling up the lack in her intra-psychic space. Also, the lineage gets reaffirmed and validated by the socio-cultural model. That way it creates an enshrined mother–son dyadic symbiotic attachment that the husband/father can only envy from a distance. The daughter's position is marked by an absence–presence existence from the initiating point itself.

Motherhood in India may often hold promises of socially clandestine pleasures, power, and worth for the woman, where her sacrifices and principles hope to find a glorified acknowledgement and authority in family and society. The caring, the nurturing, the loving, and the giving that comes with motherhood is perhaps that unique element of the feminine that finds respect in society, which otherwise, sadly, holds a painfully denigrated position of the feminine in the social reality of India. The 'inexhaustible giving' of the mother, considered a feminine cultural ideal (Deutsch, 1930), assumes a masochistic position in the Indian maternal plane in participatory fortitude governed by her own wounded narcissistic need. Denied of value in the family, the woman seeks societal/cultural worth by unconsciously incorporating the role of the 'self-sacrificial inexhaustible giver.' Motherhood seems to offer balm to the cultural misogyny of women in India who face abjection from family since childhood, leaving them with a deep sense of disavowal of their very existence. Subsequently, this negation of the self-body may indirectly endow women into reinforced masochistic positions in motherhood (perhaps an intermediate psycho-erotic dynamic investment) as their only form of sanctioned pleasure that is free of guilt, and of worth, by family and society. A glorious form of pleasure which is not possible to attain directly but to be sought indirectly through a self-sacrificial mechanism. The model of motherhood offers the option of a socially sanctified stature that is culturally familiar and readily available to the women of India. This may act as a counter-catalytic agent in the woman's own internalisation of her motherhood fantasy that strengthens her quest for self-worth through 'maternal enthrallment.' In this way motherhood helps to continue with the woman's mesmerising contribution of her body, a captivating somatic engagement to work out her life's angst, adding to the fraught narrative of the female-body in love and labour in the familial space. All this gets further reinforced in Indian society by its mythological construction and cultural exaltation of a lauded maternal imago of the Hindu goddess Durga (*Maa Durga*).

The birth of a child in a woman's life may often bring in a temporary playful space for the mother, which offers hope of worth and fulfilment after her sense of life-long rejection. It brings in an erratic sprout of life, stimulating the infant in her, which perhaps got smothered in her own childhood. This joint sharing of the provisional playful space of the infantile between the mother and the child may act as a binding, cohesive component for the dyad in the initial stage of the duo (Balint, 1959). But perhaps later it may equally hold potential for a confronting, opposing attribution instigating the possibility of jealousy, possessiveness, and competition in the mother (as may often be noticed in the mother when the child reaches adolescence and begins to claim its world). In the process, an inherently ambivalent maternal locale gets created which may seek its psychic projective journey in the mother–child dyadic space from an early stage. Needless to say, the intensity and timing of this maternal ambivalence varies and differs in the treatment of boys and girls. Due to the socio-cultural insinuations against the girl-child and the mother's own psychic projections of her own internalised ambivalence (from her mother and society at large) along with her bodily identification (with her daughter), the playful quality shared by the mother–child infantile duo finds prevalence only with the mother–son dyad in the Indian context. A heightened Hindu mythological reference to this may be found in the many stories of *Yashoda maaiya* (Yashoda, the mother) and her infant 'naughty' son, *Lord Krishna* (Krishna – the playful, loving, mischievous Hindu god who has the entire universe within him, plays a major role in most mythological ancient texts of India, including the *Bhagavad Gita* and the epic *Mahabharata*). It narrates stories of infant-Krishna's naughty pranks of eating butter from his neighbours' pots, or stealing clothes of his *sakhis* (women friends) when they were bathing in the pond, and its subsequent maternal retribution (beating fantasies) by the mother, Yashoda *maaiya*. Woven in those tales are prohibitions, instigations, and maternal retributions that merge mischievous sado-masochistic fantasies of the infant with the maternal. This playful quality then becomes the point of instigation for nuances of maternal participation in this playful act of 'infantilisation of the mother-son dyad.' Perhaps the mother's own unconscious wish of recovering and reliving her own repressed infantile desires finds equal celebration of herself in this playful act. Thereby, an unconscious surreptitious and overwhelming play of maternal symbiotic seduction starts to overrule the mother-son symbiotic space. This may equally act as a seductive insinuation for the mother's own process of internalisation, stimulating her own motherhood fantasies as much as it attempts to lure the infant-son into this perpetual maternal web of fantasy.

At this juncture, one is intrigued to imagine how this specific quality of 'infantilisation of mother–son dyad' may leave its impact on the psycho-sexual development of the growing son into adult life. One is left wondering what exactly may be the traces of the sensual and sexual characteristics that get created in the fantasy of this specific mother–son dyad in this particular cultural context. Could it be possible that the nuances of romance and sexuality in the later life of the adult man may be inherently affected by such maternal enthrallment? And would that be the ruling 'want' in male imagination that the man searches for in his 'love object'? That 'love object' with whom he dreams of building his home, but that which stands distinct from his wanting/conquering 'sex object' with whom he attains his sexual pleasure by fulfilling his desires outside the 'holy home'? That way 'dirty sex' remains out of the 'sanctified home' – which may be observed in the many clinical narratives of men who submit their difficulty in sexual performance at 'home' with the wife, that echoes an overruling notional presence of the 'sanctified maternal imago' in the internal familial space of the man. The man's internal sense of betrayal towards his maternal commitment interferes with his unacceptable sexual desires and claims that he considers to be filthy and unacceptable. Subsequently, the very same male individual who is, on the one hand, devoted and faithful towards his domestic front, his 'home' (his maternal-wife), may be equally violating, and aggressive towards the 'other woman' in his external front, on the other hand. This deceptive duality is the result of the male psychic split regarding his 'love object' and 'object-of-desire' (Kakar, 2016) This way the 'other woman' – that is, any woman who does not qualify the maternal imagination – becomes his 'dirty pit' to dump all his sexual deviance.

As often noticed in the clinical space, a probable fallout of this is the problematisation and the split between the sexual object choice and the love commitment for the adult male. His fantasy-woman gets divided into the 'milky mother,' the inexhaustible giver; and the 'other' woman being the 'devouring whore,' the insatiable, gorging woman (Kakar, 1990). As a matter of fact, Kakar (2016) draws a compelling correlation in his elaboration of the legend of infant-god Krishna and Putana, the *rakshasa* (demoness). Putana the demoness comes in the guise of a young, beautiful woman to tempt infant-Krishna and breast-feed him to kill him with her poisoned breast milk. But the infant-god Krishna sucks her milk as well as her life from Putana. The maternal body acts as inexhaustible giving machinery which the son preys upon with its insatiable sucking for its survival. The mother–son dyad is laden with betrayal, ambivalence, seduction and conflicts (with life and death, good and evil). But because Putana the demoness performed an act that is the pinnacle of maternal dedication and sacrifice, she is also considered to be a foster-mother of the infant-god Krishna. Thus, the evil that is Putana *rakshasa* (symbolically the combined imago of the seductive insatiable gorging woman and the maternal) had to die and the all-encompassing omnipresent 'good lord' survived in the form of God Krishna. In this way, the male stays firm in his singular commitment to the maternal and in servitude towards the family in a continuum to his 'illusion of unity' from his childhood fantasy of the ideal mother–son bodily-dyadic bonding. The male continues in his life-long effort at renouncing his own unacceptable voracious sexual and physical desires, and purifies himself by flooding his 'filth' (i.e. his sexual fervour) onto the 'other voracious woman.' And the inexhaustible (for)giving mother not only forgives her immortal infant-son for his every act of blunder and cruelty in life, but also for his sexual infidelities and sexual aberrations – all in semblance to infantile playful acts in the maternal (for)giving eyes. This further gives the man the unsaid consent of the maternal agreement in this dual pact, and thus may feel justified, even righteous in continuing his trailing expedition of conquesting women in his life. That way the purity of the mother–son duo's commitment to each other continues to overrule the masculine intra-psychic space and the socio-cultural dominance of patriarchy stands confirmed in society. In such situations it may be observed that the male may often go through an internal resistance to the integration of this split of his fear of defiling the ideal mother-figure with his eruption of hidden desire for the 'vagina dentata,' that is his fantasy of a devouring vagina with teeth that castrates his male virility (echoing fear of the Putana). This paranoid fantasy formulation is perhaps the consequence of a primitive symbolism of a mutual mother–son participatory pact that gets further invested with the man's own aggressive and sexual drives in later life. The internal split in the male imagination finds overt externalisation in the denigration and brutal treatment of the 'feminine' in reality in the Indian site. While the maternal worship of the woman in the form of goddesses continues to dominate the Indian male imagination and socio-cultural values. The man psychically chooses the culturally offered familiar safety-net of his primal maternal-fusion, his familial heritage, keeping intact his omnipotent, innocent, infantile psychic mechanism secured by the eternally inexhaustible (for)giving mother.

Myths

i 'The Ganesha complex,' India – Sudhir Kakar
ii The prohibition of 'Don't Look,' Japan – Osamu Kitayama

A myth is a cultural rite of passage that narrates the stories of its community fantasies in a symbolic manner, echoing the shared beliefs of its people. It is a tale that unfolds the magical power of gods and supernatural beings, representing archetypal characters, all of which teach the people of the mortal world the morals of fair and unfair, good and evil, reward and punishment. It grapples with existential uncertainties of universal concerns. In the East, the foundations of myths are deeply rooted in its people and its belief system since it is more a communal, filial culture than the individual culture of Western society. Children grow up listening to epic stories from various sources – starting from their grandmothers, to comic books, to popular television/media productions, audio-visual series, audiobooks, and so on. With the contemporary changing of socio-economic phenomena, and the blooming of technology in urban life and in nuclear family structures, the medium of such mythological deliberations is altering. But the element of magic inherent in such narratives finds even more of an overwhelming magnitude with the addition of technological illusion. Myths re-produce primitive beliefs that transform into rituals that act towards cultural cohesion, invoking a common shared practice. It acts like a binding force to hold the community together, providing a commonly shared sense of identity. The quality of timelessness inherent in mythical lore enhances the omnipotent presence of its magical charm all throughout its time span. The very structure of mythical stories bears the mark of ultimate catharsis in the unfolding of its narrative, lifting the veiled sense of 'soil' (sin/dirt) that is camouflaged as playful, miraculous material for the infantile imagination (often portrayed as passionate and aggressive bloody imageries, or scenes of wars, or aching struggles), which is meant to be overcome by the protagonist in the story. That way it teaches the reaffirmation and validation of truth and honesty in mortal existence that wins and survives the end of all the bloody wars. The recounting of story-telling, which is the very essence of a myth, with its archaic fervour and belligerence embedded in its characters, equally adds to the nuances of the infantile web of fantasia, its very own internal 'fairyland.' The people of the community are like the infant children of that civilisation who identify with the divinity of the mythological characters, giving them a magical sense of omnipotence – an innately shared suppressed desire of all members of a community across time. The cultural need to clasp such chronicles with mighty certitude may be an unconscious requirement for cultural defence to pursue a singular, common act for its binding communal identity using the 'pleasure principle' against the climate of a difficult, resisting 'reality principle.' Simultaneously, it is a shared identity of a community that was constructed from their own autonomous, indigenous imagination against all external, foreign, and colonial invasions, and the uncertainties of reality that a country has to undergo. The omnipresent power of myths, along with the seductive element of magical fables, makes it possible to travel across generations and time.

(i) Ganesha complex:

The Ganesha complex is a theoretical exposition by the eminent psychoanalyst Sudhir Kakar from India, who has worked extensively on Hindu myths; he elaborates on the Hindu mythological story of goddess Parvati (or Uma), the wife of Shiva, and her two sons, Ganesha and Skanda. The story goes like this – in a playful context, Parvati told her two sons that whoever among the two brothers went around the universe first would be rewarded by their mother with the floating mango in the stream. Hearing that, Skanda immediately got on his peacock and began his journey around the universe. While Ganesha, who rode the rat, took a while to ponder over what his mother may have actually meant by this, and in response to this quest he circled around his mother, worshipped her, and announced to his mother that he had just gone around *his* universe. Undoubtedly Parvati, his mother, was very pleased with this answer and immediately rewarded her son Ganesha with the promised mango.

Kakar in his paper, 'Hindu myth and psychoanalytic concepts: The Ganesha complex' (2005), elaborated on this mythological narrative to highlight Ganesha and Skanda as representations of two oppositional psychological positions in the wake of the oedipal conflict in the Hindu Indian male. It is a tug-of-war between the independent, autonomous, adventurous Skanda who leapt on the very aspect of exploring the world; and Ganesha, the perennially longed-for-son who renounced his dilemma of separation–individuation (Mahler, 1963) and chose to remain inseparable in his devotion to his mother. Ganesha's immersion into the maternal-fusion eternally secured him with his maternal symbiotic attachment, gaining her undeniable protection of him. Thus, the infantile status gets heightened, binding both the mother and the son in its playful infantile psychic space, symbolically resonating a singular enmeshed existence. Skanda was punished due to his choice of individuation and thus was deprived of his mother's bountiful gift-of-love. Ganesha, on the other hand, was rewarded with the return of the eternal mother's 'milky breast' (the symbolical mango). The male omnipotent fantasy finds reaffirmation in the mother's surreptitious tempting role of the building this maternal mesh. One is left wondering if the cultural validation and exaltation of such Ganeshas in a community paves the way for the intricate patriarchal architecture to covertly invoke the woman into the motherhood fantasy, counter-feeding its phallic web of masculine imagination that binds the woman into a maternal-feminine imago, who is the embodiment of the lavish and the plentiful, the infinite, as in the mythological characters. The heightened cultural glorification of this maternal-fusion acts as a clandestine partner to patriarchy itself. However, this does not imply the 'pathologisation' of this condition on its culture, but rather to be read as a cultural diversity of rearing practices that need to be appreciated and contained by the analyst for it to find its release from its psychic captivating state in the patient and understood in the clinical space, leading to the foundational fabric of identification and trust that is necessary for the progressive therapeutic engagement of the analytic dyad.

(ii)   The prohibition of Don't Look:

Osamu Kitayama from Japan took the story of *The Crane Wife* (Bodkin & Spirin, 1998) from the Japanese folk tales to develop his theory of the prohibition of 'Don't Look' (refer to Chapters 1 and 2). The story of *The Crane Wife* is of a devoted crane-animal-wife who made her husband happy and rich by weaving precious cloth from feathers that she plucked from her own body. The husband was prohibited from looking at her while she was weaving. But he broke the prohibition only to find his beautiful, bountiful wife turn into a crane and flee in shame (Kitayama, 2010).

The plucking of feathers by the wife from her own body was a self-sacrificial act that was equally self-damaging, but which brought happiness and prosperity to the family at the cost of the gradual diminishing of her own body (leading to total vanishing/dying). A quality that echoes a continuing equivalence of the inexhaustible giving mother in the woman. The husband has been characterised as an innocent child who with his onerous demands on his maternal-wife was blind to his inexhaustible giver till she fled, vanished, died. The quality of the 'animalisation' of the wife from the woman of 'idealisation' in the husband's imagination reveals his incapacity to perceive the mother-like figure as a whole object that further prompted him into his infantile nature of robbing the mother's breast of all its goodness. The prohibition acted as an unsaid rule exercised on the dependant person in a love situation, in other words in the situation of *amae* (Doi, 1989), where he is forbidden to see the inevitable painful process of separation–individuation involved in a dynamic symbiotic relationship. This is the working of the prohibition of 'Don't Look' on the mother–son symbiotic bonding. In this way, it re-emphasises maternal enthrallment and the return of the maternal-fusion that evicts all possibilities of the separation-individuation to take shape. This infantile position further protects the male from his internal paranoid split between the 'idealised' giving mother and the 'animalised' gorging woman.

The husband was punished for transgressing the prohibition of looking into the wife's secret behind her inexhaustible giving and was thus left with the guilt of killing his love object (symbolically depicted by the fleeing of the crane). Hence, to maintain the status quo of the inexhaustible nourishing arrangement, the husband had to remain in enslavement, a counter-feeding mechanism that was created by the very smothering inexhaustible giving nature of his love object itself. Any betrayal of that fusion would entail a total expulsion of the love object itself – it appears like a silent threat to the son of eviction from maternal love. At the same time let us remember that all such myths were creative inceptions of the male fantasy, mostly crafted by men themselves. The final 'flee' or death of the maternal-wife is also an act of absolute inevitability by the creative genius of the male imagination, the author, that equally warns the woman to announce her finality if she fails to sustain her web of mysterious relentless nourishment around the impassive, innocent, helpless 'infant-man.' That way the prohibition played a dual role in its application – the bell of warning was both for the 'infant-husband' and the 'maternal-wife.' The seductive element in the prohibition created a sense of secrecy around the woman which only added to the imagination of the mystical nature and vulnerability of the woman. It further ignited the male imagination of the 'other' in the woman, while keeping alive his devotion for his bountiful maternal-wife. And here lies the bed of ambivalence and split in the man regarding his worshipable mother/wife, and the object of his desire – the disdainful 'other woman.' This further creates an almost culturally inves-ted infantile position for the male in the Japanese imagination, quite similar to the Indian situation, both immersed in the devoted maternal-fusion state of frenzy. Here lies an interesting correlation between maternal enthrallment, patriarchal insinuation and cultural valuation for the fraternisation and rein-forcement of 'maternal-infusion in males' in both societies.

'Timelessness' of myths and its rupture in time

The quality of timelessness in myths is characterised by the enduring nature of powerful symbols and universal themes that connect people across gen-erations (as exemplary in the case of Japan and India in discussion here). The narratives of myths get reiterated, re-constructed, and re-emphasised time and again as they continue to travel through their oral deliberations and transi-tions across ages and cultures. As time moves, culture also goes through its transformations imbibing the essence of being in a state of flux. Accordingly, its symbolic relevancies also go through transitions complementing the cul-tural flux of its fluidity, corresponding to its changing time and its evolving, redefining environmental contextual indications. The repeated renunciation, and retelling of myths, allows it to evolve over time which opens up the probability of its changing adaptations within an altering society and time (as may be observable in the prohibition of 'don't look' as well as of the Ajase complex in both the societies in discussion here).

Confronted with such incestuous fantasies of the symbiotic bonding, as discussed above, Kitayama talks about the need for the 'prohibition,' – in the myths, and in human life – to eventually be broken. The mythological, cultural prohibitions need to undergo revision with time (Part II of the book elaborates on this). While the prohibition needs to satisfy the infantile demands of the infant child, it equally needs a cultural maturational moment to break the primal web over time for the evolutionary journey of the individual, and humankind in society. As Kitayama further exemplified – unlike the oedipal taboo, which is meant to be kept, as in most Western societies, this maternal prohibition of the mother–son symbiotic attachment in the East calls for a rupture but only over time. It is also its mark of distinction between a 'taboo' and a 'prohibition.' It is only with this rupture at the time of the symbiotic phase that the individual's capacity to be alone may be experienced, which subsequently assists in its 'true intimacy' with another (Winnicott, 1965). This is a paradoxical implication in the developmental phase of the separation–individuation process, but it is an equally essential process for the disenchantment of the magical symbiotic knot. This helps in profaning the discontent in the once considered to be sacred, omnipotent, worshipable mother–son dyad. It opens up the realm of reality for the evolving adult male to navigate through. And thus, provides opportunity for an alternative narrative formation along with an evolving psychic transformation for the age-old male imagination. Simultaneously it accelerates the floodgate of sexuality in him, making it a very complex pathway into his adult future.

The male protagonist's animalisation of his love object reaffirms his incapacity to incorporate the whole object, splitting his own unacceptable sexual fantasies and aggressive drives into the object which he eventually kills (*The Crane Wife, The Fish Wife, The Clam Wife*). It would be an interesting twist in the treatment of such myths if today's changing mother/wife/woman refuses to 'flee,' die, but instead glares back to refract the age-old 'male gaze' back to the man, enforcing him to witness his own fantasised projections, both sexual and aggressive that lead to the death of his love object. Perhaps then will begin another different and new narrative of the real flesh-and-blood woman, along with the man. Both will then stand liberated from the mystical web of mythological imagination, and patriarchal constructs of the phallic order. The new chronicle of the woman would voice her abjection, her sufferings, her disavowal, her claims, her pleasures – all that will give her an entity of being included and contained by the phallic order. The woman will become her own active agent to recreate and re-cite her own histories for the emerging new 'myths-in-fluidity' of a contemporary time.

Maternal-fusion – a phallocentric cultural and religious claim, and the 'disavowed woman'

The novelty of a cultural dogma lies in its capacity to metamorphose the essential characteristic inherent in the concept of maternal-fusion in the mother-son dyad, and invest it for political triumphs, for example in religious practice and devotion, as well as for national patriotism. The history of colonial subjugation in India only adds up to the essence of the maternal-fusion in the deification of the motherland for its sons who willingly gave up their lives and sacrificed for the mother-nation. Built on the concept of maternal-fusion, it finds a larger scope of utilisation for the benefit of a nation-construction. Needless to say, the undercurrent of such patriarchal structures, in conjunction with the socio-cultural glorification of motherhood as a cultural mechanism of self-sacrificial maternal roles for the nation's women, equally corresponds to confirming the holy and devotional submission of its sons for the greater motherland. This aspect of the devoted sons/disciples (of a community/clan) becomes the dominant admirable and aspirable cultural value of a nation, generating a climate of an enigmatic passionate maternal enthrallment with the motherland that is awe-inspiring for all. Whereas the woman's identification and internalisation of the glorious maternal of the nation prepares the ripe ground for the eternal sacrifice of her individual entity for constructing the cultural artistry of an enthroned motherland. And here lies the success of the politics of a patriarchal national ideologue that surreptitiously entices both the target and the convict in its own oppressive mechanism of a deified 'nationalism' and devotion for the maternal and the motherland. Of course, this had its own beneficial application in resisting colonial rule in India with its due victory in enticing the collective/community into its seductive, passionate, enchanting dogma of the nation. In the construction of such a national, cultural imagination of the woman, there is a subtle and surreptitious merge of this concept of the women with the *Devi*-concept, a heightened maternal goddess complex, along with the motherland of the country, who is forever the inexhaustible (for) giving mother. One may observe the elusive unifying mechanism of national politics, cultural, religious beliefs and symbols drowning the embodied woman.

In the hierarchy of the individual male emotional investment, the man's filial duty and his national commitment go hand in hand. But lost in this patriarchal discourse is the woman's chronicle of her individual self-sacrifice, creating an impact of a total disavowal of the woman – a dismissal of her entity in reality altogether. As in mythical construction, her existence is validated by only upholding the 'son of the nation.' It is an abjection of her entity, her body, and thus her sexuality – casting away all her subjectivity in totality. Only motherhood as a reproductive mechanism of patriarchy finds due corroboration in this grinding architectural design of the phallic order. Subsequently, fragmentation of the woman/feminine from the maternal leads to the objectification of the woman, and her body, and thus emphasising the 'othering' of the woman gets levied by phallic desire. By embracing the role of motherhood, the woman secures the safety measures offered by patriarchy for her survival. In this sense, motherhood is not only a biological act of bearing children for the woman in India but equally serves as an instrument of survival and social worth for the woman against patriarchal domination. Subsequently, society feels equally reassured by the women's submissive compliance to motherhood in maintaining social doctrines and confinement. The idealisation of the maternal role shields the male from his own fantasised terror of the female sexual appetite – a counter-reaction to his imagined threatening female sexuality. The male imagination of heightened maternal nurturing assists him in mitigating his fantasy of ravenous female sexual desire in his male imagination. The centrality of this male discourse, a phallocentric schema, becomes the ruling national cultural doctrine that reinforces the national stereotypical construction of motherhood in women and culture – a re-production, a mass-production of manufacturing motherhood and mothers. Both the countries under discussion here, India and Japan, stand as specimens of such political ideological formulations. However, contemporary Japanese culture is at a challenging juncture where its women are rejecting the traditional roles of marriage and motherhood. This brings hope of an emerging new and different chronicle of today's woman, which is in the making, daring a reconstitution of a national, cultural imagination.

As may be observed, often such national values intersect with religious morality, making each other a counter-feeding mechanism to promote a pseudo-integrated sense of a certain cultural notion of a country. The national symbols, cultural traditions, and rituals intertwine with religious elements, making it impossible to distinguish national doctrines from religious faith and cultural values. At the same time, such intersections may also have a confrontational impact on community cohesion where there is a vastly diverse social matrix comprising many different religious symbols and practices, as in the Indian context. The devotion to the nation is expressed in similar ways of religious fervour with rituals and ceremonies that evoke a sense of sacredness. The nation, religion, and culture become inseparable. In the process the language of pluralism gets lost, making way for a gradual stealthy evolution of a singular dominant hegemonic cultural ideology which is very different from the vast reality of pluralism (as in the case of India with its dominant Hindu religion, and culture). And thus, gets fabricated a deeply rooted, intersecting and dogmatic narrative of a culturo-religious and political doctrine that gets established as an integrated national ideology and a cultural imagination of a country, as is evident in the case of India too.

Clinical vignette

Debesh was referred for therapy by his psychiatrist who was treating him for depression and peripheral anxiety for over six months. Debesh was a 40-year-old man who was a teacher by profession; he was single and lived with his parents.

He was their only son. He took good care of his ageing parents. He was of an artistic temperament and loved music and literature. Debesh lost his biological mother when he was 7 years old. Thereafter, his father married again after a year, primarily to have someone to look after his son.

The initial years after losing his mother were very difficult for Debesh. It was painful for Debesh to even merely look at his *notun maa* (new mother), as he used to call his stepmother. It took a number of years for them to become emotionally connected. Over time Debesh started feeling much closer to his *notun maa* than to his father. As a matter of fact, he started feeling very guilty about his attachment to his stepmother, which was not only much stronger than it was with his biological father but also became his own discomfort with his growing wish to forget his biological mother, even to avoid having any object in the house prompting her memory. He just wanted both his biological parents should leave him alone with his *notun maa*. She was immediately available to him and he felt contended with his *notun maa, notun* (new) world.

After a year of therapeutic work together with Debesh, he felt much lighter and freer in his expressions:

D: I still can't understand why I had to unnecessarily go through so much pain and guilt for no reason as such! Why should I feel guilty about loving my mother – just because she did not give birth to me does not mean that I cannot love her like my real mother, right?

(His need to hold onto his *notun maa* was acute after having lost his biological mother.)

D: Especially since she has always been so nice to me (breaks into laughter). She was not like what you grow up reading about stepmothers in fairy tales! I kept on thinking that she was being nice to me just because she was new (*notun*), waiting till her true colours finally came out. I kept waiting for that eventuality! But it never came (laughs aloud!).

A: It seems like you were disappointed by that.

D: It's funny you should say that! But I actually did feel so! Can you believe it, I couldn't find any reason to hate her! I couldn't find anything to complain about her to my father. I wanted *baba* (father) to scold her for me! I thought maybe that way she would not like *baba*, and then we could be close together. But I didn't get that chance …

Though there is something else that I need to talk to you about. I know this is something I can only talk to you about, nobody else will understand it. But I can't seem to make myself do it … have been thinking about it for some time, I keep suffering because of it …

A: What is stopping you from saying it when you know that it is only here that you can talk about it?

D: I find it difficult to pronounce those words, to hear it myself … I feel ashamed …

Debesh continued,

D: Whenever I am somewhat close to *notun maa*, something happens to me … I seem to get some kind of a partial erection (followed by silence) … I then quickly leave the room, distract myself and then gradually it goes away. I try to avoid getting close to my mother, or being alone with her because I am scared that 'it' will happen to me again … 'It' doesn't happen always, just sometimes … on and off …

At one level Debesh's guilt was due to his sense of betrayal towards his biological mother for loving his stepmother. At another level, it was because of the arousal of his sexual feelings and fantasies regarding his stepmother (his partial erection). He was caught up on his route to claiming individuation by his growing strong oedipal desire for his stepmother. Debesh was failing in his effort to distinguish between his feelings of love from his feelings of desire for his mother. Thereby feeling psychically trapped between these two contrasting, but related, wishes of his that were internally trying to seek unity in one object, his mother. His resistance in wanting to see his internal conflict, his own internalisation and the following excitement of cultural insinuations of maternal-fusion as well as prohibitions, gave birth to his inner sense of guilt and consequent need for punishment. He was left in confusion with his arousal of erotic love for his primary love object and his filial love for his mother, both getting enmeshed into one body in his imagination, which further blurred all inner boundaries in him. The gradual analytic effort was to initiate opening up his sexual fantasies to the 'analytic third' in session (Ogden, 2004), only after sufficient transferential attachment had set in the analytic dyad. Thereby creating an opportunity for transferential fantasies of similar imaginations within the analytic dyad, and in the process of this evolving analytic dyad to strive for the 'prohibition' to be broken over time, without guilt, in his psychic fancy.

A well of masturbatory fantasies and other sexual fantasies erupted over time, which Debesh confirmed he had feared to even imagine earlier, let alone enjoying the pleasure of exploring his own body. Over time Debesh appeared to be able to accept his own sexual fantasies for his stepmother and overcome his internal prohibition of articulating it. His guilt seemed to dilute with time as he could examine, along with his analyst, his fantasy of a mutually seductive participation of both him and his mother in the mother–son dyad that had captivated him for so long. Perhaps one may be able to find the conceptual journey of the symbolic working of the Ganesha complex through its transition into the prohibition of 'Don't Look' in its gradual unfolding process in the analytic work with Debesh. Later in sessions, Debesh could see how he tried to re-produce similar 'romantic' situations enacted in the analytic space as well – by singing songs for me which he used to do for his mother in the evenings when sitting on the balcony of their house. The analytic space became his symbolic playful space within the dyad, interchanging in fantasy the mother–son dyad and the analytic dyad. He recalled those lovely summer evenings that he spent with his mother on the balcony when his father was travelling for work. His mother was very fond of his 'sweet' child-like voice and asked him to sing for her. His mother's clandestine longing for his child-like innocence, 'entrapped' in his 'sweet' voice, bound him into an enmeshed dyadic existence for decades. With the help of the analytic third, Debesh could gradually emerge from his enchanted state in the maternal-fusion, and search for 'true intimacy' in his evolving fresh self that he began to be interested in gradually. Needless to say, before arriving at the threshold of his newly found love object, the analytic dyadic space was charged with Debesh's exceedingly romantic-erotic fantasies revolving around the analyst. That was a point of reflection for him – his seeking for someone in reality with whom he could enjoy such romantic-erotic engagements in actuality. However, once he was outside the filial enmeshment with his *notun maa*, he equally realised his deep sense of loneliness engrained in him, stifled in him, ever since his biological mother had expired and saw his father find his life partner while he stood all alone. Debesh's severe sense of abandonment and betrayal by both his parents took us to his psychic lane of solitary existence with no love for him. Consequentially it lead us to his clinging to his internal fantasy of a bountiful, inexhaustible loving object in his imagination, his primary love object, his biological mother – that found its overt projection in corporeal stimulation/manifestations in his fantasy of his *notun maa*. The shock of having lost his biological mother at last found words of release from that throttled pain of years. It was like a psychic rebirth that brought Debesh out of an intensely emotionally enmeshed, entangled womb to the world. And that was another phase of our analytic journey.

Over time, this transition made a deep impact on Debesh whose capacity for sublimation and integration brought about a harmonious blend in his personality. Debesh's world was no longer confined within his familiar symbiotic walls but opened up to a new world of affect, attachments, and anxieties. His inner world felt alive with his own designs. It would be a mistake to think that the process of individuation in the Indian communal context attempts to separate the individual from the community or family. Its effort lies only in liberating the individual from the captivating condition of the maternal-fusion which finds cultural reaffirmation making the journey of individuation all the more painful and guilt-laden. This dual process perhaps makes the adult journey more complex since both community/filial life and the individuation process for the individual continue to exist side by side simultaneously. Debesh continued to look after his parents and appreciated his mother for treating him as her own, while his own emotional romantic-erotic life slowly started unfolding leading him to search outside his filial domain.

Conclusion

The exploration of cultural invocation of maternal-fusion in males in both India and Japan unveils profound insight into the intricate dynamics of family, tradition, and socio-cultural designs. As mentioned above, it is a nuanced observation of the interplay between nation, religion, and culture that finds a collective deliberation of a singular, overarching national ideological and cultural design (particularly for India). By delving into these cultural narratives, we not only deepen our understanding of gender roles and familial bondings in community living but equally recognise the enduring power of the phallic order in procreating patriarchal engineering. This further preys on desiring the maternal imagination within cultures determining individual identities, behaviour, along with collective consciousnesses across diverse cultural landscapes. The invocation of maternal-fusion continues to remind us of its timeless significance in being an essential fabric of socio-cultural constructs (in Eastern societies like India and Japan). A phallocentric discourse that is deeply ingrained in cultural norms and beliefs perpetuates gender stereotypes impacting individual development, fantasy and collective cultural imagination. However, an interesting challenge to this phallocentric discourse is thrown by the mythological constructs of complex maternal characterisations like Putana (from Indian mythology as discussed earlier here) and Vaidehi (i.e. Idaike from the Ajase complex, Japan – taken from the Ajatashatru Buddhist myth that originated from India but later got transported to Japan). Later, Chapter 11 will elaborate on maternal ambivalence and betrayal towards the child, the male-child in particular, thereby problematising the entire concept of maternal glorification, simultaneously indicating a more authentic narrative of the female experience. At the same time it equally questions and explores the contradictory male sadistic creative imagination of the 'evil-woman' combining elements of the 'femme fatale' and the archetypal 'witch' into its maternal characterisation, who has to pay with her life for her 'anomaly.'

References

Balint, M. (1959). *Primary Love and Psychoanalytic Technique* (pp. 82, 85). London: Tavistock Pub.

Bodkin, O. & Spirin, G. (1998). *The Crane Wife*. San Diego: Gulliver Books.

Bose, G. (1949). The genesis and adjustment of the Oedipus wish. *Samiksa*, 3 (4), 222–240. Kolkata: Indian Psychoanalytical Society.

Chodorow, Nancy. (1978). *The Reproduction of Mothering*. University of California Press.

Deutsch, H. (1930). The significance of masochism in the mental life of women. *Int. J. Psa.* 11, 48–60.

Doi, T. (1989). The concept of *amae* and its psychoanalytic implications. *Int. Review of Psycho-analysis*, 16, 349–354.

Kakar, S. (1990). *Intimate Relations: Exploring Indian Sexuality*. Chicago: Univ. of Chicago Press.

Kakar, S. (2005). Hindu myth and psychoanalytic concepts: The Ganesha complex. In *Asian Culture and Psychotherapy: Implications for East and West* (pp. 76–84). Honolulu: Univ. of Hawai'i Press.

Kakar, S. (2016). The engulfing mother in Indian mythology: Masculinity & conflicting desires. *ANTYAJAA: Indian Journal of Women & Social Change*, 1 (1).

Kitayama, O. (2010). *Prohibition of Don't Look: Living Through Psychoanalysis and Culture in Japan*. Tokyo: Iwasaki Gakujutsu Shuppansha.

Minsky, Rosalind (1996). *Jaques Lacan, 'The Meaning of the Phallus' (1958) in Psychoanalysis and Gender*. London: Routledge.

Mahler, M. S. (1963). Thoughts about development and Individuation. *Psychoanalytic Study of the Child*, 18, 307–324.

Ogden, T. H. (2004). The Analytic Third: Implications for psychoanalytic Theory and Technique. *Psychoanalytic Quarterly, LXXIII*, 167-195.

Slote, W. H. (1992). Oedipal ties and the issues of separation-individuation in traditional Confucian societies, *J. American Academy of Psychoanalysis*, 20 (3), 436–453.

Tseng, W.-s., Choo Chang, S., & Nishizono, M. (Eds.). (2005). *Asian Culture and Psychotherapy: Implications for East and West*. Honolulu: Univ. of Hawai'i Press.

Winnicott, D. W. (1965). *The Maturational Process and the Facilitating Environment: Studies in the Theory of Emotional Development*. New York: Int. Univ. Press.

Chapter 8

Vicissitudes of transience in Covid times – reflection on 'shame culture,' India

Jhuma Basak

Introduction

The Covid pandemic left humankind at large with a harrowing impact of death, disease, infinite sense of loss, isolation, and scepticism. The Covid outbreak brought forth the sheer impermanence of human life. It equally brought out the terrible angst and loneliness of human struggle for life. For an analyst, like me, this specific juncture of time enabled me to attempt a humble reflection on human life, death, uncertainty, and solitude. It led me to ruminate over the concept of transience – a Japanese philosophical and psychoanalytic approach – and the circularity of time in motion within the larger orbit of life.

In 1990 Charles Hanley stated:

> At the core of the being of each person there is a solitude in which he is related to himself. Truth resides in this solitude … The ground of genuine analytic work in the analyst is his attitude of respect for this solitude.
>
> (p. 382)

But what happens when this solitude itself becomes a state of incarceration enforced by external agency, as during the pandemic? The situation of the pandemic brought about a psychic cage of loneliness where one lost all sense of relatedness with external reality, the predominant being that of *Thanatos*, death and suffering that enveloped the immediate environment, a strange, shared phenomenon across the world. One felt bereft of all subjectivity, and meaninglessness in life crept in.

Humans are meant to live together in harmony in society – unfortunately, Covid brought about a contagious impact on fellow beings that implanted the fear of spreading germs across human connections. It had the potential to create greater discord and discrimination within human society, especially on such diverse grounds as in India – a country which already has such an age-old history of forsaken divides and bigotry in terms of caste, religion, class, ethnicity, and gender. The situation prompted a sad reawakening of the 'uncanny' in us, projecting our very own hidden fearful fantasies of the 'other'

DOI: 10.4324/9781003501930-9

to justify the already existing discriminating prejudices in India. The unsettling feeling of all familiarity transforming into strange unfamiliar territories affected human relations most profoundly, bringing about an unusual sense of estrangement within oneself and around the rest of the community.

Amae *and transience*

The concept of transience in Japanese psychoanalysis is deeply rooted in the cultural and philosophical context of Japan. It draws its inspiration from traditional philosophies, particularly from the Buddhist notion of impermanence or *mujo* where every presence/existence is subject to constant transformation. Transience works silently in object transition, which is a tangible physical movement, while by itself it aids in a psychic transformation. It liberates humans from their unyielding attachments in life, both material and abstract (like desire itself). Accepting the impermanence of life assists in cultivating the imagination of a simultaneous dual presence of life and impermanence/death within our consciousness while we continue to remain in the continuum of our lifecycles. The attempt here is to look at the nuances of reclaiming transience in cultural and individual existential practices at a point of human crisis when confronted with harsh veracities of survival, like in the recent pandemic.

Let me begin with the Ajase story – a mythological reference, originally from India (refer to the Introduction here) leading to the subsequent Japanese psychoanalytic concept of the Ajase complex by Haisaku Kosawa (1939). It was later expounded by Keigo Okonogi (1979). Interestingly Ajase is also known as Ajatasatru from Indian Buddhist mythology, meaning 'one who has no enemies.' The Ajase complex is an Eastern viewpoint on matricide, complementing the Western perspective of patricide in the Oedipus complex. The locus of its narrative is founded on the mother–child conflictual, piercing, emotional entanglement (in particular the mother–son dyad). It deals with complex dynamics of ambivalence, resentment, and contrasting passionate emotional embroilment for both connectedness and independence in Ajase. The birth of Ajase itself was rooted in the maternal acrimony and betrayal of Idaike (his mother, also known as Vaidehi in the Indian reference), who herself was struck with dreadful anxiety fearing the loss of her husband's love. Idaike's rancour was based on her grievous lament of losing the love of her husband, which perhaps found a displaced release in her helpless son. Her bitterness and prenatal rancour provoked the desire for matricide in Ajase. But over time, with her maternal maturational process, Idaike overcame her own resentful limitations and looked after her sick son to heal him with bountiful love/*amae*, endowing the seed of reparative guilt in the mother–son object relationship (Klein, 1975). *Amae* is a non-verbal feeling of love, both submissive and receptive in nature, experientially a dependant state of love that typically signifies a child's affectionate reliance on parental love 'to depend and presume upon another's love' (Doi, 1989). The reparative guilt in Ajase grew from the repentant feeling of being forgiven by his mother, which is distinct from the guilt arising out of the fear of punishment, which is persecutory guilt. Thus, Ajase could initiate the course of reparative guilt within himself towards his mother. Subsequently being supported with *amae*, having gained his primary narcissism, Ajase's latent ground for reparative guilt was prepared to carry forward the quality of generosity. Over time both Ajase and Idaike moved from an infantile state of dependency/*amae* to a developed quality of *amae*, of inter-dependence, within the symbiotic relationship, responding to the inherent effective potential of transformation in the concept of *amae*.

According to Kitayama's inference (Kitayama, 1998), the state of *amae* is transitional, locating it midway between 'one-ness' and 'separate-ness' – that which is interpolated between the enmeshed ego of the mother–child dyad and the later progression towards the separation–individuation process. The intrinsic dynamic feature of *amae* gives it the probability of a transitional element that can travel from individual to individual, generation to generation, implying the significance of the momentum in time and the quality of circularity in time. And this is *amae*'s central transformational potential. As Idaike could forego her resentment towards her son, similarly Ajase could equally express his compassion towards his mother in the circular motion of a rotating time. With mutual grace, they both traversed through the initial stage of infantile *amae*, from dependency to inter-dependence, to its mutually maturational potential of both complementing and containing each other.

Reflecting on the quality of transience working through *amae* within an object relationship, helps to create the ground for absorbing the transitional phenomenon of an object within object relationship dynamics. Transition is a phenomenological description of movement, while transience is purely an emotional counterpart of the transition complementing it. In facing death, it initiates the process of mourning by helping the transitional object to become emotionally transient, thereby internalising the essential *jouissance* of the object and containing it within the self as a continuum of the life-drive itself, propelling vitality in life's trajectory. To have transience as a philosophical and cultural attribution creates further ground for strengthening ego-insight and it then releases reparative inclination for the community as a cultural practice. It helps to experience mourning in death and loss, and not necessarily be captivated by the bereavement of the object leading to melancholia with unresolved conflicts leading to self-deprecation. While Japan is confronted with a history of environmental losses through countless earthquakes and the horrifying impact of the atomic bomb, India has battled enormous losses in its history of numerous foreign invasions, political crusades, and climatic calamities and famines. In such collective loss and trauma of both natural as well as man-made catastrophes, transience may attempt to build internal resilience and assist in transiting from one point of life to another, to transit from one phase of life to another phase. And in that way the self's cohesion towards life-drive stays preserved in the larger orbit of its lifecycle.

Mentalisation and Transience in self & community

Through a psychoanalytic lens, mentalisation implies the capacity to reflect on one's thoughts, mental states, and intentions to experience them as mental representations. And in this process, the goal is to integrate affective and cognitive processes which may further help to relate internal and external realities. This way it attempts to create an uninterrupted system of relative and unified coherence in one's thought process corresponding with affective dispositions. The capacity to imagine the other person's state of mind and feelings which elicits an empathic connection with the other is a vital human capacity of mentalisation (Fonagy & Luyten, 2018). The consolidation of this depends heavily on the early relationship between the infant and its caregiver, and progressively on the individual's aptitude for containing internal symbolisation through the process of mentalisation. It simultaneously has an almost cyclic response to the enhancement of inter-subjective reflection and deepening life's insightful experiences. Kohut, 1971, from the perspective of self-psychology, emphasised that transience highlights the *fluid* nature of self-experience and the ongoing process of psychological growth and development of the individual human psyche. Environmental anchors may equally act as catalytic agents to facilitate the process of 'epistemic trust' (Fonagy & Luyten, 2018) in the individual, especially in societies where object-relational bondings feel thwarted by overwhelming socio-political and environmental conflicts and coercions. Often cultural and environmental attachment mechanisms may assist, even substitute, as a collective continuum of this foundational trust in humankind. The rich inheritance of symbols and suggestiveness embedded in different languages and varied cultures assist in acting as a potential cultural container for collective mentalisation and offer reparation and resilience to the community. Mentalisation helps one to reach out of one's entranced solipsistic subjectivity and relate with the outer world in order to bring back reinforced meaning into one's own subjectivity – a self-enriching cyclic mechanism. The chief function of mentalisation lies in its capacity for symbolisation, and eventually the reconfiguration of the subject's relation to the object. Mentalisation thus brings about a unique converging point of thought, reflection, symbolisation and affective disposition. It may further act as a catalytic agent in the ego's effort to adapt, especially during a critical traumatic locale. For example, as witnessed in the Covid situation when our inner subjectivity was faced with an external reality of a harrowing fragile time of death and devastation.

The dynamic abstract quality of transience implies an inherent longing for what one has left behind while simultaneously helping to move ahead in life's journey. It silently assists in object transition, a tangible physical movement along with psychic transformation (Freud, 1916). In this sense, it concurrently reflects on the past along with a forward movement into the future that takes place all in a singular stroke. In Kitayama's study of the Japanese *ukiyo-e* paintings ('pictures of the floating world,' often found in woodblock prints, Kitayama, 2003) one may be able to locate a certain treatment of this to-and-fro movement between the two worlds, comprising the real world that we live in and the abstract cosmic world of our imagination. In poetic creations the nuance of the symbolic lies between what is uttered and what is implied, thereby creating possibilities of metaphoric inferences, hence dynamic inter-pretations embedded within the edifying structure of the poetic creation itself. It uses the symbolic in connecting the micro individual with the macro abstract of a universal design. Other creative forms like the musical creative forms of *Bhatiyali*, an old folk form from Bengal (India) and Bangladesh, where boatmen sing about their lives on the water, floating on the ebb and flow of the rivers. The word *bhatiyali* comes from the word *bhata* in Bengali, meaning ebb or downstream. The rhythmic flow of the music reminiscences the gentle movement of the boat on the water. The soulful and allegorical quality in the layered rendition of the music creates an abstract, sensual and symbolic connection for the community with the macro/oceanic expanse of the cosmos, fostering a sense of unity within the larger universal lifecycle (Tagore, 1913). This cultural framework comprising the capacity of 'aesthetic experience' enables the psychic processing of grave anxiety into creativity, a constructive life-enforcing act, that takes place at the inception of the depressive position in the psychic structure (Klein, 1935). This assists in cul-tivating ego strength and trust within the individual, reinforcing the intuitive foundation for faith in the unknown and the mysteries of the universe. It uses both transience and transition to offer a collective, cultural reparation and containment for the uncertainty faced by the boatmen, fishermen and common man in the water and in life. The musical quality acts as a 'transi-tional phenomenon' (Winnicott, 1979), an ephemerality of transience faced by the boatmen in water. This way life's preservation continues to reside in the intrapsychic space giving hope which subsequently provides ego strength to navigate through obstacles faced in external reality. It offers the metaphorical inclusion of the concept of mortality in its lifecycle. With the annual torrent of rain and deluge that Bangladesh faces every year, it is quite unfathomable how its boatmen and fishermen still find the courage to set sail every day with the hope of life and sustenance in such tumultuous rivers. It is only with the unconscious internalisation of such collective-mentalisation processes and transience phenomena that a community can survive its trials of constant coexistence of life and death faced in daily existence in this singular lifecycle.

The conjecture may be that the highly symbolic and abstract potential inherent in cultural beliefs and practices may prepare the very ground for the mechanism of mentalisation to be initiated by the community. Mentalisation employs transience bringing about reparation to perform its task of transition of the lost object, thereby assisting in the transformational process of its own subjective position. And in this affective manner it attempts to attach the two worlds in this existing lifecycle. It symbolically provides the human subject with a connecting psychic bridge between its internal world of imagination and its shared external uncertain reality which together helps in life's dynamic progressive movement. The Eastern philosophy with the belief in the soul – its interminable, immortal existence – and its metaphysical journey through the two worlds in this very lifetime acts as a comprehensive quality of mentalisation and transience working together for the eternal floating and travelling self in juxtaposition against the impermanence and fragility of reality-time. This creates the magical notion of an infinite life force in spite of an individualised limited mortal survival in the existing reality of a limited life-span. The Covid outbreak produced a ghastly experience of the outright insubstantiality of life where the quality of transience in engagement with mentalisation could help humankind sail through such unpredictable periods of existence.

Caste sectarianism and 'shame culture' in India

During the recent pandemic there was an alarming 'psychic spread' of dirt and filth that cast over India adding to its already existing ground of a highly discriminated social reality. As if the Covid pandemic brought about psychic contagious dread in its people along with its terror of physical contamination. A severe paradoxical sense of dirt and purity resides in the Indian social and psychic structures from ancient times. The antiquated system of caste division of the country adds to the prejudice rooted in the community (Thapar, 2002). That way the very entity of a 'low-caste' individual has to combat shame and indignity from birth itself. The basis of a 'shame culture' plays a powerful role in segregating its people into different strata of society. A shame culture not only regulates social norms and behaviour of its community but equally builds powerful unshakeable archaic cultural and national idealised objects/ superego structures. There is the benign self-experiences of internalisation of self-defect (in extension to the body under the hierarchical structure of the caste system in India), leading to a mortification of being exposed/disclosed, resulting in the morbid fear of humiliation. Subsequently, it influences and interferes with all interpersonal relationships. Shame culture further uses psychological coercive measures of ostracisation to divide its people into authoritarian extremism. In that sense, the shame culture acts as an inherent clandestine resistance to the formation of epistemic trust in an individual and in the collective which is a necessary foundation for the development of mentalisation in later life. In such a plane, often the survival mechanism of a psychic split gets undertaken, and a primitive nature of doubt, mistrust, and consequent projections may overrule its climate. Other psychic defences that may be often used to protect the 'depleted self' against a climate of such shame are the ploy of pathological narcissism and disassociation. The feeling of a 'well of emptiness' may further prompt the crushed subjectivity to often search for collective identification in order to hold itself together and build a sense of belonging through community connections for its survival. More often than not it may lead to blind and dogmatic religious beliefs or magical faith in superstitious ideas, fundamental political ideology as well as authoritarian cultural and national typecasts. However, perhaps a more refined and creative pathway lies as an alternative artistic provenance of a country that formulates the greater enveloping cultural climate of the country. The aspired link with the community may temporarily help the individual ego to gather its seemingly sublimated functional potential, but its foundation may still continue to remain essentially fragile. In this way, such a complex shame cultural matrix may inadvertently foster the procreation of fragile ego structures while at the same time paradoxically try to provide a collective holding environment through its available mechanisms of cultural defences, reparations, and transmutations.

The concept of '*misogi*' is a Japanese practice of ritualistic cleansing of the body with water that Kitayama referred to in his elaboration of the mythological tale of Isanami–Izanaki. It is 'to wash away with water the filth from the Land of the Dead that contaminated him' (Kitayama & Ogimoto, 2022). Kitayama calls this state 'mythological thought patterns,' which determines the Japanese perception of acute uncleanliness or impurity. Thus, dirt becomes a taboo that gets further internalised by the subject situating the prohibition in the internal psychic locale of the subject's existence. This internal conflict with dirt and purity compels one into external actions of various cleansing and discriminatory practices all simultaneously. As Kitayama elaborated, mysophobia embedded in such 'mythological thinking' found dreadful expressions during the pandemic that further problematised the 'shame culture' in Japan.

As we may know, there is a dual ground of unholiness and piety rooted in the socio-cultural matrix of India as well. The underlying principle of such strange stringent concepts of the unsanctified and the virtuous, all together, in the Indian site may find its root way back in its ancient Sanskrit scriptures, like the *Manusmriti*, also known as the *Manava-Dharmasastra*, or the Laws of Manu, which is an authoritative book that charters duties, rules, values for the practice of Hindu religion by the community. *Manusmriti* was a metrical text that defined the social strata of India according to the Vedic scriptures (sacred Hindu religious text since the 2nd millennium BCE) based on people's *karma* (work) and *dharma* (duty, also religion). It may be noticed that in the very construction of *Manusmriti* itself that governance and religious faith has acted in a conjoined manner for the country from ancient times. Thus, human faith in divinity and one's sense of duty to daily tasks became coordinates of each other. As if, for the people, the law and order pronounced in running a society came as a direct dictate of God's will itself, thus it became the ultimate verdict for mankind. During the colonial period in India, *Manusmriti* was considered a legal text of reference to later construct the foundational code for Hindu Law. This division of the social structure separated communities based on tasks performed by them, keeping in mind the smooth running of order and regularity in society at large, which counter-produced an invariable strong foundation of hierarchy and discrimination in the social structure.

The Hindu legend is that the trinity of supreme divinity, *Trimurti*, comprising *Lord Brahma* – the creator, *Lord Vishnu* – the preserver, and *Lord Shiva* – the destroyer, hold the cosmic functions of creation, preservation, and destruction of the universe, embodied in a *Triad of Deities*. The quality of this legendary trinity comprising birth, life, and destruction of Indian divinity finds similar resonance in the Japanese concept of the triadic characteristics found in its mythical texts (like the Izanami–Izanaki story in Chapter 2) comprising passion, birth, and death in its narratives. Both echo an extraordinary sense of emotional embroilment as a mythical background for its cultural reference that further prepares the field for Eastern turbulent, dramatic and highly passionate states (as maybe often experienced in our clinical experiences with patients). In the Indian context of the *Triad of Deities*, the feminine endowment of giving birth is surreptitiously masked by having *Lord Brahma* as the creator of life (unlike the maternal deity Izanami of Japan). The Indian *Triad of Deities* covertly echoes its bisexual rumination by having a paternal deity, *Lord Brahma*, as the creator of life. This acted perhaps as a pretext for the cultural concept of '*ardhanarishwara*' (half male and half female bodied united in one body, i.e. *Lord Shiva* and his wife *Goddess Parvati*, an imagination that expanded into the heterosexual marital couples' concept of union), which happens to be the foundational cultural terrain of Indian sexuality that nurtured its cultural imagination of bisexuality from ancient times. Bisexuality as essentially an inherent fluid complementarity between traditionally defined male-female energies or identities. Perhaps the later centuries of colonial rule had its impact of turning such indigenous cultural imaginations of the Indian panorama into an imitative, imperialised, 'civilised,' Western existence that erased all its ethnic culturo-specific sexual imaginations for fear of being termed 'primitive,' 'dirty,' and 'uncivilised' by the 'white' West. It is quite evident then that the Indian cultural imagination is essentially a very complex structure that necessitates repeated historical examination for its continual reinterpretation and redefinition.

According to the fable, it is the divine manifestation of *Lord Brahma*, the creator, that gave birth to the allotment of society into four major divisions comprising the *Brahmins* (priests and scholars – the highest), the *Kshatriyas* (rulers and warriors), the *Vaishyas* (tradesmen and landowners), and *Shudras* (peasants and labourers – the lowest). The 'Untouchables' were right at the bottom, or outside the caste structure itself. Later they were called the 'Harijans' – children of God – by Mahatma Gandhi, 'the father of the nation.' The post-independent era considered such a coinage with much scepticism due to its very patronising impression that echoes the basic didactic ground of discrimination engrained in the psychic space of the 'elite class.' Over time the representations from minority communities, like the Tribals, added to the growing Dalit-voice, amounting to a very critical and sensitive socio-political, compounded caste-dynamics in the socio-cultural demography of the country.

Indian Caste System

Brahmins
(priests)

Kshatriyas
(warriors)

- Vaisyas
(merchants)

- Shudras
(peasants)

- Dalits
('untouchables')

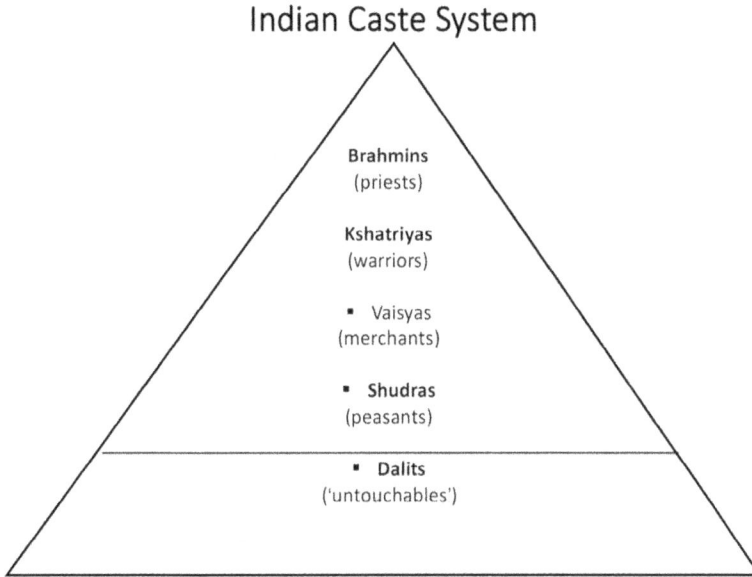

Figure 8.1 The caste pyramid

The caste system creates a landscape of entrenched prejudice and mutual discrimination within the country. It became the foundational tool for the 'uncanny' in projecting our own hidden fearful fantasies of the 'other' to further justifiably discriminate the already existing differences in the Indian national panorama (comprising 28 States and eight Union Territories). And in this way, it can 'abject,' cast out, the unacceptable 'foreign' elements in us, as often seen in the treatment of marginalised groups of 'low-caste' people, women, homosexuals, minority religious faith-holders, and so on, which became the target of a defective mechanism of the socio-cultural political practice in Indian society. This process of 'sectarian thought patterns' brings out the 'animality' in us, mixing violence with unruly fortitude. It abjects anything that is considered to be non-conforming, dirty, or impure – be it sex, or people, or women. The mysophobia embedded in 'mythological thinking' in Japanese culture resonates similar exposition in the 'sectarian thinking' in the Indian context, prompting immeasurable discrimination and unfairness among its people. Cleansing rituals in Hindu practices that follow religious morals, in sanctimonious social ceremonies like marriages, births or after death, unfortunately echo such internalised mysophobia in the daily existence of life in India. Such 'sectarian thinking' runs deep in the Indian psyche due to its passionate devotion and commitment entrenched in a co-existential and cooperative mechanism comprising ancient texts of religious faith and the governing duty of the nation. It is frightening to find that sectarianism can hold such a rooted controlling frenzy that it can transmit collective hysteria in the community (as was widely visible in the ruthless unreasonable treatment of 'migrant labourers' by 'other upper-class masters' in India during the pandemic). Sectarian imagination gets fed from all sectors of the socio-cultural parameters of the country. The stormy Covid period not only brought about the angst of the annihilation of human life itself, but equally perhaps of human conscience and empathy from society. One of the greatest challenges of such external threats was that it had the potential to rip apart human conscientiousness and the capacity for mutual compassion, and leave one with only one's own solitary timid existence. It had a direct impact on the collapse of all human ability for mentalisation and related compassion. It brought about the 'animality' in us that sought 'other' minority sectors in the community (like the Muslims, low-castes, migrant labourers) to dump its unruly infantile reawakening of the uncanny. It shook the apparently cohesive united ground of the country, leaving its people helpless in front of such a gigantic trial of humankind. This is perhaps where psychoanalytic insights like transience and mentalisation may help us to regain that hope within us to remain grounded within the community, with human bonding, to find mutual empathy and generosity in spite of such shuddering times.

Clinical vignette

Working with loss, shame, and sectarian thinking

Rupa came for therapy immediately after the pandemic lockdown, almost right after the clinic opened up for in-person treatment. Rupa's father accompanied her to the clinic who was himself 75 years old with frail health. Rupa was the only child of the family, 32 years old with a daughter of 6 years. She had recently, and very suddenly, lost her husband to Covid. At that time Rupa was living with her daughter in her father's house. Her father insisted she consult a psychiatrist who further recommended her for therapy along with medication (she was prescribed antidepressants). Rupa's father reported that Rupa had stopped going to work, hardly looked after her daughter, had disrupted eating and sleeping, and she would lie in her bed for hours and cry. She was in a state of shock, equivalent to a breakdown – it was not even two months since she had lost her husband. Rupa's father also reported that he found her to be repeatedly washing her hands with soap, and if he asked her why she was doing so she would reply – 'I must stay clean or else you will all get contaminated and die like Samir' (her husband). She held herself at fault for Samir's death. That is when Rupa's father insisted she come with him to the clinic. Before Rupa's husband passed away, she used to live in a joint family with her husband and daughter along with her in-laws in their house. After her husband's death, the in-laws asked Rupa's father to take Rupa back to his house along with her daughter. Rupa's in-laws accused her of the death of their son due to Covid.

(i) Background

Samir, Rupa's husband, was her university friend. They studied together for their graduate qualifications during which period they fell in love with each other and proposed their wish for marriage to their respective families. Samir's family was initially resistant towards the marriage – Samir was from the 'highest Brahmin caste,' and Rupa was from a 'low-caste.' Besides, Rupa's family's financial standing also did not match up to Samir's family status. They knew the families may bring all this up against their marriage proposal, but Samir with his youthful strong belief stood strong next to Rupa at that time. He admired Rupa's inner determination to fight against all social obstacles and stand up for her dream of being educated and having a career. Samir's parents opposed the couple formation because they could not accept Rupa for her low-caste and dark complexion. They apprehended that their son's children would not have fair skin, a mark of a high-caste Brahmanic genealogical lineage, which would be a matter of shame and disgrace for them in their societal repute. The history of caste segregation along with the country's colonial legacy continues to spread its taint of racial discrimination across time and boundaries of class, educated/non-educated and urban-rural sectors. Samir convinced his family of how Rupa was a very 'good girl' from a good, middle-class educated family, and she would 'listen' to her in-laws and look after them well. This persuasion only closed the rupture for a short time. Though underlying this, one wonders if he was echoing his own camouflaged wishes regarding his would-be-wife.

The couple were happy to be finally married against all the odds. Rupa's father was happy with his daughter's marriage as she was getting married into a 'good Brahmin, educated family' – it brought him an element of upward social status showering superficial prestige upon his family. He tried to compensate for all his 'daughter's lapses' by giving a huge dowry which he was very proud of. All this seemed to successfully, superficially, cover the 'shame' internalised by the father and the family at large.

After a year of marriage when Rupa gave birth to a girl-child, it shattered the in-laws' dreams of an ideal progeny of a male heir for their only son. The loving celebration of a newborn was merged with such emotional entanglement of unfairness and prejudice that the environment for 'dead mother' syndrome (Green, 1996) was broiling simultaneously in Rupa. The in-laws' pressure for a second child, and a male-child, added to Rupa's deep distress, unhappiness, and rising conflict with Samir. On top of that, she had her own internal struggle with her newborn daughter who she imagined brought about so much misery and disturbance in her life – unconsciously holding similar accusations like her in-laws against her; also equally echoing repressed internalised voices of her own mother's ambivalence against her. Samir's silence through all the unfairness inflicted by his family left Rupa feeling deeply hurt, betrayed and angry – why could Samir not stand by her and be vocal like their courtship period?

(ii) Covid phase

With the pandemic and lockdown, Rupa's household chores increased in volume. Regular domestic help was not available during the lockdown, which added to her chores of sweeping and mopping floors to cooking for the family, including teaching and looking after her daughter. On top of that, she had her own work to do (she was a primary school teacher). She was the only one who could leave the house for medicines or groceries to fill up the fridge. She had her worries regarding Samir – he was a smoker so she did not want him to be exposed in any way; she would even stock up on his cigarettes so that he did not have to go out at all. Her way of loving her husband resonated with her unconscious wish of controlling and smothering him – perhaps a passive indirect way of oppressing him, something that her in-laws were inflicting upon her. After getting back home with the groceries she would immediately rush for a shower, put her clothes for wash, use sanitisers for all the newly bought things from the market, and even sponge-wash her daughter as well, since she was closest to her physical proximity. As she narrated, in spite of all her precautions she could not stop herself from being infected with Covid. She strictly isolated herself and became even more particular with her 'cleansing rituals' – her frightful anxiety was 'What if Samir's parents were infected? They are old, their immune systems are so weak as it is, what will I say to Samir?' She felt she alone was liable for keeping them safe; she held herself at fault for catching Covid. Her ingrained sense of shame in her 'body-defect' (being a 'low-caste woman') found an extension into the 'Covid frenzy' that seeped out in symptomatic outbursts in her reaction to it. Rupa's years of long unconscious aggressive wishes against her in-laws were turning into anxious spells of Covid mania. A paradoxical reality of dirt and purity that was internalised within her resulted in clashing 'sectarian thinking,' which often baffles our reasoning faculties and creates grounds for disturbing internal dissonance. Subsequently, unconsciously we fall into the cycle of splitting and loathing the self into 'othering' with prejudices and biases – which may often get expressed in overt externalised acts of care and anxiety for the 'other' (Rupa's 'frantic care' of her own body, her daughter, her in-laws during the pandemic). Interestingly unconscious participation in such rigid sectarian, communal thought patterns, contradictorily gives the 'false' feeling of being connected to the community at large. This further generates a 'false sense of security and belonging' at the manifest level, while at the same time it continues to maintain its parochial segregation within the community at the latent level.

After Rupa recovered from Covid she was completely shaken up to find her husband diagnosed with Covid. She was particularly alarmed due to his smoking. Samir's symptoms were much more severe than hers and he had to be immediately hospitalised. It was not easy for her to find an available bed in a decent hospital, as there was no support from family or friends for such running around or back at home for domestic chores. Once Samir was in the hospital, she had no way of reaching out to him or meeting him – her only information about her husband's status were the periodical updates via messages that she received on her phone from the hospital. Back home she was torn apart both emotionally and physically – her distress with her in-laws heightened as their heartless blaming increased, holding her responsible for their son's Covid condition, which she infected him with. Their belief system and their related sense of reality were deeply rooted in an age-old inflexible fanatic thinking structure. At a time of such huge grief of losing their son, it was impossible for them to perceive a reality that was free of antagonism. The overwhelming state of the Covid reality and the home environment, as well as Rupa's own feeble health, all together made it an impossible situation for Rupa to hold onto her inner sense of coherence. Her frantic state of washing hands seemed to have started from that time. Her inner anxiety, and vicious ambivalence, were trying to seek release, relief, in her judicious washing of her hands, in an effort to cleanse off her anger against her in-laws, her helpless state against destiny, and her induced sense of guilt. Rupa's locality and house were cordoned off due to being a Covid zone, but at times she desperately managed to sneak out to run to the hospital and stand outside for hours, hoping that she may be lucky enough to be allowed inside to see her husband. This angst to bring her husband safely back home was internally more driven by her shattering fear of being proven in reality of her 'infectious' being to her in-laws. And like this, after about ten days, all of a sudden Rupa got the information of her husband's unfortunate demise on her mobile.

(iii) Discussion

The initial sessions were mostly filled with long silences, weeping, and occasional verbal exchanges. Rupa was heavy with a sense of unreality of the entire situation – her husband's death, not having seen him during his illness or even after he expired, her entire experience of the Covid account, and finally her in-laws holding her responsible for their son's death and asking her to leave home with her daughter – all appeared so surreal to her, like a bad dream. The multiple traumatic experiences in such a short span of time altogether left her in a state of overwhelming shock – almost in a state of non-action, like an autistic retreat. The last that she saw of her husband was when she was running in desperation to get him admitted to the hospital. After which hardly being able to speak to doctors, let alone seeing her husband, and not knowing what was happening to him – all of this compounded her mental state. And then all of a sudden his death was announced to her – she was not even allowed to see his body. According to government norms of the State at that time, all Covid deaths were cremated *en masse* in a specified crematorium, away from civil habitation in order to avoid cross-contamination. The only thing she remembered from that period was her desolating state of helplessness and her inner silent accusation against her husband's reckless irresponsible smoking, his total disregard for her safety, and survival – he never cared for her, he just did whatever he wanted to, how could he leave her alone to fight everything! How would she ever explain the rationale behind Covid to her in-laws. Their orthodox and prejudiced world-views held her 'callousness' to the cause of their son's death. Did she too, at least partially, blame herself equally for her husband's death?

The dependable, holding principle of the therapeutic exchange helped Rupa to gradually express her conflicting inner thoughts. That way one could approach the ground for her anxiety leading to the symptom formation (of washing hands) which consequentially, and hopefully, lead to a symptom-free state when they were sufficiently articulated, worked through, and then set free over time. It appeared that the externalised action of her washing hands symbolically acted like a stepping stone for therapeutic intervention in her intrapsychic space – possibly a way for me to carve out an engagement into forming a dyad with her in her then-critical condition. At that point, the symptom acted like the only symbolic externalised tangible act of conviction for Rupa. Paradoxically the symptom acted as a tool for Rupa to unconsciously enter her well of solitude where she alone could reside with her symptom, the very act of which equally kept her feeling alive. It emphasised her capacity for self-agency even if it were in an inverted manner, however feeble it may be, of her inner effort towards mentalisation against a paralysing deadness both inside and around her. This was a point of hope for both Rupa and the therapeutic situation. The external loss of her love object, her husband, shook up Rupa's internal world creating a core vacuum, and setting forth a temporary collapse of her capacity for internal mental mechanisms – the external symptom was palpable that she could see clearly to hold onto. Thus, the symptom of washing hands may be seen as a necessary tangible reality, signifying a symbolic transition in nature, something for her to hold onto with desperate effort for the time being. Thus, the continuation of the symptom as a living element along with her – the externalisation of the act which kept her internal self alive. Perhaps it acted as an unconscious hope, key to her capacity for mentalisation, fiercely trying to bridge the two worlds to initiate the process of internalisation of an enormous, unfathomable reality-force like the loss of a part of herself and her love object in an environmental death that enveloped all around her.

R: I must stay clean, I must wash my hands always … if I did that well enough then perhaps Samir would not get Covid; he would still be alive.

A: Is that why you keep washing your hands?

R: Maybe … it's like a reminder to myself – *(a reminder to punish herself for Samir's death, or a reminder of that intense moment of helplessness which was also the last point of togetherness shared between them – I wondered).* I don't know why, but I like to wash my hands, it somehow makes me feel calmer, as if am closer to Samir.

Her symptoms may echo a punitive action while at the same time it connected her with her lost love object.

A: I can understand what it means to you … while this stays with you, maybe we could also explore other ways which may make you feel equally closer to Samir. That way you will have more ways of being close to him.

The unconscious choice of the symptom of washing her hands for Rupa may equally take us to her deep sense of being unwanted, 'impure' due to all the sectarianism that she has grown up with, faced in real life, and internalised as well. The rigour of washing itself equally helped Rupa to lighten her aggression, but only temporarily, thus the need to perform the act again and again. Rupa's own paralysed state implied her inner need for love and affection which, at that juncture, was not possible for her to offer to her daughter. She had moved into an infantile state of dependency where the visible reminder of her daughter's need for love was intolerable for her. Significant time for healing was necessary before Rupa could reclaim her status of mutual inter-dependency to be able to pour into the mother–daughter relationship yet again. During this period the therapist's role of holding and empathy were crucial for Rupa's recovery of her sense of self.

Almost about six months into our therapeutic work together, one day Rupa came for her session and started showing me Samir's photograph with her and their daughter. She could talk more freely about her husband without breaking into tears or silence. Similarly, another two months later, she stepped into the therapy room one day, smiling, and before sitting down she asked me to look at her shoes and said – 'these are Samir's! And now I can walk with him anywhere I want!'

A: So where do you want to go with these?

R: (she thought for a while and said happily) Maybe I want to go to the restaurant where we used to go before we got married.

So, the shoes helped her to look at a loving past, a freer past with Samir, a more loving and freer time in her life. It was acting as an external object of transition that was helping her to initiate the process of mentally travelling to and fro, staying in that internal dynamism of transience that was subsequently helping her to internalise the object-loss. Gradually it helped her to travel back and forth, narrating memories of love and longing from their initial days of courtship when they were in the university together. At the same time, she expressed her shattering disappointment with Samir after marriage when he failed to stand up for her against her in-laws' unfair demands and accusations against her.

Rupa needed a tangible object in reality, like Samir's shoes, to hold onto because losing her husband not only meant the traumatic loss of a love object in her life but more importantly a part-loss of her own self that was invested in that object relationship for years. Rupa's gripping feet over Samir's shoes to walk over the world was a life affirmative action, claiming the reality ground. This was also the time that temporarily she started smoking, something that she used to do occasionally during her college days with Samir and their friends. Her smoking brought about a range of intense associations – it brought about her immediate connection with Samir, wearing 'his shoes' and smoking 'his cigarettes' gave her a familiar sense of feeling Samir within her body. It vibrated her anger against his irresponsibility, as if by blowing off that smoke in her through those cigarettes she could counter-retaliate against him in his very language (of smoking). At the same time, it brought memories of a 'freer time' in her life when she was happy with life, Samir, and unrestrained time. It acted in many layers – it was also an equal effort to control and conquer the element of dread and morbidity that was overruling her internal mindscape. Overcoming her painful reality with the tools of Samir (his shoes and cigarettes) helped her in transition in reality while at the same time they assisted her in processing her internal loss through transience. Very slowly Rupa was moving towards claiming life for herself.

Over time in therapy, she started increasingly voicing her own dissatisfaction with Samir and her marriage, her sense of feeling betrayed by Samir, and the unforgivable unfairness of what her in-laws have made her (and her daughter) go through. With the release of her suppressed aggression her sense of guilt was also gradually freeing her. Long sessions of acute anger against her in-laws, parents who failed to stand up for her and against such injustice, and society in general – all took us through a pathway of her helpless rage against an engulfing reality. The mother–daughter inter-dependency gained a renewed life-engaging energy through their painting together in the new painting class that they had both enrolled for. In this way, the reclaimed love/ *amae* in the mother–daughter object relationship was attempting to absorb the transitional phenomenon of their common lost love object. Thereby, simultaneously creating ground for the internalisation of the love object to allow transience to grow inside, resonating resilience. One could say that this was the beginning of 'stirring up a hornet's nest' for Rupa.

Conclusion

According to the philosophy of transience, life is itself in a state of transience in this mortal realm – as if it is on its own journey from this world of reality to another world of ephemerality. This allegory of life's trajectory not only echoes the Indian spiritual lineage of an eternal travelling soul but equally resonates with an Asian tenet of its belief factor in afterlife. In other words, it appears that the task of life itself may be to initiate the feeling of transience in humankind as it simply passes through this world – transforming life from a conflictual emotionally entangled beginning to a gradual progress towards transience over time and age. The philosophical development of transience leads to the finding of a correlation with evolutionary human resilience that subsequently acts as the reservoir of sustenance for the fragile human ego. It is in this context itself that the psychoanalytic reading of transience and mentalisation plays its role in deciphering how these various aspects contribute in connecting individual consciousness to a larger order of the universe, uniting it with the consciousness of all other existence that is both living and non-living entity, thereby altogether resonating the creative life-drive of the universe.

References

Fonagy, P. & Luyten, P. (2018). Attachment, mentalization, and the self. In W. J. Livesley & R. Larstone (Eds.), *Handbook of Personality Disorder*. New York: Guilford Press.

Freud, S. (1916). On transience. In *Standard Edition*, Vol. 14. London: Hogarth Press.

Green, Andre (1996). The dead mother. In *On Private Madness* (pp. 142–173). London: Karnac.

Hanley, Charles (1990). The concept of truth in psychoanalysis. *Int. J. Psa.*, 71, 382.

Keigo, Okonogi (1979). Japanese psychoanalysis and the Ajase complex (Kosawa). *Psychotherapy & Psychosomatics*, 31 (1–4), 350–356.

Kitayama, O. & Ogimoto, K. (2022). COVID-19 and Japanese tragedies: Looking forward to our happy endings. *Pers. Comm.*

Kitayama, Osamu (1998). Transience: Its beauty and danger. *Int. J. Psycho-Anal.*, 70, 937–953.

Kitayama, Osamu (2003). Japanese mothers and children in pictures of the floating world: Sharing the theme of transience. In Elsa Blum, Harold P. Blum, & Jacqueline Amati-Mehler (Eds.), *Psychoanalysis and Art: The Artistic Representation of the Parent-Child Relationship* (pp. 289–299). Madison: International Universities Press.

Klein, M. (1935). A contribution to the psychogenesis of manic-depressive states. *Int. J. Psa*, 16, 145–174.

Klein, M. (1975). *Love, Guilt and Reparation and Other Works* 1921-1945. The Hogarth Press.

Kohut, Heinz (1971). *Kohut, Heinz: The Analysis of the Self: A Systematic Approach to the Psychoanalytic Treatment of Narcissistic Personality Disorders*. New York: International Universities Press.

Kosawa, H. (1939). Two kinds of guilt feelings – the Ajase complex. In *Japanese Contributions to Psychoanalysis*, Vol. 2. Tokyo: Japan Psychoanalytic Society, 2007.

Doi, Taeko (1989). The concept of amae and its psychoanalytic implications. *Int. Rev. Psycho-Anal*, 16, 349–354.

Tagore, Rabindranath (1913). The Relation of the Individual to the Universe in *Sadhana: The Realization of Life*. Macmillan & Co. London

Thapar, Romilla (2002). *Early India: From the Origins to AD 1300*. Berkeley: Univ. of California Press.

Winnicott, D. W. (1953). Transitional objects and transitional phenomena: a study of the first not-me possession. *Int. J. Psychoanal.*, 34, 89–97.

Part 2

The triadic tryst

Chapter 9

Being drawn into a primal scene

Osamu Kitayama

Considering the back through 'dramatic psychoanalysis'

As I wrote in my *Introduction to Dramatic Psychoanalysis* (Kitayama, 2007), in Japanese we often describe a person's external and internal life in everyday communications by using drama metaphorical expressions. As the playwright Masakazu Yamazaki pointed out in his Japanese book *The Dramatic Japanese* (Yamazaki, 1971), the life of the Japanese people, as shown by the concept of the 'fleeting world' or *ukiyo*, is dramatic in some ways. Strictly speaking, however, drama performed before God must be a different experience from drama performed in Japan before people in the world. In the former, it is through a monotheistic faith that God tends to be seen as the absolute authority. In Japan, however, even if our audience is divine, we have 8 million of them, and we cannot rely on them to respond seriously. This difference leads to the former being described as a 'culture of sin' and the latter as a 'culture of shame.'

On the other hand, according to the dramatic viewpoint of psychoanalysis, the plot that a person plays out has been written in early childhood, and the repeated performance of the role that he or she has acquired, and through interpersonal relationships, is adopted as his/her personality. Nowadays, moreover, clinicians show less resistance to having therapeutic relations described in dramatic metaphors. This may be because the significance of 'play' (both literally and signifying 'a piece of drama' in English and German) has come to be highly regarded.

A psychoanalyst's theory of Japanese culture therefore has a great advantage since, as the Japanese people's repetitive behaviour is studied in Japanese, our Japanese readers can easily confirm the dramatic viewpoints that are used for clinical psychoanalysis. Figuratively speaking, our ways of living, of hiding our true faces with makeup and masks, can also be understood easily from the dramatic viewpoint of psychoanalysis. In particular, of the things that are *namagusai* (maybe having a 'fishy' odour, and being half-rotten), only those that have been thoroughly processed end up being released, moved by the feeling of *sumanai*, which implies both 'an apologetic feeling,' and 'impure or not yet processed.' Not only in everyday life but also in psychoanalytic

DOI: 10.4324/9781003501930-11

therapy, psychological resistance appears in places where inner unprocessed truth is difficult to express in words. I therefore wish to focus on these difficulties and describe what is in the back, beneath the surface, discussing the mind of 'dramatic Japanese' as well as 'dramatic psychoanalysis.'

Being an animal despite being a human being

An easy-to-understand example of parents' duality of front and back, as viewed from a child's perspective can be seen in *Spirited Away* (directed by Hayao Miyazaki, 2001), an animated film by Studio Ghibli. In the movie, a girl looks at her gluttonous parents and sees them as pigs. At the base of a process in which the girl experiences, together with her parents, the duality – while being human beings who look calm on the surface, we are actually animals that smell of blood (*chi*) – lies a situation which I pointed out in Chapter 6: the proponent of the Ajase complex, called the Japanese habit of having their children sleep between them, or, in other words, the mother sleeping next her child in bed and also sleeping together with the father, with the child in the middle.

In *shunga*, or erotic pictures that flourished in Japan from the 17th to 19th centuries, the situation is depicted, where the mother, who is sleeping with her child, is combined with the father who is about to have sex with her, like this picture by Utamaro (see Figure 9.1). We can find many of these pictures in

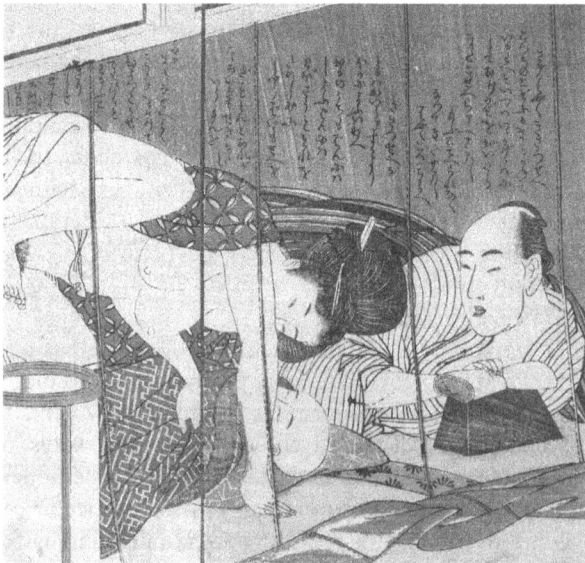

Figure 9.1 (Edited) *Ehon Hanafubuki [Pornographic Shower of Cherry Blossoms]* (1802) by Utamaro Kitagawa.
Source: International Research Center for Japanese Studies (Nichibunken), Kyoto.

the art book by M. Hayakawa (2000). As she uses her body and role as a mother and a wife dichotomously depending on the two-sided situation, the child ends up repeatedly undergoing, during infancy, this 'graphic' experience of the threesome sleeping alongside each other. Many children personally experience the two faces of their parents and their duality in the form of 'sleeping together with their parents.' We are all familiar with a child witnessing the primal scene, of his or her parents engaging in sexual activities, through numerous *shunga* pictures in Japan (Kitayama, 2021).

On looking at my studies of *shunga*, Okonogi used to say personally that this was related to none other than the Ajase complex (Okonogi, 1978, 1979). In the story of Ajase which Kosawa and his followers[1] used as their foundation, Ajase, the son, learns that his mother covered her body with honey and secretly visited her husband (Ajase's father) in prison to feed him. Ajase becomes enraged and harbours a murderous intent. In the image described in *manga* by Yōsuke Tamaru (1989), the mother resigns herself to her husband, who is Ajase's father, saying, 'Go on, help yourself to the honey covering my body.'

The 'filthy' or 'fishy' image of a father licking the mother's body, coated with honey, in the same way as his son, is an important climax in the family participation-type sexual experience. Disgusted, the child thinks that the betrayal was made by his mother, and thus directs his anger towards her. I believe that bedroom circumstances are behind this tendency of anger being directed at the mother but not towards the father. This is what Okonogi refers to as the culture of parents sleeping with their child in between, like the Chinese character for 'river,' (川) and the state of a triad comprising the mother, the child, and the father experiencing sleeping together (Okonogi, 1984).

Shunga *or erotic prints, comic pictures*

Japanese culture possesses numerous prints and pictures in a rich variety that depict sexual intercourse between a man and a woman. Although I have eliminated them from my citations of pictures, *shunga* or erotic prints that show the genitals in gigantic form, fully attest to our sexual thoughts. As indicated by the fact that they were also called 'comic pictures,' these prints, edited to reduce anxiety, fear, and a sense of guilt, invite maniac laughter among their beholders.

Interestingly enough, many Japanese *shunga* prints depict children as observers and participants in the parents' sexual acts. Prints of this type, in which children take part, are rare throughout the world. This may attest to the fact that children in Japan have many opportunities to become drawn into a primal scene. The artistic convention of putting small animals, such as cats and dogs, in places where they can watch these acts, may suggest the beholder's animal-like mindset (see Figure 9.2).

For example, a picture from *Ehon Hanafubuki* by Utamaro (see Figure 9.3), depicts the mother, who is sleeping with her child, moving parallel towards

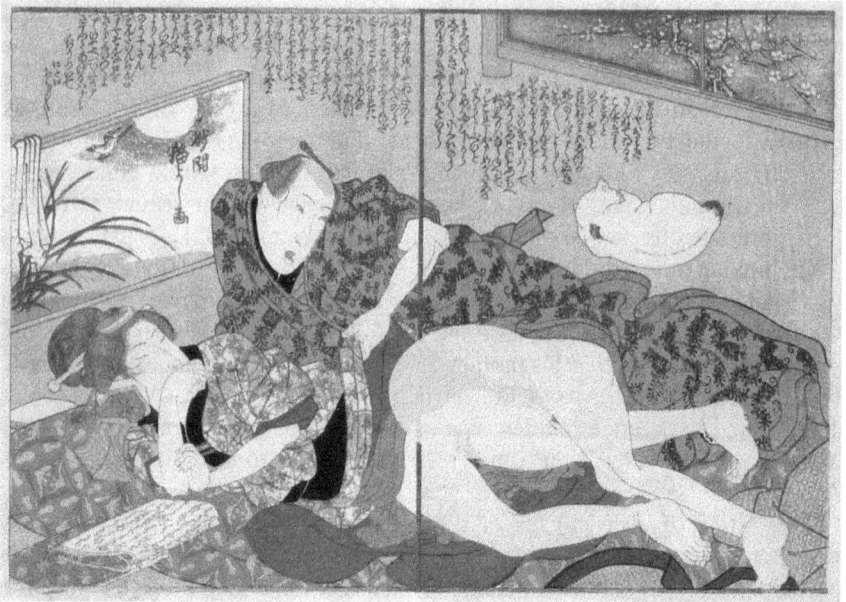

Figure 9.2 (Edited) *Hana Goyomi [Flower Calendar]* (1835) by Kuniyoshi Utagawa.
Source: International Research Center for Japanese Studies (Nichibunken), Kyoto.

Figure 9.3 (Edited) *Ehon Hanafubuki [Pornographic Shower of Cherry Blossoms]* (1802) by
        Utamaro Kitagawa.
Source: International Research Center for Japanese Studies (Nichibunken), Kyoto.

the father. By having the mother doubling her body, or her role, as both a wife and a mother, the child, who has been elevated to the same position as the father by sleeping together with him and co-existing with him, risks becoming drawn into the parents' sexual activities.

Seen from a classic psychoanalytic viewpoint, this sort of situation might delay the oedipal triangulation in which the child competes and clashes with the father. Moreover, the parents and the child come to co-exist in the primal scene at an extremely close distance. As depicted by Harunobu in his *shunga* (see Figure 9.4), sudden disillusionment and exclusion occur within a triangular relationship as the child discovers his parents' coitus proving his mother's duality.

The print shows the co-existence of child-rearing and sex, or 'this and that,' not the dichotomy of 'this or that.' Harunobu's observations led him to illustrate, in the child's facial expressions, his negative emotions of having been 'left out in the cold' from the three-body relationship, and literally left out of the cosy mosquito net (made from hemp fibres for protection against the ubiquitous mosquitos). If things were going well, without any serious involvements, this might be regarded as a comic scene. At the same time, however, the child's agony caused by his exclusion likely causes a clinical problem as well. From the perspective of child-rearing support, Reiko Baba

Figure 9.4 Ketsudai Kumimono [Unnamed Set] (ca. 1769) by Harunobu Suzuki.
Source: E. Chiossone Museum of Oriental Art, Genova.

(2021), a clinical psychologist, said that, since the mother is being coveted by her husband on one side and her child on the other, she should enjoy her popular status more. Taking into account the pathogenicity of the primal scene, however, things may not be that simple. I feel that we must discuss the emotional confusion that was described in Freud's report on 'the Wolf Man,' such as anxiety, fear, and eeriness.

Taboo and mythical thinking

As far as Japanese stories go, triggers of tragic disillusionment associated with a child's growth are concentrated in the duality and the two-facedness of the mother object and the child's parents. Examples of disillusionment, which overly focus on the filthy aspects of ideal things, occur when one is suddenly made to confront his/her parents' filthy truths. A typical example of this is the myth that describes the birth of Japan, of the Father God peeking inside, only to find the rotting body of his beloved Mother Goddess. According to the description found in the *Kojiki*, a record of ancient matters and mythologies of Japan, the Father God broke the prohibition of 'Don't Look,' was chased after by ugly females, and went to the 'filthy Land of the Dead.' He had the sensation that, having seen things that are filthy and ugly involving his wife's half-rotten corpse, he, too, had become filthy. Although this ugly scene is not easy to describe, if it were depicted in a modern sense, it would look like this illustration (see Figure 9.5).

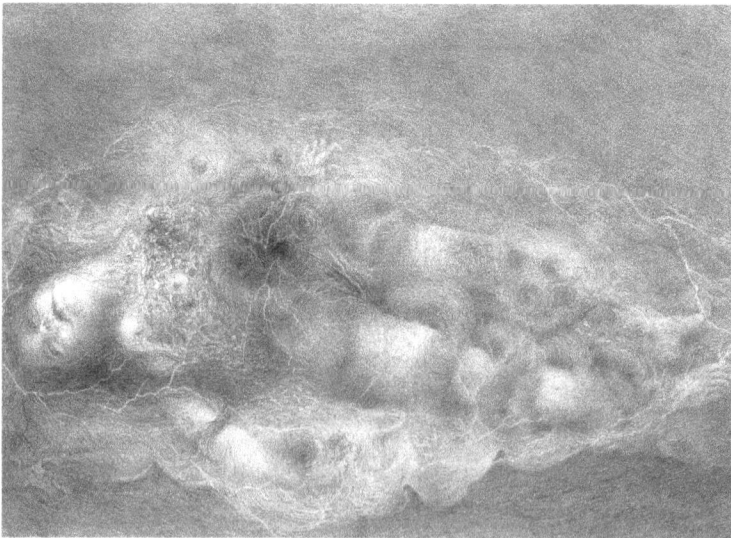

Figure 9.5 Ehon Kojiki: Yomigaeri – Izanagi to Izanami [Picture Book Kojiki: Resurrection – Iza-nagi and Izanami]. Illustration by Jin Yamamoto (story by Michiko Ryō) (2015), Tokyo: Kokushokankōkai.

With this mythical thinking as the basis, we have dreaded death, tried our utmost to avoid coming into contact with it, and cleansed our own filth by washing it away with water. If this continues and grows worse, it leads to a tragic ending, of eliminating even the self and making it disappear. This is why the story of the prohibition of 'Don't Look' serves as a deep psychological insight into the serious discrimination and isolation seen in our society. This was also seen during the COVID-19 pandemic: the Japanese people's deep mysophobia, or fear of filth, powerfully reinforced their compulsion to conform to other people's expectations.

For people of all ages and places, however, regarding death as a taboo and trying not to see it has been a perfectly natural practice, and a reflex of sorts. The corpse of someone you love is especially difficult to look at; we automatically look away from it. Still, in the tragedy of the prohibition of 'Don't Look,' everyone breaks this prohibition. Instead of being a taboo that absolutely should never gets broken, it is a taboo to be broken when the right time comes.

In the tragedy of Izanagi–Izanami, the death of a female protagonist was seen by a male protagonist who had violated the prohibition; she then had no choice but to leave the real world. No matter how much they are loved, the dead disappear from the stage. To make an intercultural comparison of mythologies, as did the mythologist Matsumura (1955), while many in other countries depict the dead as objects of fear, those in Japan depict the Land of the Dead as 'filth or impurity.' In other words, it is characterised as raw, rotting filth. On the surface, moreover, the male God Izanagi and Yohyō, the husband who stands there stunned when his wife, Tsū, who was a crane, leaves him in the story of *Twilight of Crane*, appear totally passive towards their fate despite having themselves invited their own tragedies; they don't seem to regret having broken the prohibition.

However, the principle of the elimination of non-humans cannot be said to only be a problem on the male side. For example, in a Japanese folk tale called *The Monkey's Marriage*, a woman who marries a monkey had planned to kill the monkey from the start, but she has no sense of guilt for this act. Elimination of non-humans is an absolute must: a crane is a crane, and a monkey is a monkey. At the same time, however, the creatures are objects we love dearly, so this duality of love and murder cannot be swallowed 100%, and causes a feeling of unfathomable uneasiness. It is liable to cause indigestion and nausea, so to *sumasu* (cleanse or eliminate) this *minikui* (ugly or 'difficult to see') and filthy object, we need to purify, exorcise, and cleanse it, just as Izanagi did.

The question of whether the ways of Japanese sexuality within the context of Japan's culture are the same as, or different from, ways in other cultures, and if so, how, must be asked with care. The author's discussion of the prohibition of 'Don't Look' (Kitayama, 2010, 2017) focuses on the taboo of people 'not wanting to see,' and 'not wanting to be seen.' It is also deeply involved with the 'Japanese people's resistance' to the sexual theory of psychoanalysis. I have examined this theme in Japanese, published my thoughts in English, and had them investigated both in Japan and overseas. However, I believe that this is still not far enough, so I wish to ask for help from other clinical researchers.

Especially concerning the clinical issue of the primal scene, meaning a child's witnessing his or her parents' sexual activities; it should be no surprise that this tends to be taboo even in academic discussions. However, in the myth that describes the birth of Japan, the death of the maternal deity, which the paternal deity witnessed by breaking the prohibition of 'Don't Look,' was due entirely to their past sexual intercourse. In other words, the story of Izanami and Izanagi, who got married on Onogoro Island, had sex, and created various deities and different countries, and the maternal deity Izanami then giving birth to a fire deity, and dying after having her genitals burned, suggests a direct connection between the parents' coitus and the mother's death (see Figure 9.6).

Also in the story of *The Crane Wife*, which uses the same prohibition of 'Don't Look,' we can see the possibility that the piercing of the crane-wife with an arrow at the beginning of the story may symbolise a sexual act, and the loss of a mother object due to the exposure of the injured crane can be interpreted as a 'death while engaging in a sexual act.' Furthermore, the wounded appearance of the revealed crane-wife is interpreted in Chapter 2 as a displacement for the birth scene of the parturient mother with her legs spread (see Figure 2.2).

Stories of prohibiting a male figure from looking at the death of his beloved female partner can not only be seen in Japan but also sporadically in other cultures around the world. One of the most famous is the Greek story of Orpheus being told not to look at his dead wife Eurydice as he rescues her from the Land of the Dead. The husband breaks this prohibition by turning around to look at

Figure 9.6 Ehon Kojiki: Yomigaeri – Izanagi to Izanami [Picture Book Kojiki: Resurrection – Izanagi and Izanami] Illustration by Jin Yamamoto (story by Michiko Ryō) (2015), Tokyo: Kokushokankōkai.

his wife who is following him and ends up losing her as she is drawn back into the Land of the Dead. We find no major cultural differences in the tragic setting of the prohibition of 'Don't Look' in which the audience and the readers witness, together with the husband, the death of the wife as a result of the exchange of love between a man and a woman. One thing that should be noted, however, is that, while Japanese mythology maintains the final tragedy and the notion of *minikusa*, or 'hard to see' (a homonym with *minikui*, meaning 'ugly'), stories with happy endings similar to those that are popular in the Christian world such as *Beauty and the Beast* and *The Frog Prince* may be said to be, more correctly, recent fabrications or editing, or, in other words, defensive elaborations based on beautification and idealisation of 'the miracle of love.'

A participation-type primal scene

In one picture of *Azuma Nishiki* (c. 1812) by Hokusai, the father approaches the mother, pressing her to choose 'this little kid (= the father's penis) over that little kid.' Here, the man's penis has the same rank as the child, and the 'little kid' which, in Japanese, signifies a penis, is clearly getting drawn into the sexual act. You can find a similar situation in the picture by Eisen Keisai (see Figure 9.7). Moreover, a novel by Hiroyuki Itsuki (1989) depicts a child taking part in his parents' sexual intercourse, as if it were a festival of sorts:

Figure 9.7 (Edited) *Ehon Midaregami [Sexy Pictures – Messy Hair]* (1815) by Eisen Keisai.
Source: International Research Center for Japanese Studies (Nichibunken), Kyoto.

> In his dream, he [Shinsuke] was making love to Tae [his stepmother], together with his father [Jūzo]. Tae was responding to both Jūzo and Shinsuke while cooing like a pigeon. With Tae's white body in between, the two intertwined their arms, exchanged smiles, and vigorously moved their bodies alternately from the front and the back. For Shinsuke, this certainly did not carry an obscene image. He felt it was like a refreshing, vibrant festival that further strengthened the solid bond among the threesome of the father, the son and Tae.
>
> (*Seishunno Mon [The Gate of Youth]*, 1989)

Instead of a witness-type primal scene, this novel testifies to the potential of a participation-type primal scene, of a child joining his father to engage in sexual intercourse with the mother. I myself have heard patients narrate their manic participation experiences in my clinical practice. Here, with generational differences and exclusions having been ignored, all the participants had become monkeys and experienced intense excitement.

Thus, our psychoanalysis should transcend its idealisation and romanticism, and instead discuss the participation-type primal scenes that are likely to occur under diverse conditions. Specifically, however, discussions that cover too diverse a scope are expected to occur; the potentials of various pathologies that accompany the family's sleeping together during one's infancy, cannot be grasped in their entirety, or sorted out, simply by referring to a person's individual clinical experience alone. We must also emphasise that this culture of sleeping together nurtures not only pathology, but also the Japanese people's *amae*, or interdependence, or a sense of solidarity (the Japanese word is *tsurumu*, meaning 'to get together'), with a feeling of security and peace of mind.

Needless to say, as Freud wrote, a young child's experience of interpreting his parents' sexual intercourse as something violent and animal-like, may be a phenomenon that transcends culture. So, even in Japanese culture, I believe that eyewitness information such as 'my mother is being killed by my father' is something we often hear. And, based on cultural searches such as those described above, I would like to limit my clinical material in this chapter to eyewitness testimonies, of 'the murder of a mother by the father' in both a boy's and a girl's case. To this, I would like to add the potential of 'active participation in a primal scene' because of the family sleeping together. I then believe that we can expect to see a situation in which phantasy and reality become mixed together, causing two traumatic involvements such as those cited below.

1   The possibility that a child, who identifies himself with his father, rapes his mother alongside his father. The child will also have a part in his father's matricide; merely looking on as a bystander would likely constitute collusion.

2   The possibility that a son and a daughter who identify themselves with their helpless mother who is being killed in a passive fashion, feel that they are raped or killed by the father, together with the mother.

Therefore, in the latter half of this chapter, I would like to describe two patients who talk overtly about a primal scene. In both cases, the patients describe their helplessly witnessing the murder of the mother by the father. I will also be discussing not only anxiety, the fear, and eeriness caused by being drawn into it in a visual way, but also emotions felt by the witnesses such as disgust/hatred, contempt, ugliness, and filth. I would like to stress that, physically, one often experiences dizziness and nausea accompanying the spinning and rotation of 'becoming drawn into it.'

A male patient: 'fainting'

This was a 55-year-old businessman who talks about 'having been excluded' throughout his life. The reason for his coming to my office was that, although he had achieved success in his business, he had broken down, personality-wise, and wanted to rethink his life. Specifically, he complained that he was not sufficiently respected as an organisation man, and it was quite difficult for him to become popular because of his strong opinions.

For a long time, he was in another psychological therapy but ended it after he changed jobs. He had lots of interesting things to talk about in diverse fields; his associations were rich, and, from the initial stages, he described a whole series of dreams. Because the content of what he spoke about was extremely rich and diverse, and since the subjects of his conversations tended to wander, I adopted a restrictive setting of once-weekly sessions, done face-to-face.

He idealised me with a passive attitude. While this was helpful in forming a therapeutic alliance for doing search work, he always adopted a self-depre-cating attitude, and would never speak assertively or say aggressive things.

He continued to recount masochistic episodes, such as being bullied ever since he was small, and being punched by his younger brother and laughed at. His grandmother repeatedly talked about her expectations of him, that he should be hired by a good company and move up the hierarchy.

The relationship between his mother and his father, who had taken over the family business, was confusing: their relationship looked both good and bad. What the patient always recalled was a scene that took place when he was about 4 years old, of his parents arguing. A hellish scene of his father, a drunkard, attacking his mother, shouting, 'I'm gonna kill you,' and strangling her, was one of the patient's most traumatic memories. The patient, who was still a child at the time, was thinking over and over, 'I'm sorry, I'm sorry (for not being able to help you, Mother),' and then eventually fainted. He said that when he came to, he was in an ambulance (he was unsure who had called an ambulance).

What he repeatedly recalls in parallel to this incident took place when he was around 6 years old: a scene in which his mother was about to be dragged out of their home, coerced by an acquaintance, while his father was absent. Here again, the patient simply trembled, unable to do anything despite his mother resisting and seeking help before his eyes.

In the end, it became clear that the patient had become drawn into a *minikui* scene, and, when unable to take it in, he fainted. The scene that he could not endure was a phantasy in which his mother was being killed or raped, and what he had recalled as an incident that should be added was something that had taken place years ago, when he was a little child, sleeping with his mother lying beside him. Because the bedroom was small, and the family used just one *futon* mattress, the father was sleeping on the opposite side of the same *futon*. The patient said that his parents' feet were entangled and crept about, which he found eerie. Even after he began to be taken care of by his grandmother in another room, he occasionally spotted the grandmother peeking at scenes of the parents having sex. He therefore said that, although a little child, he, too, appeared to have gotten involved in this snooping activity. Later, despite knowing that fierce quarrels and lovemaking exist in a married couple like the two sides of a coin, he himself was unable to consider 'loving each other' and 'quarrelling' co-existing in his mind.

To 'filthy and ugly' incidents from his memory such as these, a reconstruction of trauma occurred in the patient as a little child: He felt dizzy and helpless, and, confronting the imaginary results of seeing his mother killed – which in fact might have been possible – he fainted as if he himself had also been killed. Looking at them once again now, even his ugly primal scene experiences had become *gucha-gucha* (messy), he pondered the *zubu-zubu* (stuck deeply in mud), the fact which he had been drawn into sexual acts and murder by 'nosing around' in his own sinful form. Then he had no choice but to admit the repetition because of being hopelessly helpless.

Afterwards, the patient began saying that parents have two sides, the front and the back, and that, while they argue in the front, they have sex in the back. He admitted that he, too, had two sides, the front and the back. He added, 'The fact that I'm coming here to you is also a behind-the-scenes story, you know?' Verbalisation and reconstruction such as these, being 'held' or supported by a therapeutic framework, helped to maintain his sanity as an intellectual being. It appeared, however, that the problem of disillusionment with me was being put off by his idealisation.

A female patient: 'I feel nauseous'

This was a 50-year-old housewife who worked part-time. Her husband, the same age as her, operated a store. The patient was a mother to multiple boys and had enjoyed fairly good health. Several years before coming to my office, her father died of an illness, and, one year later, she lost her mother due to an illness. During the following years, the patient had lived her life normally. Gradually, however, she began going frequently to the hospital where her mother had died, lamenting intensely that she wanted to die. I thought that her symptoms were hysteric in nature, but soon a mechanism began operating between her dazed state and sanity which I had no choice but to diagnose as 'severe dissociation.' Treatment began as once-a-week psychotherapy, with the sessions moving on to four times a week after about 18 months.

From the early stages of treatment, she talked about her primal scene experience that she could not speak of to anybody else. 'When I was small, I was sleeping with my father and mother. It appeared to me that my father, by having sex with my mother, was trying to kill her.' She said, in tears as if spitting it out, 'Along with my mother, my father raped me, his daughter, with his penis. At the same time, being helpless, I felt that I would be killed, and wanted to die,' and continued to talk about her involvement in primal scene experiences.

After marrying, moreover, she held a negative attitude towards having sex. She felt as if she was being made fun of by her family, and there was countertransference on my part also, of wanting to tease this woman.

Although she sometimes exhibited intense regression, I was able to 'hold' her during our sessions. She came to the sessions on time, left the office more or less on time, and paid the fees without fail. Along with androphobia and the fear of being penetrated by a penis, she hated overweight men and men who left their noses exposed while wearing a face mask. Countless numbers of times, she brushed away, with her hand, the imagined filthy contacts.

Her attitude clearly became rebellious after the third year. She focused on the fact that I merely listened to what she said without taking any notes for record-keeping, and began talking about her persecutory phantasies, of being made light of by me. Sometimes, she mentioned weekends and long holidays, and could not help telling me, 'After I leave the office, I bet you flirt with your other patients.' However, despite accusing me of most likely looking down on her, she then reversed her attitude and revoked her comments numerous times with apologies.

Eventually, the part of her that remained a small child (a boy) with halted growth and development, slowly appeared and took centre stage in how she spoke as an individual with a dual personality. Around the time that 'Peter Pan' began to make news as a separate personality, the patient accidentally skipped several steps while going down the stairs at a train station, fell, and broke her fingers. At a session during this period, while listening to her free associations and allowing my attention to float while continuing to understand her ways of being, I heard a little boy, sitting in a corner of the couch, looking dissatisfied and mumbling, 'Oh yeah? I don't think so ...'

Because of this episode, I started to interpret her division/splitting between a boy and a girl. I must say that it took many years until the considerably serious division/splitting of the two children – a boy who asserted himself and made fun of others, and a girl who retracted this and apologised – came to be mitigated, allowing them to co-exist more harmoniously. Needless to say, the gradual process was important. What is more important, however, is that the sexual aggressiveness of the separate male personality of this passive woman, and the division/splitting of the two people, had derived from her traumatic experience of viewing a primal scene.

Later, the patient and I laughed out loud when she protested to me, saying 'You must be flirting with your other patients,' then retracted her outburst and apologised, embarrassed: 'I've said something I didn't mean at all: I'm sorry.' Gradually, she became able to accept my interpretation, 'You must actually be the one who is making light of others.' For example, it was about the fact she was brushing away sexual intercourse and erect penises by becoming 'nauseated by them and vomiting'; I also pointed out that her having trouble remembering and mastering my interpretations and the understandings that I had conveyed to her, was because it was incomprehensible to a little girl, and also because 'the little boy inside you is spitting them out, so you cannot remember or master them.'

One thing that eventually became clear about this was related to the fact that, in the process of the patient coming to fear her parents' sexual intercourse, she became even more scared after watching rabbits engaging in sex, doggy-style, from the back. In other words, she appeared to have 'animalised' human sex, and thought that 'Every one of them is a beast.' One of the reasons she dreaded sex more than anything was that she, as a little boy, would be raped, get castrated and die as a result.

She admitted that she regarded sex as 'a low-level matter,' and sometimes gained insight, 'Since you watched your parents having sex, you regarded them as animals and mocked them. These animals, made furious by being mocked, came to attack you. These events are all occurring in your head.' Thanks to transference and its dramatisation, the patient came to apologise, 'I'm sorry for saying things I didn't really mean,' and admitted also that a phantasy of me, 'flirting with my other patients' was in her mind at the same time.

I felt scorned by her, so I had to tolerate my irritation. I then conveyed to her, 'I believe the reason you spit out my interpretations when outside my office is because you hate thinking about me as a person who examines and treats other patients.' Saying 'I can't believe that you are thinking about other things, even during sessions,' she had no choice but to admit that, even though I worry about different patients, I listen to her story at the same time. The patient was therefore now becoming able to allow and tolerate, little by little, the fact that, beyond the 'mutual killing' of a man and a woman, she can see them snuggling and flirting, despite becoming confused, not understanding what exactly is going on as a whole, or, in other words, experiencing spitting them out in her head.

The reality of sleeping with the father, together with the mother

Conscious memories have become easy to understand, thanks to *Nachträglichkeit*, or deferred action, and its subsequent elaboration. Despite this, early-stage primal involvements are more 'mixed-up' things that cause dizziness and nausea, or are still undifferentiated and cannot be understood, so they were *minikui*. Here, I'm tempted to refer to the 'swamp' that appears at the opening of a Japanese myth. This is because of the description in which Izanagi and Izanami lowered the *nuboko*, or the heavenly spear, into a sea of mud, and stirred it, 'curdle-curdle,' round and round. When they raised the spear from the ocean, drops of seawater fell from the spear, dripping steadily, and formed an island. Onogoro Island was the place where the nation was created through the deities' sexual intercourse. This is none other than what speaks symbolically about copulation and conception. In the beginning, it must have been the 'overwhelming unknown' (Fenichel, 1945) that had been swirled.

Moreover, I recall what A. Green referred to as 'the dead mother' (Green, 1986). What is interesting about the things that our Izanagi–Izanami myth depicts is the problem of 'looking at' the 'dying mother.' Yes, she seems to be dying, but she might survive. Their fates are 'unknown' (= *wakaranai*, in Japanese, which signifies the inability to understand, as well as the condition of being undifferentiated). And, needless to say, for a patient to escape the sexual 'swamp' that he or she has become drawn into, and to survive, two things become important: The 'survival' of the analyst and the therapist himself (Winnicott, 1969), and not getting involved when talking to a child who had been excluded. Gaining such externality and objectivity from us analysts as a bridging third, the male patient whom I reported about above came to look at the original family while keeping a distance from them, referring to them as the 'naked tribe.' The female patient, for her part, became able to think objectively, 'People in the old days did not regard this as harmful.'

A 'fishy' swamp

In folk tales, animal nature and death are depicted in easily understood, culturally refined forms as things that must be avoided. However, in the case of a primal scene that an infant witnesses, the triadic experience becomes something that is unfathomable, nauseating, or incomprehensible. From what I understand from my clinical experience with some psychologically disturbed people is that, during infancy, the primal scene, where all sorts of 'this and that' – sort of opposites – humans and animals, mother and father, the front and the back – get mixed-up is extremely *minikui*. Many patients who were drawn into a primal scene during infancy describe what they perceive as tangled-up scenes, and use muddy words in Japanese, such as *gucha-gucha* (messy), *gocha-gocha* (mixed-up), *gucho-gucho* (soggy and soaking wet), *zubu-*

zubu (stuck deeply in mud), and *doro-doro* (muddy). They also recall it as something that causes nausea. However, there is a possibility that primal experiences may refer to the 'primordial, organic mix-up' that is seen before the establishment of a clear-cut awareness that regards it as 'filthy' or 'fishy.'

If the spear which the Mother Goddess and the Father God stirred, 'curdle-curdle,' round and round in the origin myth of Japan is the penis, then the swamp is the mother's womb itself. Many of us may not remember seeing or hearing about it directly. However, many of us may have seen or heard of this as a physical experience.

Then there is a statement in Shūsaku Endō's novel *Silence* (Endō, 1989), that Christianity does not take root in Japan, since our country is a 'swamp.' I believe there is a deeply rooted meaning and reason for this. The Japanese people's experience of crisis, such as wars dragging on ('stuck in a muddy marsh'), and when the ground becomes liquefied because of an earthquake, is liable to be revived as the familiar anxiety associated with a muddy, blood-smelling swamp and its *minikusa* (ugliness and the difficulty of looking at it) that dwell in the minds and bodies of people who live in this country.

Expressions of impurity

The themes of 'the mother who is killed' and 'the death of the mother,' which are likely to appear in clinical problems, also exist as the background to the figure of the masochistic caretaker that I have been discussing for some time. When treating masochistic caretakers, represented mythologically by the crane-wife who tries desperately to serve the people around her, I am aware of the importance of their sadistic extroverted anger. There is the possibility that the mythology of the Mother Goddess losing her life after having sex and delivering a child may have created a prototype for female passivity and masochism. Past case reports (Kitayama, 2009) show that the outward expression of anger, jealousy, and hatred/disgust, that Izanami manifested, act as a major turning point in treatment. However, in the tragic tale of Dōjōji, in which Kiyohime, smitten by the handsome priest Anchin, kills him in a jealous rage, a woman's anger is regarded mythologically as something filthy and ugly, and is expressed in the form of the incarnation of a snake.

I personally think that, if the feelings of shame and dislike towards 'filthy and ugly things' that lurk in a swamp become refined, they become *sumanai–mono*, or things that are impure, unprocessed/uncompleted, or probably a sense of guilt. If you rush into processing things, *kegare*, or uncleanliness, which has the dual meaning of filth and sin (*sumanai*, or being sorry), is evaded, as if it were a bad substance. It may motivate the action of repayment (as dedications and monetary donations), or even suicide. It was only recently that a certain religion adopted this donation mechanism, which was brought to light as a serious social problem in Japan.

Sumanai is unfinished

When we try to understand the 'swamp' that is lurking inside us, a duality of the front and the back emerges, as well as associated failures/disappointments. The reason is that, in most cases, they have caused an endless feeling of unfathomable uneasiness. Still, in order for 'I,' who faces such failures/disappointments, to survive, I must tackle the challenge of processing contradictions and impurities, such as the back in relation to the front. Needless to say, intellectual unification and integration are certainly not an easy task.

In this sense, what makes us neurotic in terms of our Japanese language is the practice of using taboo words and different words for different situations and purposes. According to the psychology of socialised taboos in Japan, the objects that are being avoided and hushed up are concentrated in fishy, 'filthy' events involving blood, such as child delivery and menstruation ('red' impurity) and death ('black' impurity). I may be repeating myself, but what motivates avoidance of this taboo is not the psychology of a thing being 'absolutely dreadful and terrifying,' but the psychology of *kegare*, or uncleanliness, such as something being ugly and filthy that must be detested. If we consider this in reference to the anthropologist Douglas' *Purity and Danger* (Douglas, 1966), it is something that cannot be classified, something that cannot be understood, and something that cannot be put in order.

Uncovered eros and death give power to psychoanalytic practitioners who handle the theme of taboo, to receive various sorts of remarks from the patients. It is important for therapists, who serve as receptacles for these remarks, to continue to stand 'where the reviews/evaluations are mixed,' such as actors in the past simultaneously being hailed and ridiculed, sometimes being regarded as 'riverbank beggars.' Contradictions and impurities tend to get muddy, being mixtures of the front and the back, and of black and white. However, the significance of these things that cause unfathomable uneasiness, is that they easily become *sumanai*. If a person leaves these *sumanai* things as *sumanai* or unfinished, part of it becomes the psychology of our survival and creativity. We exist, first and foremost, where we hold in our minds the impurities and contradictions of the 'unfathomable swamp' without spitting them out, and savour them as the concerned party without running away from them.

What the mythology of the creation of the islands of Japan depicts as 'filthy and ugly' is the difficulty of 'seeing' a dying mother. However, although these mothers are on the verge of dying, they may very well survive: they are *wakaranai* things (in Japanese, they signify things that are both unfathomable/incomprehensible and cannot be clearly categorised) that wander between life and death. In this *wakaranai* place, bipolarity overlaps in the categories of father and mother, the front and the back, a man and a woman, humans and animals, penis and vagina, and life and death. They copulate, mingle with each other in a dramatic fashion, melt together, and most likely form what appears to be a fishy swamp.

Conclusion – where is women's 'tragedy' heading?

Based on the cultural studies and clinical examples described above, I have shown the likelihood of, and the pathology of, people in our culture frequently experiencing participation-type primal scenes, of a child sleeping together with his or her parents and getting drawn into the parents' sexual activities. As facts relating to the Japanese language that underpin these claims, it may be possible to point out the presence of obscenities such as calling the penis of an adult male, 'son,' and the meaningfulness of the proverb, 'badgers in the same hole' which is equivalent to 'birds of a feather' or 'partners in crime' (Kitayama, 2021). Many people laugh at these associations; for some patients, however, they may bring to mind the intense dizziness and nausea they felt when becoming involved in these situations.

Ukiyo-e researchers state that Japanese *shunga* artists depict genitals in exaggerated form, as if to 'show them off.' I personally feel that this concerns not only a child's problem; I believe that there may be parents who try to draw their children into the primal scene. I also feel that, regarding these lively and boisterous 'festivals and parties,' many patients experience excitement that they can never feel they have talked enough about, in addition to the indigestible death and horror.

The tragedy of the 'prohibition of "Don't Look"' depicts the critical experience of an actor who performs in a theatre called Life, watching the disappearance of two separate realms, the dissolution of the crucial boundary between the stage and the backstage dressing room, and suddenly sees the two mixed-up. This is why I believe that a theory of culture that is based on the duality of people's daily life, such as the front and the back, and *honne to tatemae* (what you say as opposed to what you really think), is crucial to acquire a dramatic perspective in clinical practice in Japan.

The tragic tales of marriages between humans and non-humans that show, in particular, a dying mother and an injured woman being excluded and leaving this world, reflect the history of our having forced the human duality of being both humans and animals mainly onto women who were said to have 'no home of their own in the three worlds' (such as past, present, and future). This has an aspect that may be described as 'abuse of the mother.' Now that this sin is gradually being revealed, I feel it perfectly understandable that the Japanese are having sex less frequently, fewer couples are getting married, and the number of babies born continues to sharply decrease.

Note

1 See the papers in the special issue on the 'Ajase complex,' *Journal of the Japan Psychoanalytic Society, 4* (2022).

References

Baba, R. (2021). Personal communication. In Kitayama, O. (2021). *Haburaretemo Ikinokorutameno Shinsōshinrigaku [Depth Psychology for Survival Despite Being Excluded]*. Tokyo: Iwanamishoten.

Douglas, M. (1966). *Purity and Danger: An Analysis of the Concepts of Pollution and Taboo*. London: Routledge and Kegan Paul.

Endō, S. (1989). *Chinmoku [Silence]*. Tokyo: Shinchōsha. (Original work published 1966)

Fenichel, O. (1945). *The Psychoanalytic Theory of Neurosis*. New York: Norton.

Green, A. (1986). The dead mother. In *On Private Madness* (pp. 142–173). London: Hogarth Press.

Hayakawa, M. (2000). *Shunganonakano Kodomotatchi – edosyominno seiishiki [Children in Shunga – Sexual Awareness in Ordinary Edo People]*. Tokyo: Kawadeshobō Shinsha.

Matsumura, T. (1955). *Nihonshinwa no Kenkyū [Sudies of Japanese Myths]*, Vol. 2, Part 1. Tokyo: Baifūkan.

Itsuki, H. (1989). *Seishunno Mon [The Gate of Youth]* Part 1 (revised ed.). Tokyo: Kōdansha. (Original work published 1970)

Kitayama, O. (2007). *Gekitekina Seishinbunsekinyūmon [Introduction to Dramatic Psychoanalysis]*. Tokyo: Misuzushobō.

Kitayama, O. (2009). *Ooiwotorukoto Tsukurukoto [Uncovering and Making Covers]*. Tokyo: Iwasaki Gakujutsu Shuppansha.

Kitayama, O. (2010). *Prohibition of Don't Look*. Tokyo: Iwasaki Gakujutsu Shuppansha.

Kitayama, O. (2017). *Teiban Mirunanokinshi – nihongo rinsyōno shinsō [The Prohibition of Don't Look: The Depth of Japanese-Language Oriented Clinical Practice (Standard Edition)]*. Tokyo: Iwasaki Gakujutsu Shuppansha.

Kitayama, O. (2021). *Haburaretemo Ikinokorutameno Shinsōshinrigaku [Depth Psychology for Survival Despite Being Excluded]*. Tokyo: Iwanamishoten.

Okonogi, K. (1978). The Ajase complex of the Japanese (1). *Japan Echo*, 5 (4), 88–105.

Okonogi, K. (1979). The Ajase complex of the Japanese (2). *Japan Echo*, 6 (1), 104–118.

Okonogi, K. (1984). Kakukazokukara nettowākukazokue [From nuclear families to network families]. Reports by the Housing Construction Institute. *Modern Housing Research and Promotion Fund*, 11, 19–29.

Tamaru, Y. (1989). *Ajase-Ou [King Ajase]*. Tokyo: Daisanbunmeisha.

Winnicott, D.W. (1969). The use of an object. *International Journal of Psycho-Analysis*, 50, 711–716.

Yamazaki, M. (1971). *Gekitekinaru Nihonjin [Dramatic Japanese]*. Tokyo: Shinchōsha.

Chapter 10

Music heard when one jumps into a swamp

Osamu Kitayama

Being drawn into a primal scene

In his paper entitled 'From the history of an infantile neurosis' (Freud, 1918), which is the case study of 'Wolf Man,' Freud described the case of a patient who developed neurosis after having witnessed, during infancy, his parents engaged in sexual intercourse. Freud called the witnessing of the parents engaging in sexual intercourse the 'primal scene,' and analysed it in detail as a cause of neurosis.

If we think back on Japanese culture, we know that it is a common practice for young children to sleep side by side or with his/her parents, especially during infancy. There is therefore a greater likelihood that a child will be exposed to what Freud calls 'the primal scene.' In the West, parents and children usually sleep in different rooms, so the term 'primal scene' seems to anticipate a situation in which a child secretly witnesses the act through a partly opened door, for example. In Japan, however, the child sleeps in the same room as the parents, so he or she is liable to not only 'witness' it, but also inevitably become 'drawn into it,' and become psychologically involved.

As I have reported in the past, we often encounter cases during clinical psychoanalysis in which this experience has affected the patients' minds in different ways. Japan's *ukiyo-e* pictures, especially *shunga* or erotic prints, which were also called 'comic pictures,' often depict a child sleeping with his or her parents in various configurations. We find here a culture that allows the beholders to casually enjoy these prints, suggesting that a rich continuity exists between pathology and culture. In this chapter, I would like to stress once again the need for an academic study that examines, with a broad perspective, the culture of a family sleeping alongside each other, forming the Chinese character for 'river,' or 川.

Let me remind you, however, that I personally am able to discuss this subject without much hesitation. This is not just because of my intellectual curiosity and awareness of the issue from a clinical perspective. It is because since my youth, I have been engaged in composing and performing music that includes love songs, and, because this process serves as a 'purification device,' I am able to think and talk in a relaxed way about the darker and more complex sides of love.

DOI: 10.4324/9781003501930-12

Growing up near a train station

Let me now discuss my past of having grown up in a house near Kyoto Station. I will focus on my deepest and most complex memories of this time. I was the eldest son of a doctor of general medicine. My family ran a clinic in front of Kyoto Station. The front of the station was a busy place, lined with hotels and a post office, and, amid the overflowing crowds of travellers and station workers, there were also prostitutes and wounded veterans who stood sorrowfully, playing melancholy music.

The station plaza was also a kind of live museum where all sorts of worldly things came together. It almost resembled an amusement park. Today's Kyoto Station looks like a battleship, but the one I remember, two versions before it, was an elegant wooden structure. The sight of this station being destroyed in a fire in 1950, right before my eyes, is the most shocking memory I am able to describe in public within socially acceptable limits.

There was also a hotel in front of the same station that was used by the US Occupation Forces, about three minutes from my house. That was where I witnessed American culture being brought into our country. I sometimes heard jazz and country music being played from the hotel, both live and on the radio. I believe that I was influenced by the fact that the blues and songs expressing the sorrow and grief of black people and low-level workers who were at the base of those types of music. At the same time, I became aware of the fact that playing music brings about a momentary feeling of liberation. Along with this, 'Give me chocolate' was the first English sentence I learned. I also got a taste for success: I once ran after a US Army jeep that was heading for the hotel, and, knowing that it would slow down at the next corner, I approached the jeep, said those magic words, and was given the sweet chocolate that I craved.

Another intense, unforgettable experience in my youth was seeing how differently the members of a certain class of people, who were discriminated against, were being treated. In fact, the discriminated area spreading in east and south of Kyoto Station was the 'biggest taboo in Kyoto' despite being in my neighbourhood. I became increasingly curious about the complex and forbidden parts of the world. For example, Kyushu University Hospital, with which I became involved in later years as a university professor, stands near the sea in East Ward, Fukuoka City, where this type of discrimination was common in the past. In the sense that both the hospital and the surrounding community deal with *namagusai* things, or things with a 'fishy' odour, I have been aware, ever since I was small, of the 'continuity' between medicine that deals with 'unnormal' things, and the 'unnormal' community, being located next to each other.

I also wrote about this in my autobiography, *A Camel without a Hump* (Kitamaya, 2016), but there was an incident that took place during my childhood that I can never forget. My father was arrested and taken into custody by the Military Police (MP) on suspicion of having performed an abortion on a Japanese woman who had become pregnant with a soldier's child. My family and I felt extremely helpless. This developed into my own meaningful memory that connects to my study of the primal scene in this book associated with 'my father's crime.'

While singing, 'I ended up dying' …

A major event during my young adulthood that I must mention is my unexpected debut in the entertainment industry after I started college. My friends and I formed a group of three called the Folk Crusaders, and released a song, 'Kaettekita Yopparai' ('The Drunk Who Came Back to Earth from Heaven'); the English title is 'I Only Live Twice'); the song started with the line 'I ended up dying' (Kitayama, 2017).[1] The record, which sold 2.8 million copies in Japan from 1967 to 1968, an unprecedented number in those days, touches on the taboo of death. The Japanese lyrics contained numerous voiced consonants with 'heavy' sounds such as *ji* and *da*. At the same time, the song highlighted the aspect of young people's confrontation with their fathers' generation. Our contemporary folk song subculture in those days sent messages about peace and equality, and many men grew their hair long. Their looks were criticised for being effeminate. Even today, if you look at the lyrics that I wrote, you cannot help getting the impression that they are effeminate. However, I still view this in a strongly positive light. In those days, we were mocked by being called 'rotten, like a woman.' I became interested in learning what would happen if a woman became rotten, and since then I have been led to the story featured at the opening of the *Kojiki*, in which the Goddess Izanami is banished as she decays away.

After the Folk Crusaders disbanded, we created numerous songs, with long-haired Kazuhiko Katoh and Norihiko Hashida composing the music, with me writing the lyrics.[2] Unfortunately, Katoh, who remained active with a myriad of creative endeavours, ultimately chose to take his own life. I believe that, if the song had not become such a huge hit, he would not have died while still in his 60s. At the core was the conflict between the mass and the personal, or between the group and the individual. We have continued to live, still deeply involved in this paradox, for 40 and even 50 years. To this day, I am still involved with this paradox. Through records and radio culture, we achieved a level of fame that we certainly did not deserve; at the same time, from our mass media experience, we derived no satisfaction at all and a feeling of unreality. We found ourselves in an empty and futile state in which only our names floated about, with no attention whatsoever given to our physical existence or personal presence. We ended up repeating the same thing, both in name and substance, and eventually developed a sense of puppet-like emptiness. We even felt that we had been victimised. I feel that this was why I, a medical student at the time, ultimately returned to medicine, which deals directly with people's real and personal lives.

Encounter with psychoanalysis through play

However, I have not quit performing music. It remains my hobby to this day and helps me stay healthy. Music has become one of the places where I belong. On the other hand, I have numerous opportunities to communicate directly with people such as you, the reader, and to give lectures and presentations. I sometimes feel that the 'me' who plays music and sings songs is the more real, genuine me, than the 'me' engaged in intellectual thinking such as this. The fact that an expressive activity called 'play' such as this has become the key concept of my life, begins with the awareness that I am referring to my activity as 'play' in English. Record players, CD players ... all performers are players. I personally love baseball, and those who play baseball are also players. On the other hand, I became troubled by the suggestion that this 'engaging in play' might contradict my practising medicine. This is because I was subject to criticism that I, a musician and an entertainer who was simply 'playing around,' was not qualified to return to medical school. I felt that I was being discriminated against.

However, there is a theory in the world of psychoanalysis that supports play as a method of treatment. For example, child psychoanalyst D. W. Winnicott asserts that play is the goal of treatment; it is also a method of analysis. I encountered his writings in London when I began undergoing training in psychoanalysis. As his most representative book, I must cite *Playing and Reality*. There is also a famous paper by Freud entitled 'Creative writers and day-dreaming' (Freud, 1907). We find that Freud understood the significance of play, but regarded adult play in a rather negative light.

Needless to say, Freud talks about taboo, as seen in *Totem and Taboo* (Freud, 1913), and discusses the issue of sexual desire and death. Moreover, with the understanding of neurosis that is based on the love triangle theory, mentioned alongside a concept called the Oedipus complex, Freud took up, as a universal human task and challenge, the struggles that enable someone like me to reveal my thoughts like this in front of an audience, urging my opinions on others. This is none other than the deep psychology of *Kaettekita Yopparai*, and the content of the lyrics – a drunkard was having a ball in heaven, finding that 'here, alcohol tastes great and the ladies are pretty'; then a scary god comes and kicks him out of heaven – described as a typical Oedipal story. I felt that the world that the song depicts is the Oedipus complex itself; I was impressed that Freud himself had foreseen the song being a hit. I was attracted to psychoanalysis and eventually dived into it.

I therefore believe that psychoanalysis has enabled me to allow play and other cultural activities to coexist with medicine. According to Winnicott's theory, play is about living between one's inner impulses and external reality, positioned on the middle ground and bridging the two sides. Adults also gradually learn to enjoy this as a form of culture. Moreover, psychoanalysis handles things that have been repressed, called the unconscious, or the reality of a person's inner mind. This was also about the deep psychology of taboos. So, in this way, these theories of psychoanalysis increased my awareness of the issues concerning discrimination, as well as my experiences with play, music and culture. The clinical practice of psychoanalysis became my life's work.

Masochism in Japanese culture

After starting the clinical practice of psychoanalysis, at a relatively early stage of my career, I discovered a certain group of patients and published a paper about them written in English. Like the female protagonist in a play called *The Twilight of a Crane*, these people, whom I termed 'masochistic caretakers,' worked hard, damaging themselves in the process, and suffered from a sense of guilt that had been imposed on them. Searching for references to masochistic ways of living and thinking in the Japanese language, I find that the following have become everyday words and expressions: – 所懸命 (working extremely hard), 粉骨砕身 (giving one's all), 必死 (acting desperately), and 命懸け (risking one's life). Although these deep-rooted masochistic tendencies and excessive sense of guilt are components of negative therapeutic reactions that get in the way of psychoanalysis, they are broadly shared in the Japanese culture of shame in the form of *harakiri* (ritual suicide by self-disembowelment using a sword) and the *kamikaze* suicide fighter pilots during the end of Second World War. This warrants special attention on the part of analysts who practice the 'uncovering' method. This is because the sense of guilt that has developed as an introversion of anger, or masochism that results from the redirection of aggression toward the self, is liable to become activated in Japanese culture. On the other hand, a negative therapeutic reaction, if used in a narrow sense, is a concept that is extremely difficult to use, but is commonly resorted to in psychoanalytic treatment because the patient cannot avoid experiencing short-lived regression and aggravation to improve his or her symptoms.

As Freud stated (Freud, 1923), if a therapist talks to a patient with hope, and expresses his/her satisfaction, he/she conversely aggravates the patient. I, too, am unable to successfully present a neat solution to this. However, this is an important perspective for making psychoanalysis 'take shape,' and, at the same time, there is a perspective which I have long emphasised and applied, called the 'dramatisation of transference,' which means to take the perspective of looking at therapeutic relations and a person's life as a drama. In particular, I believe that 'figuration,' in terms of conceptual understanding taking shape, is extremely important in that our understanding of the self-progress to the point where a static shape changes to a dynamic shape.

The front and the back of Japanese culture

There are also countless characteristics of the Japanese language when looked at from a global perspective. To psychoanalysis that emphasises language and verbalisation to ensure third-party-style clarifications, the characteristic of the Japanese language that stands out, above all, is, as was discussed in Chapter 6, that we are living a double-level semantic relationship of using hard *kanji* characters and loose *kana* characters. This double structure makes one more aware of the duality and the splitting tendency of the self, such as *honne* and *tatemae* (what you say, as opposed to what you really think; one's honest feelings versus one's official stance), and the front and the back. This consequently makes it easier to tell jokes; conversely, patients suffering severe symptoms are liable to be swayed by the language's ambiguity, and as a result experience confusion of thoughts and make misstatements.

The conscious memory of the primal scene experience, which becomes a problem in the case report I describe below, has become easier to understand, thanks to its after-the-fact rationalisation and subsequent elaboration. The early-stage primal experience itself, however, is an 'unfathomable' situation that causes dizziness and nausea. As stated in Chapter 6 and below, it generally turns into a watery state, like soft mud.

The reason I want to focus on the 'swamp' that appears at the outset of the Japanese creation myth is because of the scene in which the gods Izanagi and Izanami together lower the heavenly jewelled spear into a sea of mud and stir it round and round, causing it to curdle. On pulling it out of the ocean, drops of seawater that drip from the spear pile up to form an island. It was on Onogoro Island that a nation was created through the deities' spectacular sexual intercourse. This symbolically and powerfully describes an image of copulation and conception. In the beginning, it must have been the 'overwhelming unknown' (Fenichel, 1945) that was swirling around.

The onomatopoeia of mucinous voiced consonants[3]

In the tragedy of the prohibition of 'Don't Look' described in the latter half of the myth about the birth of the country of Japan, what depicted as 'filthy and ugly,' is the difficulty of looking at the dying mother. This mother, although dying, might perhaps survive. She is in an 'unfathomable' state (the Japanese word for this is *wakeno wakaranai mono*, which also means things that cannot be understood, as well as the condition of being undifferentiated), of wandering between life and death. Regarding this 'unknown' state, in the primal scene, two opposing poles overlap, such as a father and a mother, front and back, a man and a woman, people and animals, the penis and vagina, love and violence, and life and death. They get mixed together, in a dichotomy of 'neither this nor that.' They melt together to become a liquid form, of 'either one will do.'

Furthermore, in Japan, negative reactions are liable to occur in psychoanalysis, particularly towards interpretations that accompany sex and death. I believe this is due to a deep-rooted tendency to regard various experiences associated with sex and death as filthy foreign substances that need to be washed away through rituals such as exorcism, purification and cleansing. There is also the myth about the creation of a country that shows the Mother Goddess, together with the Father God, engaging in repeated sexual intercourse and child delivery, and dying thereafter. The tragedy of a father leaving the mother to die without helping her is extremely interesting if seen from the primal scene perspective of childhood.

In addition, it is because of the external reality of a humid climate and islands surrounded by water that the Japanese people's bedroom sleeping status is typified by a family of three sleeping alongside each other like canned sardines. Moreover, the fact that the scenes of sexual intercourse are called 'wet scenes' in Japanese theatrical terms must be because sexual intercourse is accompanied by the physical phenomenon of bodies becoming 'wet.' This is why we end up with so many water-related images and metaphors, such as mud and swamps. Along with these, according to my clinical observations, complex experiences that are difficult to digest, and nauseating things that have a 'fishy, half-rotten odour,' can be physically liquefied and washed away. The onomatopoeia of mucinous voiced consonants that accompanies mucinous tactile sensations is liable to occur in interactions between a mother and her child, as well as in exchanges between a man and a woman. This must be because they are sounds associated with physical exchanges and sexual activities that involve the mouth/lips, the excretory organs, and the genitals, etc.

Case study: the primal scene and rape

I would now like to discuss the case of a patient who taught me about the above in an easy-to-understand fashion. The patient's treatment was initially held once a week. After about a year and a half, the sessions were increased to four times a week, focusing on free association using the couch. Although the course of treatment was long, covering more than ten years and 1,500 sessions, I would like to summarise the course by dividing it into episodes. The following accounts are the later developments of the female case described in Chapter 9. Because some of the material overlaps, I will not repeat my overview of the case. I have modified the content and the passage of time from the perspectives of privacy protection and ease of understanding.

From the early stages of treatment, the patient talked about her primal scene experience that she was unable to tell anyone about. 'When I was small, I used to sleep with my father and mother, the three of us. When my father was having sex with my mother, it looked to me as if he was killing her.' And, along with her mother, the patient was raped by her father with his penis. At the same time, she felt that he would kill her since she was weak and powerless. While crying almost as if spitting something out, she said that she began to think that she wanted to die, and continued to narrate her involvement-style primal scene experiences. She also talked repeatedly, seemingly embarrassed, about her fear of men and the penis, as well as the fact that she had actually been raped by someone she knew and became pregnant. After getting married, she was negative towards engaging in sexual intercourse. It appeared that her family looked down on her. There also was a countertransference occurring within me, of wanting to tease her.

The patient also talked about her ambivalence towards breasts. Since her mother could not produce enough breast milk, she forcibly weaned the baby – the patient – who cried for it, by applying mustard onto her nipples. At the same time, when the patient opened up her heart to other people, she said that her boundaries weakened and an object with a pointed tip would enter her body. So, at first, I was worried about the risk of her developing severe regression and taking her own life. On the other hand, she came to the office on time, matter-of-factly, left more or less on time, and was somehow able to 'contain' herself during the sessions.

The back and the front

She talked endlessly about being a victim. She cried uncontrollably and belittled herself. From around the second year, she talked about a certain awareness she had developed. 'Dr. Kitayama, I finally realised that there is someone named *A* inside me, and that this *A* is mean and trying to make the other person angry.' However, this feeling of the presence of an alter ego was not that strong. Along with her fear of being penetrated by a penis, as well as her dislike of fat men and of men in general, I occasionally saw her brush off the possibility of filthy contact, numerous times with her hands. However, I myself was like a mother figure to her, and her acting out relating to mysophobia, or fear of filth, was hidden, at least during the sessions. ·

An alter ego named Peter Pan

Soon, as her alter ego, the part of her that had stopped growing and remained a child (in terms of gender, it was a boy), slowly emerged, in the centre of her conversations, as an individual with a dual personality. Around the time that she began to speak about her inner Peter Pan, his acting out occurred, which was something I had worried about: when going down the staircase at a train station, she jumped down several steps, fell, and broke her finger. During this period, when I listened to her free associations, I heard her, in the 'corner' of the couch, utter in a dissatisfied tone, 'Really? I'm not too sure about that ...' At first, I thought that I had heard her wrong, but when I listened more closely, I understood that she was definitely uttering complaints about my interpretations. This was when I learned, for the first time, that there was another person inside the treatment room. Even though I interpreted this, and made her confront it, she herself remained completely unaware of it.

It was around the third year of treatment that her attitude became clearly rebellious. She focused on the fact that I merely listened passively to what she said and did not make any record of her treatment, and began saying, 'You don't care a bit about me,' and 'I bet you'd dump me without a thought, right?' This was as if she could not help describing her fantasies about my victimising her. Sometimes, prior to weekends and long holidays, she would also burst out with things like 'When I'm not around, I bet you flirt and make out with other patients.' Despite making these critical comments, she would immediately switch her attitude and take back her remarks, saying 'I'm sorry, that was just a joke.'

Progression and regression

At the beginning of the fourth year, with her dependence progressing, *A* continued to deteriorate. Hysterical hallucinations appeared, such as: when she boards a train, she is surrounded by men who display their penises; she said 'Men stick their penises into me; a needle gets inside; legs go in.' I made the interpretation, 'I think you want to connect to somebody, so unpleasant things get inside,' and tried to continue a meaningful dialogue, but she merely replied, 'I know,' and ignored my words, giving no response whatsoever.

On the train, her experiences of fear of filthy, smelly men increased, and she would get up and change seats. Seeing that I remained slightly sceptical about her abnormal experiences outside, she became angry, but apologised in the next session, saying, 'I'm sorry for being rebellious.' Even when I connected her anxiety to her treatment, she always said, 'Yes, I know.' On the other hand, by seeing me as her 'surrogate mother,' she developed peace of mind. I continued to watch over her major personality shifts between anger and being apologetic.

Becoming mixed-up and messy

Before long, two selves began to appear during the sessions, switching frequently. A period of confusion, as if she was being fooled and deceived somehow, continued for several years. These two selves were eventually called *A*, a female, and *B*, a young boy. They were more like a dual self than a dual personality. I learnt that the two were in a confrontational relationship: while *A* depended on me, *B* interfered with this relationship of dependence. *A* was an adult and apologises since she accepts what I say and 'understands' it, but *B* does not understand, refuses to accept it, and rebels against me. He unleashes abusive language against me, but quickly takes it back, so I become confused and tired. These exhausting sessions continued, but, despite completely acknowledging this switchover of personality, the patient herself refused point-blank to acknowledge it and became even more confused. This irritated me at times.

She acknowledges her fantasies but denies that they are such

From around the sixth year of treatment, the patient began to acknowledge that her self-transformation was triggered by her being suddenly scared when fantasising about bad things. Still, a self that said, 'No, it's not a fantasy; I'm not doing this because I like it,' appeared. Along with this 'acting-in,' however, she no longer experienced the divergence, while being outside, of having men's legs penetrate her body or being able to see men's penises. She thanked me for saving her life. However, although her symptoms improved, they also worsened to the same degree. She also became especially rebellious. Indeed, it appeared that these two selves were not so much showing division or divergence as collaborating to confuse both the treatment and me.

A boy and a girl

I continued to interpret the splitting between her boy and girl selves. A very wide split was seen, with the boy asserting and ridiculing, and the girl withdrawing them and apologising. It took many years for the two to be able to coexist. This slow process was, of course, important. What was interesting, however, was that I was able to hypothesise that the split between the two – the passiveness of the girl and the aggressiveness of the different, masculine personality – had their roots in the traumatic primal scene experience itself.

The climax of the mixed-up, messy experiences

It was around the seventh year that the quick transformation of the patient's divided self occurred from her free associations related to accounts about the penis and death. It all appeared too obvious, though it compels me to describe it as always being the same. *B* then began saying that she was scared, even though there was nothing to be afraid of.

> I don't know why, but I suddenly become sad and that makes me cry … I can't explain it … but it's different from usual. The sky over there, the air over there, and the flowers … they look strange. Why do they all come rushing in on me?

The patient was driven into a corner. Each time a new problem was solved and we rejoiced about it, *B* had nothing to say, and she began feeling that he was causing trouble for me. Situations emerged, such as *A* coming to the waiting room first, and *B* leaving the office. Instances of my *zukkokeru* (slipping up, or my becoming surprised with the unexpected that turned out to be extremely funny and made me laugh) increased, in a *zuru-zuru* (slithery) manner. Positive relations changed to negative ones, and I sometimes tried to chase after the one who was trying to go home. This sort of mix-up and confusion marked the climax of her treatment.

Acknowledging the self-contradiction that has become embodied, and groaning

And so, the pattern of contradiction, of *A* wanting to go but *B* interfering with her, took shape, and the patient came to confront the repetition of achieving peace of mind followed by its destruction. When she became aware that the same mouth was saying contradictory things, I began to hear her groan like an animal. This continued for about two years, and I felt that a sense of history had developed, in that she was repeating the same type of things.

Her fear of the penis, rape, sex, and death regressed, and another type of fear slowly began to creep into the relationship: fear in the absence of anything to be afraid of, and fear that *B* would make me, the mother figure, angry.

Contempt

In contrast, what gradually became clear was that, in the process of the patient becoming afraid of her parents' sexual intercourse, she witnessed rabbits having sex from the back, doggy-style and that made her even more afraid. In other words, she regarded human sexual activities as animalistic, and felt 'They are all bestial, like dogs.' The reason she was afraid of sex, more than anything, was that the patient, as a boy, would be castrated and die.

She also admitted that she regarded sex as despicable. She occasionally began talking about her insights, such as 'I made fun of my parents who were engaged in sex by calling them animals, and now the animals that I made fun of have become angry and attack me. This is all happening inside my head.' Thanks to transference and its dramatisation, the patient was able to say, 'I'm sorry for saying things I didn't mean.' There were also times when she admitted that she had the fantasy, inside her heart at the same time, of me flirting and making out with other patients.

The devil is a nuisance, an interference

Although there were many outlandish, ridiculous dreams, gradually, more realistic dreams came about. 'I'm trying to go see you, Doctor, but I am somehow blocked, which makes me anxious.' Regarding this, she came to accept my interpretation, 'The devil in you is getting in your way and blocking you,' and she laughed at this repetition.

Here, concerning this case of severe borderline personality, I understood that two entities existed within the same mind: the patient who clings to me, which Fairbairn (1944) calls 'the exciting object' that causes feelings of excitement within a person, and an 'internal *saboteur*' who interferes. *B*, who is the main subject, was figured, or given shape, as an 'internal *saboteur*,' and the patient, too, began to acknowledge its presence.

'You're the one who's looking at things superficially'

Swayed by her beating around the bush, saying one thing and meaning another, I felt as if I was being made fun of, and became irritated. Later, there were times when, after accusing me of likely flirting and making out with other patients, she reversed her stance and said, embarrassed, 'I'm sorry for saying something I didn't mean,' and we both burst out laughing. Eventually, there were moments when the patient took my interpretation, '*You*'re the one who's looking at things superficially,' in a positive light. For example, I pointed out that it was about her becoming nauseated by images such as sexual intercourse and erect penises, and pushing them aside. I added that the reason she is unable to acquire, as her own, my interpretations and her understanding of the things I had conveyed to her was because, although the girl in her becomes 'confused and lost,' the boy inside her is spitting them out, and thus she cannot acquire them as her own.

The interpretation of 'throwing things into the gutter'

Along with the subsequent progress in treatment, there was a process in which, while achieving a satisfactory relationship of dependence upon me, or especially when she confirmed this, she became aware that she ended up thinking directly the opposite, especially outside the sessions, such as 'Dr Kitayama is absent,' and 'Dr Kitayama would absolutely not come to help me.' In the course of this, I began to feel that *B* himself would 'throw *A*'s accomplishments into the gutter' ('gutter,' in Japanese is *dobu*), so I used it in my interpretations. Looking back, I now think that the use of the voiced consonants in the word *dobu* makes it possible to understand the patient's negative therapeutic reactions.

I then conveyed to her that the reason she spits out my interpretations when outside the sessions is because she hates thinking about me examining other patients. She said, 'I can't believe that you are thinking about other things, even during sessions with me,' but she eventually had no choice but to admit that, even though there are times I am concerned about other patients, I still listen to what she has to say. The patient therefore became able to tolerate, little by little, the fact that one can see a couple's 'flirting and making out' beyond their 'killing each other,' even while feeling an 'unfathomable uneasiness,' or, in other words, spitting it out inside one's mind.

She also required a period during which *A* and *B* were mixed together, or, according to the patient's account, a period of 'unfathomable uneasiness' which in Japanese is *dara-dara* (sloppy and dragging on), *guzu-guzu* (slow and dilly-dallying), and *zuru-zuru* (slithering and dragging on). The patient managed to live rather than die because I existed; but the more she felt grateful to me the more her gratitude and sense of guilt were thrown into the gutter, outside the sessions. When she became *B*, she felt that I refused to be with her and offer help, and she negated me. The more she negated me outside the sessions, the more she came to the office to apologise and thank me. These behaviours were repeated. Although she rejoiced that she had become better thanks to me, at the same time she became stricken with anxiety, hurling remarks such as 'You hate me, don't you?,' 'You're not waiting for me, are you?,' and 'You probably think it's better for me not to come.'

It was a boy

Moreover, the reason she required four-times-a-week analytical treatment for more than ten years was that Peter Pan, *B*, and the devil who claimed a dwelling place inside her body, and stayed on as a little boy. In this process, the patient once again became aware of a series of traumatic experiences: the use of mustard to wean her from breastfeeding; in the primal scene where her mother was 'killed' by her father, she 'abandoned' the mother, leaving her to be killed but, at the same time the patient was also killed; and the rape that had occurred when she was around 20 years old. The patient said, 'I think *B* held a grudge against it; he sulked and was jealous; he also had intense penis envy.' In this context, even in her therapeutic relationship with me, she repeatedly experienced the anxiety of being abandoned and the fear of being kicked out, confusing my remarks of 'Let's quit (saying stupid things)' with 'Let's quit treatment.' She also experienced conflict and the confusion of logic that sometimes occurs with homonyms.

A sloppy, slithery sensation

If considered from the time at which the patient achieved considerable calmness and stability, I believe that being 'thrown into the gutter' is verbalisation by the analyst who shared sorrow and anger, and, at the same time, the confusion of thoughts and the miring of the relationship. A chaotic and confusing mix-up continued, such as the patient entering the treatment room by saying 'good-bye,' instead of 'hello' which is what she should have said. This caused laughter on both sides, and these slimy, slipped-up experiences were repeated for many years.

However, with the pattern taking shape of *B* interfering despite *A* wanting to express her gratitude, the patient herself began to confirm that *B* was a heinous villain who made nothing but false allegations. And, since the patient was familiar with English, she began calling *B* a 'devil's advocate.' The fact that *B*, who had no place to belong, either in the patient's body or in reality, had 'no choice but to die,' and that he was extremely jealous, took shape. And so, instances of getting the two mixed-up continued to decrease, and the patient acknowledged that, if she said one thing, the other would immediately say something else, and thus *A* and *B* became able to encounter each other.

'Throwing things into the gutter' and laughter

In the 12th year of treatment, the patient brought in a joke: 'A man saw a woman walking in front of him who was putting up a beautiful umbrella. He went past her, glanced at the woman's face, and remarked, "Ah, who cares? You're just an old bag! (You don't need to be worried about being sexually assaulted.)"' This clearly showed that *A*, who states her *tatemae*, or public stance, and *B*, who reveals his true feelings, began talking to each other, including about the patient's relationship with me. So, I told her from the back, 'I think it's the same as my telling you, from the back, that it's okay.'

And the patient, who rarely said positive things, remarked, without later taking back what she had said, 'The words you told me that I cannot forget are "throw things into the gutter." I recall them and cannot help laughing.'

Confrontation with the boy

The conversation between *A* and *B* continued. Listening to them, I became very aware that the teaser whom I had initially noticed inside me was *B* himself. I understood again the fact that *B* was a boy and had an imaginary penis, therefore this boy was impelled to be mean to me, a dependable figure, and to *A* as a girl too. And I thought at the same time that she was able to withstand a serious confrontation. So, I faced up to mean *B* and interpreted 'You think you have a penis as you wanted to fight against your father, but you are teasing *A* about her female body instead of me, due to your not really having a penis.' This was accepted better than before and gradually pushed *B* back and reassured *A*, little by little. However, during this intensive process, I identified myself with 'injured' *A* so much and my voice unexpectedly became tearful at *B*'s irresponsible defiance, and then the patient became responsively sorry for me when she heard my tearful voice. Saying that she had done something that could not be undone, she never became overtly *B*, even when she sometimes spoke up for *B*'s opinions. I think that her personality had been integrated more than ever before, but there was no more laughter and no more music. Now I admit that my 'injured femininity' or my internal crane-wife, which I inherited from my mother and others, got activated with *B* dramatically when I cried a little internally. Of course, I did not fly away.

Towards the end: voicing along with a rhythmic *gucha-gucha* (mix-up)

Looking at the difficult situation internationally, I find that, as Kernberg (1983) pointed out early on, the Fairbairn theory that describes the splitting of the object differs from other object relations theories in that it puts, as its basis, the ego's need for dependency. And, in terms of the theory of this technique, while grasping what Fairbairn refers to as the two bad object relationships comprising the exciting object and the rejecting object, it is possible to conceive of a therapeutic response of supporting the dependent ego that lives in the conflict between the two objects. Here, we can make use not only of the dichotomic understanding of whether the object 'is good or bad,' but, at the same time, we can also put to use the dependence of the ego, or what Doi refers to as *amae*, as well as the ideas of 'holding' and 'management' (Winnicott, 1958). In one of my reports, I believe that I was able to present the workings of supporting the ego of the patient exposing the ambivalence of rebelling despite being dependent, and living where the content becomes mixedup. The content is 'a mixture that is incomprehensible and unfathomable,' and the analyst is held, inside the treatment together with the patient, with things that had been dispersed because of nausea and disgust.

An infant's triadic experience in the primal scene becomes an 'unfathomable' or incomprehensible event that is quite nauseating. What I can tell from my clinical experiences with sick people is that, if seen from the outside, the primal scene that contains a mixture of human beings and animals, mothers and fathers, the front and the back, life and death, and other 'this and that,' is an ugly and filthy thing. Many patients who had become involved with the primal scene during early childhood describe this experience, using onomatopoeia of voiced consonants such as *gucha-gucha* (messy and chaotic), *zubu-zubu* (drenched and deeply immersed), *doro-doro* (thick and muddy), *guzu-guzu* (slow and dilly-dallying), and *beto-beto* (sticky), and also recall it as something that is accompanied by nausea. There is a possibility, however, that the original experience itself may be a rhythmical, primordial, and organic unity.

In clinical situations, moreover, at places where two different poles get mixed together and make the circumstances appear as if 'either is okay,' if, together with time, the *gucha* (mild messiness and sloppiness) of voiced consonants, is repeated rhythmically to form a state of *gucha-gucha* (a fullblown mix-up), then, gradually, a sense of play and music develops inside me. If *ge* becomes *ge-ge*, if *boo* becomes *boo-boo*, and if *doro* (mud) becomes *doro-doro* (thick and muddy), then, along with the second beat that follows the first beat, and like a back-beat and hand-clapping, there is an 'image of someone following after me' (Kitayama, 2019) or the pleasures of mutual interaction such as interjections and call-and-response, may accompany them.

Nazumu, or 'becoming familiarised with' mud

On the other hand, what motivates reflexive avoidance of a taboo is not the psychology of something being terribly scary, but rather the 'psychology of filth,' that something is ugly and unclean so that it should be avoided and the taboo should be respected. Considering this, using for reference, the figure I showed in Chapter 6, the 'mud' which I refer to is found at the centre of the drawing, and is something that cannot be categorised successfully, something that one cannot understand, and/or something that cannot be successfully categorised or placed in order. What should be noted, however, is that this drawing depicts my ideological bridging when Winnicott's intermediate area theory has been learned and mastered. Here again, readers are encouraged to perceive the fact that *watashi* or I = *watashi* or bridging, and therefore the '*Bridging I*' that experiences this, is experiencing a rhythmic movement between binocular vision and double vision, of seeing one object becoming two, and two objects becoming one.

In a previous report, I used a clinical case study to describe how negative reactions, while dealing with the emotions of contempt and neglect of 'looking at things superficially,' become dramatised into a liquid state in the form of 'throwing things into the gutter,' or how they are embodied by metaphorisation and dramatisation. At the same time, however, an understanding of culture and rhythm provided leeway to the therapist and enabled the articulation of circumstances, so, in that context, I was able to fit the difficulties within a set scope and hold/contain them.

Moreover, sexual love and death give psychoanalytic clinicians, who handle their taboos, the power to serve as a receptacle of being told 'this and that' from the patients. It is important for therapists, who 'touch on' various taboos, to continue to stand in a rhythmical manner where they 'receive mixed reviews,' or, in other words, remain the object of ambivalence, just like actors in the past who were referred to 'riverbank beggars' and who were praised and degraded in quick succession. Between idealisation and contempt, contradictions and impurities tend to get murky, with opposites such as the front and the back, and black and white getting mixed together, and the significance of these 'unfathomable things,' more than anything, is that they do not become *sumanai* too easily. The Japanese word s*umanai* implies both an apologetic feeling, and that something is impure or not yet completed. If we were to leave this *sumanai* unresolved, some of it becomes the source of a sense of guilt, as well as an inspiration for new creative works. To begin with, we, who become involved, keep the impurities and contradictions in mind without spitting them out. We do not run away, but instead chew them and savour them as the party involved, and become used to them (*najimu*, in Japanese), together with a rhythm. This signifies that 'I' (*watashi*) exists. Also, in Japanese culture that prefers clean sounds and cleanliness, the Japanese word that is written as 泥む with the Chinese character 泥 that signifies 'mud,' is read as *nazumu*, whose meaning ranges from 'stagnate, care deeply for, and cling to,' to *najimu*, or 'become familiarised with.' As I have stated in Chapter 6, amid the confusion of negative and positive elements getting repeatedly mixed together, there is a path for us to survive until the time that we fade away from our lives (Kitayama, 2024).

Two paintings

The bottom of the psychic apparatus

Freud and his followers discovered that both a consciousness and unconscious are present inside a human being, and analysed its content using words. They also elucidated the mechanism by which psychopathology occurs by examining it and grasping it from the perspective of the whole psyche, and through this they established psychoanalysis. The upper area, called the consciousness, demands that thought be mostly organised and clear. It approves of a state where things are classified and categorised in a cut-and-dry fashion. The unconscious, on the other hand, is difficult for us to understand; we cannot control its content, either. Parts that are wet, such as mud and swamps, comprise the lower region of this unconscious, while the sense of *ukiyo*, or the fleeting world depicted in *ukiyo-e* paintings, is recognised as floating above it.

A large number of psychoanalysts have made the area of the consciousness the upper region, and that of the unconscious the lower region. However, there is something I have recently come to realise. It concerns a drawing of what Freud called the psychic apparatus, which psychoanalyst Shigeharu Maeda drew when he was young and gave to me ten years ago. Since then, I have displayed this picture in front of my office desk (see Figure 10.1). Using a touch that strongly reflects Maeda's youth immediately after the Second World War, he drew the image of psychoanalysis during the days when Freud's theories were being introduced into Japan.

The upper part is turned to the external world, and, because of sensory perception, the mind is turned outward. The group of buildings on the left side of the drawing shows the part called the conscience and the super-ego. They monitor the ego's words and actions; there even is a prison. In the centre of the drawing, we find a building called the ego. Just as I made use of the Japanese word, *watashi* or I = *watashi* or bridging, and call this the 'Bridging I,' 'I' is in the middle of the entire mind. It oversees the entirety by bridging it, achieves the balance of the top and the bottom as well as left and right, and maintains the correlation among each of its departments.

In this drawing that Maeda created, there is also *es* (a German word meaning *it* in English), which is not easy to recognise in this drawing. It is placed in the lower part, and in the lowest layer, rooted in the physical body, a 'gate to take in drives' has opened up. This must be where the navel was, the place from which people, while a foetus, absorbed nutrients while inside the uterus and excreted waste materials. Close by it, we can see a pond or a swamp. The real swamp, however, seems to be hidden in the primaeval forest at the top left. Above the pond, there is a storage area for myths, which I am interested in, and slightly above that there is a place for storing taboos. Their positioning is by no means coincidental as they are based on a psychoanalyst's associations. Pictured at the bottom on the right is what appears to be a slaughtering and

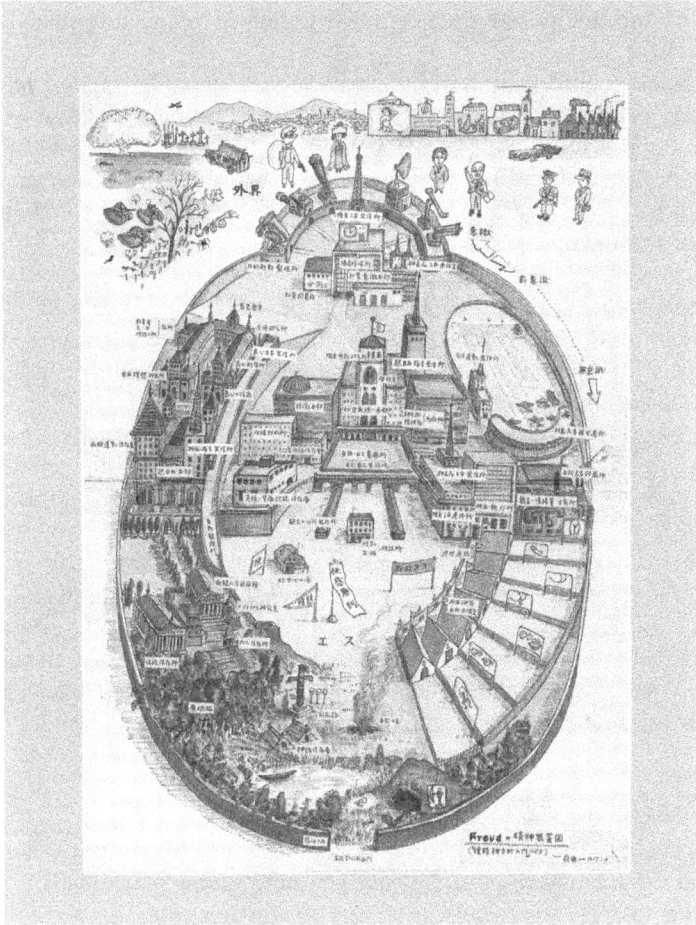

Figure 10.1 Seishin Souchi Zu [Psychic Apparatus Illustrated] (1958) by Shigeharu Maeda.
Source: the author's private collection.

butchering area where we see scattered bones. Discrimination and prejudice against this sort of work still persist in Japan. To its right, moreover, a cave is open. This hole might be connected to the Land of the Dead where Izanami rests in peace; it may also be an important outlet related to the death of living things.[4]

The thing that I can relate to the most in this drawing is where the floor underneath the ego and the region of *es* are connected seamlessly at the central square. This is where the '*Bridging I*' opens up the gate, as if looking down, and holds and contains the areas of depth-psychology, shown in the lower part of the drawing. However, if 'I' look up from below, although the path of cultural sub-limation of the burning flame is indicated with the staircase on the right, the upper part appears to have been completely roofed over, as if to unconsciously cover it with a lid.

The 'psychological swamp of innumerable determinants' which I have been describing, or in other words, the reservoir of the obscure and ambiguous, is present at the bottom of a person's mind, in this way we can say that the Japanese feel it as deep and unfathomable. Regarding this 'amorphous ego' part, Mikihachiro Tatara, a researcher of psychoanalysis, points out the fluidity of the Japanese ego as follows.

> Basic thoughts and principles that are deemed unwavering as the basic foundation of our existence are, in our country's case, often present in an obscure, ambiguous state, to a certain extent. Rock-solid beliefs, values and creeds and the like are fluid and not fixed. They sway from right to left, like a swing, and transform from one thing into another. And, in a person's lifetime, they are replaced by new things numerous times.
>
> (Tatara, 1998)

I believe that, if the mixing of people were to have the elements of *zubu-zubu* (drenched and deeply immersed) and *gucha-gucha* (messy and chaotic), there must be amorphous aspects in our minds that could always turn into a quagmire. In other words, our minds become *gucha-gucha*, or chaotic, in this melting pot, so we conclude that 'either would do.' To us, this is neither regression nor progression; it is neither homologous nor heterologous.

The earthy Izanami beneath the ukiyo, or the fleeting world

Maeda's drawing, moreover, can be looked at by mapping it onto the human body and the internal organs. We can then note that consciousness is located at the top and is facing outwards, and the unconscious is at the bottom, together with the stomach and other organs. The mind is found at the bottom of the bottom, or the navel which I mentioned earlier, and where it used to be connected to the womb. It is now rooted in our own physical body, and from there, we obtain energy from desires and impulses, then, alongside it, we excrete waste and other unnecessary things.

It is easy to see the importance of the lower abdomen if you get to know the expressions in the Japanese language involving the stomach. The idiom, *fukuzou naku* (without anything inside the stomach) means 'without hiding anything you have in mind,' and *hara ni ichimotsu* (there is something inside the stomach) signifies that there is something in your mind that you are scheming about. Moreover, in the old days, *samurai* warriors committed, with decisive resolution, *seppuku*, a ritualistic suicide done by cutting open the abdomen to prove their innocence. This must have been because one's true feelings and character were believed to have been hidden in the stomach.

In the abdominal area, moreover, while the intestines located deep inside prepare contents to be excreted, flames of unprocessed youth and energy swirl in the reproductive organs that develop during puberty. Animals are being slaughtered beside the pond at the bottom of Maeda's drawing. Because of this, the water of the swamp may sometimes become clouded with blood. If one fails to process and treat things at the bottom like these, the mass of this area floods the upper area. The odour alone may bring about confusion in the consciousness of the upper part. And so, human beings cannot live only with the brains and reason of the upper part; they alone are not everything about what people are. Therefore, even though one tries to make rational consciousness clear, there may be times when the *moya-moya* (fuzziness, a feeling of uneasiness) emanating from the smell of the swamp and desires that spring up from the bottom of the mind, may become stronger. It is therefore the '*Bridging Γ*' that exists between the upper and the lower parts, and, while appropriately differentiating both areas, bridges the entire system in a well-balanced manner, and makes it function.

In the Izanagi–Izanami myth, the former flees after seeing the latter's decaying body. Izanagi is chased after by Izanami and a group of ugly females. In the end, Izanagi deems Izanami's world as filthy, seals the boundary between the Land of the Dead and this world, and locks death under the ground. We then associate this as follows: It may be that, later, Izanami was buried underground, returned to the earth, became nutrients in the soil, and brought rich life to the land. A painting called *Kojiki Yori [From the Kojiki]* created by the artist Saori Akutagawa in 1957, inspired me to fantasise about this (see Figure 10.2). The part that is selected from this huge painting – over 13 metres wide – depicts the earthy Goddess Izanami after she has been buried underground and banished as an ugly, filthy being. In the painting, she becomes fertiliser in the soil, and bears and grows peaches and grapes. These fruits carry meaning as a talisman and an amulet. I believe this is an outstanding creative work that is based on mythological thinking. After people die, their bodies return to the earth, are broken down, become organic matter,

Figure 10.2 (Edited) *Kojiki Yori [From Kojiki]* (1957) by Saori Akutatagawa.
Source: Setagaya Art Museum, Tokyo.

and create the next new life. Here again, the voiced consonants of the Japanese language express not only our filth, but also strength as they become familiarised sounds that are 'felt in the stomach.' For example, the Japanese word for drawing is *zu*, which is a voiced consonant. It is strong, powerful and earthy, just like *zun-zun* (briskly and rapidly), *zuru-zuru* (slithery and dragging on), and *doro-doro* (thick and muddy).

In other countries, gods often exist in heaven. This is because many of us want to go back to heaven. In the myths of various countries, we rarely find gods such as Izanami who remains buried in the earth. Even when banished in an ugly form – rotten and giving off a foul smell – Izanami became fertiliser for the next generation, so she may, in fact, be like an underground guardian deity. As a filthy and ugly entity, Izanami brings about new creations while she herself contains all sorts of contradictory, unprocessed things. Izanami, who was left in the earth, becomes fertiliser, and continues to bring about new life to us who live in this gloomy, depressing *ukiyo* (憂世) world despite it being a fleeting world with an upper part of a floating *ukiyo* (浮世) world. I also want to take note of the fact that Izanami is not only an earth goddess but also a Mother Goddess. You can put unprocessed things as they are underground, including unclean, filthy things, and this also may lead to the birth of a new life. The image of a swamp completely maps onto the maternal lower abdomen, or the womb, which carries a child, bears it and nurtures it.

In the end

As I wrote, though a woman giving birth tells a man, 'Don't Look,' the man peeks and the woman turns out to be an animal. Even in one recent story (Matsutani, 1993), entitled *Tatsunoko Tarō [Tarō the Dragon Boy]*, the dragon-mother losses both her eyes in order to raise her child. All kinds of bad things happen but Tarō, the protagonist, and the blind dragon work together and fight on. Helping each other, they challenge many misfortunes of heaven and earth. In the end, the dragon becomes human and is refamiliarised with our world. Stories of human–animal marriage in Japan involve men marrying animal protagonists who leave at the end when their wives are revealed to be animals. The story of a dragon becoming human and refamiliarised was first published as recently as 1960. In this modern version, the wounded mother didn't disappear at the end. I am very pleased about the appearance of this happy ending. Having been on a therapeutic journey with these stories for the past 40 years, and having developed an understanding of the problems faced by my patients, I am pleased to be able to conclude this with this story of the mother who finally turned into a human being.

Lastly, I remember what my psychoanalyst Thomas Hayley said to me by way of interpretation, 'You became a doctor like your father, but became a musician for your mother's sake.' Indeed, there was no way for me to give up one to choose the other. And if *You*, the readers, were to tell me to choose one of the two, I would have to answer, 'I need them both.'

Notes

1 Words by T. Matsuyama & O. Kitayama, and composed by K. Katoh.
2 For a while after breaking up the Folk Crusaders, I wrote lyrics for a number of songs, including 'Sensōwo Shiranaikodomotachi' ['Children Who Don't Know War'] (1971), for which I was given the Japan Records' Best Lyricist Award.
3 In the Japanese language, voiced consonants, when used in onomatopoeia, are often said to accompany unpleasant, negative, or bold nuances.
4 Superimposing Freud's diagram of the mental apparatus on the earthy illustration by Maeda reminds me of my Old Kyoto and brings some historical associations, such as Freud's 'Vienna' which began in Leopoldstadt (Wien II), where Jews and immigrants lived. The reason why these deep-seated lands in Kyoto and Vienna became places for the discriminated is that both have the Kamo River and the Danube River, which repeatedly overflowed, so the boggy places were avoided and development was delayed.

References

Fairbairn, W. R. D. (1944). Endopsychic structure considered in terms of object-relationships. *International Journal of Psychoanalysis*, 25, 70–93.

Freud, S. (1907) Creative writers and day-dreaming. In *Standard Edition*, Vol. 9. London: Hogarth Press.

Freud, S. (1913) *Totem and Taboo*. In *Standard Edition*, Vol. 12. London: Hogarth Press.

Freud, S. (1918) From the history of an infantile neurosis. In *Standard Edition*, Vol. 17. London: Hogarth Press.

Freud, S. (1923) The ego and the id. In *Standard Edition*, Vol. 19. London: Hogarth Press.

Fenichel, O. (1945). *The Psychoanalytic Theory of Neurosis*. New York: Norton.

Kernberg, O. (1983). (Maeda, S., Trans.) *Object Relations Theory and Clinical Psychoanalysis*. Tokyo: Iwasaki Gakujutsu Shuppansha. (Original work published 1976)

Kitayama, O. (2016). *Kobunonai Rakuda [A Camel without a Hump]*. Tokyo: Iwanamishoten.

Kitayama, O. (2017). Becoming a psychoanalyst: to think about the nature of jealousy. *Psychoanalytic Inquiry*, 36 (2), 162–170.

Kitayama, O. (2019). Nihonno rizumu [Japanese rhythm]. In N. Sofue & J. Hosozawa (Eds.), *Bunka Geijutsuno Seishinbunseki [Psychoanalysis of Culture and Art]* (pp. 9–21). Tokyo: Tōmishobō.

Kitayama, O. (2024). *Munashisano Ajiwaikata [Taste of Emptiness]*. Tokyo: Iwanamishoten.

Matsutani, M. (1993). *Tatsunoko Tarō [Tarō the Dragon Boy]*. Tokyo: Kodansha. (Original work published 1960)

Tatara, M. (1998). *Hajito Iji – nihonjinno shinnrikōzō [Shame and Obstinacy – The Structure of Japanese Psychology]*. Tokyo: Kōdansha.

Winnicott, D.W. (1958). *Collected Papers: Through Paediatrics to Psycho-Analysis*. London: Tavistock Publications.

Chapter 11

Enthralled infancy in a bed of parental tryst

Jhuma Basak

Introduction

It is imperative to understand the ambiguity and metaphoric element in Japanese culture to comprehend its cultural nuances embedded in the complex elucidation of their psychoanalytic theories, like the Ajase complex (Heisaku Kosawa, 2022), and the prohibition of 'Don't Look' (Osamu Kitayama, 2010) – which is addressed in this chapter. Both Kosawa and Kitayama exemplified the symbolic ingrained in the Japanese language with mythological references from Japan in elaboration of their clinical analysis. The unfolding processes in both these conceptual developments imply a hidden decree of time during which period the psychic maturational transformations (of the reader/ beholder) would enable the capacity required to contain witnessing a catastrophic moment of breaking a prohibition along with the breakdown of one's illusion of an ideal love object (the maternal/parental object). With this perspective in mind, a re-look at both these analytical concepts may give us an opportunity to further examine the many-layered intercommunications innate in them. Subsequently, it may add another dimension to the theories compounding our present analytic discussion here. Kitayama's paper, 'Being drawn into a primal scene' (Kitayama, 2023; Chapter 9) is an exemplification of one such unfolding process that started its journey of unravelling unconscious fantasies with his work on 'The wounded caretaker' (Kitayama, 1991), taking us from the dyadic primal prohibitions to the tripartite oedipal torrents built-in within the prohibition (as discussed in the primal-scene paper of 2023). This chapter will also be looking into similar such 'play' of the tripartite oedipal collisions in Indian society embedded in the narratives of the 'triadic sleeping together in infancy' through its clinical elaborations (Basak, 2023).

DOI: 10.4324/9781003501930-13

A turbulent emotional background

Background to the Ajase complex

A conflictual, piercing, passionate emotional entanglement may be discovered in the Ajase story where the birth of Ajase itself is rooted in maternal acrimony and betrayal of the mother (Idaike), who herself was struck with dreadful anxiety fearing the loss of her husband's love (*JJPS*, 2022). Idaike's rancour stemmed from the deep sorrow of losing her husband's love and this unresolved grief manifested in her relationship with her son, perhaps expressing displaced resentment (Okonogi, 1979). This suggests a complex interplay of emotions within the family dynamics. Idaike's bitterness infused the complexity of the Ajase narrative, intertwining themes of maternal resentment, counter-provocation, and prenatal rancour. However, as time passed and Idaike underwent a process of maturation, she transcended her own resentful constraints. She dedicated herself to caring for her ailing son (who exuded a strong stench) with abundant love and *amae*, nurturing him back to health. This transformation laid the groundwork for reparative guilt, as described in the Kleinian framework, within the mother–son relationship, reshaping their bond (Klein, 1975).

Elaboration on the Ajase complex

Thus, Ajase could initiate the course of reparative guilt within him towards his mother (Klein, 1975), perhaps internalising a cyclic process of maternal forgiveness that he saw his mother act upon. Following his acceptance of *amae* and the attainment of his primary narcissism, Ajase's potential for reparative guilt was primed, paving the psychic pathway for generosity. As time passed, both Ajase and Idaike transitioned from a state of infantile *amae* (sole dependency) to a more mature form of interdependent *amae* within their symbiotic exchange. From a Kleinian perspective, this implies a psychic movement from the 'paranoid–schizoid position' (total state of dependence) to a 'depressive position' (state of mutual interdependence). Kitayama's inference that *amae* exists as a state that is both transient (psychic) and transitional (physical), positioning it between the concepts of 'one-ness' and 'separate-ness,' further indicates that it occupies a space between the enmeshed ego of the mother–child dyad along with the subsequent journey towards separation–individuation. The inherent dynamism of *amae* suggests its capacity as a transitional phenomenon that is capable of passing between individuals and across generations. This underscores the importance of time and its inherent transformative potential, which subsequently posits a lasting impact on its community over a prolonged period of time (Okano, 2019).

In the above mythical references, it may be observed a direct connection of parental coitus with sexuality, birth, and death, all three inter-connected with each other – making it a potent ground for intense emotional embroilment and involvement. However, this inner crescendo is meant to be very private in these mythologies as much as in everyday Japanese life and culture. That way it stays concealed from external visibility. Nishizono explained this inner world as *uchi* from *soto* (external world), maintaining equity between silence and articulation (Nishizono, 1998), an equivalence of Winnicott's 'true self' and 'false self.' Though the 'shameful self' may be hidden from the public but not necessarily from one's own self (Okano). The notion of the 'shameful self' suggests an internalised part of one's own self that feels ashamed and considers to be unworthy, which could be concealed from public view but weighs heavily on one's own conscience and self-perception.

Language is the symbolic route to the unconscious, and thus the query into the Japanese language (as noticeable in Kitayama's chapters here) is essential, which has a very complex structure emphasising its silence and metaphoric aspect much more than its articulation. The 'site of silence' in the Japanese language is very significant, i.e. between what is uttered and what is implied, necessitating dynamic interpretations embedded in the symbolic abstract qualities within the language (like poetry and haiku in Japan). Simultaneously, it equally adds to the enquiry of ambiguity in it. In this sense the personal, private, primal attachment with the mother, which later evolves to its love object, may be robust with a fierce emotional coil in its intrapsychic space ('feminine' quality); while the 'impersonal' code of social conduct in daily life in Japan is a triadic oedipal manifestation ('masculine' quality) that implicates this multi-layered complex bisexual suggestiveness in their daily application of language. The tension between these intimate, emotional relationships and the structured, socially detached norms creates a rich tapestry of meaning and interpretations within the Japanese culture, reflecting the intricate interplay and duality between individual private intrapsychic space and the social public norms of orderly conduct. This may further indicate generating intense internal friction for an individual in daily life in such a culture.

According to the *Kojiki* myth of the Izanami–Izanaki legend, the birth of Japan unravels Izanami's process of giving birth to different deities (which are the many islands of Japan), and giving birth to the fire deity leaves Izanami with burnt genitals. The paternal deity, Izanaki, witnessed the death of the maternal-deity, Izanami, by breaking the prohibition of 'Don't Look.' One finds an intricate and concurrent relation between the sparkle of magical birth and agonising crude death. Further in the elaboration of the story of *The Crane Wife* (see Chapter 9) that exemplifies the theme of the prohibition of 'Don't Look,' it mentions the act of piercing the crane's body with an arrow possibly symbolises a sexual act after being witnessed and exposed by her husband, bringing an end to the life of the crane-wife. It brought 'death while engaging in a sexual act' (Kitayama, 2023, p. 23) for the maternal object. By this, it suggests a simultaneous celebration of the birth of life with sexuality, and a coexisting mourning of death (of the maternal-deity/maternal-wife) in this singular act. Thus, it may appear that sexuality in these mythical expositions is loaded with ambivalence and an intense entanglement of (i) adult passionate sex, (ii) infantile childbirth, along with (iii) unsightly repulsive death associated with the act of giving birth – all echoing a powerful psychic trilateral entrapment comprising sex, birth, and death. Subsequently echoing in the backdrop of this tumultuous dramatic narration is a symbolic and compelling triadic bonding between the mother–child, and the father. It is very difficult to distinguish clear boundaries in the interrelations of such narratives – ambivalence and ambiguity play a vital role in intermingling (i) sexuality with motherhood, or (ii) infantilism with parenthood, or (iii) sexuality with infancy, or (iv) sexuality with death, as it may often get voiced in clinical contexts as well. A comparative ground of the quality of trinity comprising birth, life and destruction is equally found in the Indian divine context embodied in the 'Triad of Deities' (Brahma, Vishnu, Maheshwar/Shiva – creator, preserver, destroyer – as elaborated by Basak in Chapter 8). Both cultures evoke an extraordinary depth of emotional entanglement, serving with legendary settings of mythological references that prepare the groundwork for turbulent, dramatic, and emotional chronicles usually found in the Eastern socio-cultural climate. Such mythological recitals are essentially non-linear and polylithic by nature imparting the illusion of a kaleidoscopic visio-scape.

Triadic sleeping together in infancy – a reflection

As is well established by now, the dyadic bonding between the mother and the child (specifically with the son) is very unique in some Asian societies, particularly Indian culture. That itself echoes the probable rooted patriarchal foundation of its familial systems that embellish the exceptional heterogeneity of the mother–son dyad, specifically in the context of the Indian society (as we will also see in the clinical citations later). It contributes to the perpetuation of patriarchal values and norms, where masculinity is worshipped and desired for its autocracy and ruthless power, unlike femininity. It is in the reproduction of motherhood, a patriarchal normative manufacturing mechanism and imagination, that it finds equivalence within the patriarchal structure. Child-rearing practices in Eastern cultures, like India and Japan, ruminate the essence of a compounded trilateral involvement of the mother–child and the father, but that which mostly continues its maternal imagination in its traditional subservient role to the patriarchal dynasty. Added to this in the Indian context is the extended family framework making it a complex matrix of familial dynamics. The finer nuances of an overshadowing maternal imagination with its seductive employment into the triangulation of the family make it a compelling desire for the child to remain enmeshed in its primal pre-oedipal, pre-conflictual, yet stifling dyadic cocoon. The possibility of sensual linkage and transition from dyadic to triadic intersubjectivity may often feel throttled and crushed by such an overriding dyadic enchantment.

In view of the sleeping arrangement of the infant in Japan, Okonogi's reference to the child sleeping between the parents, implies a 'state of three-some in infancy' with the mother–child and father together in bed, adding to the complex triadic narrative of infancy in such cultures. Kitayama's reference to *shunga* or the erotic prints of Japan (Chapter 9) elucidates the cultural background for the probable indirect role of the sexual-ternary in the child's development. It is interesting to note the camouflaged triadic narrative of infancy which holds intense erotic bodily significance in the triangulation. The captivating play of *amae* in the mother–child object relationship creates the shield for less probability of oedipal rivalry between the father and the child (son) (Doi, 1971). The mother's fantasy around the son symbolically acts as an 'armour of love' around him from the father. Thus, when the father joins the mother in bed, i.e. the site of their unique 'parental tryst' which is an intimate rendezvous between two lovers' union, the inseparable mother–child/son duo is left uninterrupted in its infant-couplet. Moreover, the father may experience a sense of betrayal by the wife in his tryst with his wife, unless he portrays an evolved cultivation of *amae* to yield to the mother–child duo. This way the primal bonding of *amae* in the mother–child (son) duo offers a firm foundation for it to be free from the later oedipal sexual struggle against the father (Doi, 2005).

Here it would be interesting to draw our attention to the mother–daughter duo where the mother may fail to envelop her daughter with her fantasy 'armour of love' due to her own bodily transmissions of internalised ambivalence. This could be because of her projection of her internalised ambivalence stemming from societal patriarchal expectations, family dynamics, her own experiences of rejection of her sexuality and aggressive drives while growing up. All of which inadvertently projects itself into her daughter viewing her as an authentication of her own bodily auxiliary in external reality that reminds her of herself, her unfulfilled desires, electrifying extremely opposing emotional strings (Green, 1986). This maternal projection of annihilation is often a deeply ingrained dynamic that leads to a dreadful sense of rejection of the very entity of the daughter (adding to the collective socio-cultural practices, as in India). A combination of such individual maternal ambivalence against a backdrop of a collective cultural environment of disavowal of women makes *femininity* a challenging qualitative component to be nurtured or cherished in the Indian cultural site. Later this may further exacerbate feelings of rivalry or competition within the oedipal dynamics between the mother and the daughter. While the daughter experiences physical abjection of her active sensuous bodily engagement with the mother (Lichtenberg, 2008), she at the same time yearns for the mother's love and affection because of her identification and idealisation of the maternal body. The frustration of it leads to a heightened state of anxiety and resentment in her. This contributes to a sense of counter-torrid ambivalence in the daughter towards the mother and her own sense of femininity. In this intense triangulation for the daughter to manoeuvre the father's disengagement and his disregard may only reinforce her insecured position in the triadic familial design, magnifying her worthlessness, low self-esteem, sense of identity, desire and sexuality. It takes much longer for her to recognise the father in the intrapsychic and symbolic plane since it is overwhelmed with its desire for maternal-fusion, leading her into a fantasy space of dwelling in its 'lack,' prompting the birth of depression in her (Green, 1986). The daughter's internalised feelings of repudiation add up to her ambivalence and her struggle to assert her autonomous identity in her evolving authentic exploration of the self, its subjectivity and her sexuality in later years. The daughter's emotional journey from this triadic entrapment of disavowal in infancy to adult life calls upon a humungous effort to navigate her fiery interplay of distraught currents of affective dispositions in order to reach any stable integration of her internal self, identity, and quest for her subjectivity. Being internally caught in her torrential emotive battles, often she may tend to lose out on reality achievements in life.

The undercurrent of this silent triadic troth, stimulated by the 'state of threesome in infancy,' or in other words a 'state of co-sleeping,' creates the possible bedrock of filial pledge, a sense of almost paralysing commitment towards the family, specifically for the male. The socio-cultural practice perhaps adds to the unconscious primitive totemistic order of its commitment to the collective sense of community, and family happens to be the infant's first experience of the collective community. This may be observed to be a foundational characteristic in family structures of both Japan and India, perhaps even the East at large. There is a coexistence of the three together in such family structures, implying a subtle non-exclusivity of the couple formation (Basak, Chapter 7), unlike Western practices. This triadic coexistence is possible because it incorporates the 'this *and* that' in such Eastern societies, and not the dichotomy of 'this *or* that' – making interrelational boundaries more ambiguous and overlapping. In most Asian societies there's a prevalent emphasis on the harmony of opposites and the acceptance of paradoxes. This outlook of opposing forces acting in an interdependent and complementary manner gets encapsulated in the concept of *yin and yang* (as in Chinese philosophy), or in *lasya* and *tandav* (the tender-feminine and the bold-masculine in Indian aesthetics, *Natya Shastra*, Muni, 1951), the extension of which may be envisioned in the concept of the *ardhanarishvara*, the lord with the half-male and half-female body. Elaborating from the Indian classical aesthetics is the cosmic dance of Lord Shiva in the form of *Nataraja* that upholds simultaneously the creation, destruction and preservation of his devotees in mortal land. The idea of coexistence in such societies often revolves around integrating multiple perspectives, values, and beliefs, rather than strictly adhering to binary choices or uni-linear positions. As a matter of fact, India as a nation with diverse cultures, and languages, endorses its harmonious declaration of *unity in diversity*. This perspective fosters a greater tolerance for ambiguity and a willingness to embrace paradoxical truths implying a containing capacity of heightened emotional quotient – both individually and collectively. This may be the root of understanding the significance of fierce emotional attachments, filial vows, along with intense community attachment among the people of such societies. In the Indian child-rearing practice, it may still often be noticed that the child experiences more than a singular mother phenomenon and the child grows up with the grandmother's breast/lap or aunt's/*aya*-s (nanny's) breast/lap in addition to its mother's – all who are readily available within the household to take care of the child when the mother of the child may be taken up with other household chores. This is applicable specifically in extended joint family structures which is still the majority of the Indian familial sites, though over time nuclear families in urban spaces are increasing in number. This practice is deeply rooted in the social fabric of Indian society teaching one to navigate complicated social dynamics from an early time. Subsequently, this may implicate the possibility of the development of an intricate multiple-attachment schema that can foster a sense of enthralling interconnectedness and counter-dependence within the family and community. A delicate underlying layer of early powerful kinship bonding leading to incestuous constellations may be a likely outcome of a cultural phenomenon like this that may only add up to the idea of a compounded complex cultural site of the Indian cultural environment. The acknowledgement of the fantasy of the seductive maternal in incestuous imagination that is inbuilt into this triadic narrative may be a ground-shaking actuality to engineer for the evolving individual. The oceanic-encompassing experience of maternal-fusion may often impede the capacity to distinguish between the self and the not-self, thus incapacitating in identifying the other as well, which may later affect and impede having a fulfilling object relationship. That may call for further analytic exploration of its adult love, sexuality, and fidelity in order to understand the controversial sexual complexities embedded in the nuances of different cultural practices, though not necessarily from any 'pathological lens.' 'Psychoanalysis is not – or at least should not be – "normative" about the family model. I believe that we must above all analyse what exists, what persists or changes, how it changes, and what the consequences are' (Argentieri, in Ambrosia, 2005, p. 18).

The practice of triadic sleeping together of the mother–child, and father, as noticed in the Indian context equally corresponds to the unique cultural belief of the supremely significant status of the mother–child unit/bonding, as also described in Japanese tradition. However, as may be understood from the above argument, the quality and character of the mother–child dyadic significance fiercely depends on whether it is a boy-child or a girl-child. The triadic sleeping together equally correlates to the socio-economic plight in India as much as it is a socio-cultural phenomenon – the sheer lack of physical space to have different rooms for different members of the family is often not a choice. So, the family ends up mostly sleeping together in one big parental bed in one big room. Needless to say, the rising nuclear family structures in urban spaces with their emerging economy and evolving modern child-rearing practices that incorporate more commercial creches and domestic help within the inner family structure have their own complex narratives of child-rearing customs to unfold in time. However, it is mostly an urban practice and still not the dominant socio-cultural occurrence of family sites in India. The triadic sleeping together is a most 'natural' rearing custom for most Indian families. This is so because once a child is born into the family, the unit of the family is no longer the husband and the wife but it is the mother and the child. As a matter of fact, the husband–wife couple unit has its own challenges from its initiation itself given the extended family structure that it has to negotiate with. A 'good enough' mother must prioritise her child over her own coupledom with her husband. Thus, the mother and the child become one unit. Needless to say, as mentioned above, the birth of a girl-child has very different dynamics to cascade on the family unit altogether.

The central positioning of the child in between its parents in the bed signifies the central positioning of the child (male) in the family. Under the practice of normative patriarchal structures, the omnipotent supremacy of the male-child is both a household and a community celebration. Interestingly, the provoking ambivalence in the child is also rooted in this very middle position of the triadic sleeping together. On one hand, the child feels very secure, loved, and protected taking the omnipotent middle position between the parents (Freud, 1913); while, on the other hand, the child tends to think that it has been betrayed by the mother who by choosing the father over her child (in her choice of her partner for the primal act) in their trilateral struggle at the very site of their triadic sleeping together and has forsaken her child. Perhaps it conveys to the child a sense of duality in maternal love, its primal love object. Whereas, the mother has been left with no ambit for the couple's exclusive intimacy whatsoever given the stifling socio-cultural parameters that her combined role as a mother and wife has to endure. It appears that the mother is the common object of enmity for both the child and the father – the mother who has betrayed her child in choosing intimacy with her husband, and the wife who has deceived her husband by forming her intimate internal unit with her child. A most successful ploy of patriarchy to continue its powerful status quo in exerting control over the woman and to hold her at fault, the cause for all 'evil' in society. Later, only the quality of *amae* that holds the promise of showering forgiveness as maturational inference by both the father and the child may help in bringing about insight into the truth of the matter. Situated in between its parental psychogenic angst the child is totally consumed by its heightened stimulation, feeling both torn apart as well as tightly held in the triadic tryst. The clinical space in the Indian context may often witness such painful and fierce internal vacillations in individuals when in long-term analytic work with patients (as will unfold later in this chapter).

'Participation-type' primal scene

Drawing directly from the practice of triadic sleeping together in bed, Kitayama distinguishes the child's role in this trilateral constellation as a 'participation-type' primal scene from a 'witness-type' primal scene (Kitayama, 2023, p. 25). It is stated that in a participation-type primal scene the child *actively* joins the parents in their sexual encounter with each other. Here, *actively* calls for its clarification – for the child it does not imply its capacity to exercise *self-agency* by exercising its independent *choice* in participating in the primal bed, but drawn by the parents' enticing ring of tryst in the bed the corresponding psychosexual stimulations that it experiences in response to the joint parental stimulants. It is in the form of auditory, olfactory, vibratory experiences that the child perceives the parental intimacy. Its consequent *active reaction*, a psychobiological or a psychosexual stimulation at the very site itself makes it a third participant in the triadic act of intimacy, something that was initiated between the parents only. In the act the parents are the 'initiators,' 'doers,' while the child is the 'respondent' to their action. In that sense, conceptually it is a participation-type (active) primal scene that incorporates qualities of both active-receptive positions for the child, distinct from a witness-type (passive) primal scene. This fraught bed of sexuality may create the probable ground for a fantasy of infantile foreplay in its very early relational dynamics (Winnicott, 1971), which may further echo early sexual intimations for the child as well, creating a very complex, fertile, yet difficult developmental phenomenon for the child to manoeuvre. Subsequently, the child's mental factors intertwined with bodily stimulations (psycho-somatic) along with its propensity for provocations in sadistic or masochistic fantasies, depending on its vast identification with active or passive aspects of parental masculine and feminine qualities, or even voyeuristic trepidations, may often be a very early onset of possible pathogenesis. It may at times lead to even catastrophic developments in the later adult years of the child (as will unfold in the subsequent clinical reference here). However, this does not entail an outright 'pathologisation' of such an aetiology that occurs under diverse cultural practices of different socio-economic societies. Rather it is a plea to stay committed to an ethical reading of divergent rearing habits, and approaching the triadic tryst in the oedipal ordinance as an allegorical field comprising different symbols and metaphors according to diverse cultural habits and practices that resonate later into our complex adult sexuality.

Often it may appear that the dominant intrusive Eurocentric critic of non-Western cultures brings about an unconscious aspiration in our subjugated subjectivities the need to prove ourselves 'clean and pure' from our inherited indigenous allusions, from our 'so-called-barbaric native skin.' More so, in order to be accepted by them. In *Group Psychology and the Analysis of the Ego* (1921), Freud formulated that the modern individual subjectivity evolved out of 'disorderly' communities, thereby implying a possible subtle hierarchical psychic configuration that distinguishes the new, emerging 'reformed' ego from the 'unruly,' 'reckless herd' (Freud, 1921). But is the 'primal' the 'mark of primitivity,' implying racial ethnicity, and the concept of an individual ego the 'mark of civilisation' of the 'white west' (Celia Brickman, 2018)? Perhaps it is relevant to consider in today's time that both the primal, the individual and the collective hold a simultaneous coexistence in such Asian cultures that are equally striving for modernity within their community. Perhaps it is time for us to liberate ourselves from such 'prejudiced scientific axioms' in psychoanalytic dictum and learn with a free mind from our galaxy of diversity in human cultures and its numerous forms of oedipal constellations (Bueskens, 2021).

Clinical vignettes

Case – 1

Dia was a 35-year-old working woman who taught language and literature in a high school. She was married for eight years with a son of 6 years. She came for consultation with her growing anxiety, something that she complained had troubled her since childhood. Increasingly she found it difficult to speak, as her voice would often shake while teaching classes in her school. That frustrated her and angered her, making it difficult for her to take her classes with ease. Thus, she tried to speak very softly and as little as possible so that she could keep control over her trembling voice – something that found expression even in the sessions. It appeared almost like a hysterical quiver underlining her voice, but one could equally feel the suppressed intone in her that was waiting to pour out – as if something was eager to burst forth. She was in a constant state of jitters and nervousness. Dia wished to go for analytic treatment with two sessions a week.

Dia was sharp enough to know what was pounding inside her for which she had been suffering for a long time. She wanted to talk about it immediately since it was something that she couldn't talk to anyone about, something that she was extremely guilty about and felt terribly disturbed with it. She feared that if she could not speak soon with someone whom she believed would be able to guide her properly (in this case in the session with me) then not only her own state of mind but her conjugal relationship would be at stake (because she did not enjoy having sex with her husband, nor did she ever groan with orgasm– like she remembered her parents!), but also it may have its impact on her son due to her own suppressed desires around him! And that way she would lose all bearings of life with her loved ones. This made it possible for us to approach the subject right at the beginning of our analytic work together.

D: I cannot deal with this anymore. It has ruined my life. I am always angry, guilty, nervous – I don't know what I feel anymore. [She was evidently agitated, asking for immediate therapeutic intervention.]

Dia's narrative took us to her early days when she used to sleep with her parents in their bed, in between them. She felt her anxiety started from that time itself, though she loved her middle position in between her parents. She felt loved, special, and very secure within. She disclosed how since childhood she used to enjoy watching, and listening, to her parents having sex (needless to say at that time she did not understand it was 'sex') – it was more like the two of them would get close, 'struggle' with each other, sometimes laugh, mostly she remembered many kinds of sounds. Her parents thought that she was asleep but she would only pretend to be so. She remembered her heart throbbing when her parents would start their 'physical struggle' at night – in her mind the parental intimacy/sex appeared like a physical struggle. Though she felt anxious she even looked forward to those 'physical struggles' – as if like a 'prohibited private show' of some kind performed at night. She had an internal clear division of the 'morning fights' from the 'night struggle' of her parents. The morning fights were only verbal fights with them screaming at each other in the open, in full light. According to her at times the 'night fights' would also have some whispering verbal fights like the 'morning fights' – which became her favourite ones because those specific fights held a conviction for her. She described that when her parents had a combined physical and verbal fight at night (implying the orgasmic moment in all probability) she knew that soon the fights would be over, they would be still, and the 'night show' would come to an end and she would eventually lie still like them, falling asleep together in between them. And in this manner she would act as a co-participant in the parental sexual encounter.

Dia recalled having slept with her parents in their bed till she was about 6 years old when the birth of her baby brother in the family displaced her middle position in the bed/family, and she was shifted to the divan in the sitting room. She was not only angry with her baby brother for whom she was thrown out of the parental bed but was even more so with her mother who happily, lovingly, kept that 'ugly baby' next to her, gave it her breast, and just forgot all about her daughter. How could her mother forget her just like that, so easily? She was there next to her mother's side for all those years, much before that 'ugly baby' arrived, and her mother just threw her out of her bed just like that! And like this Dia imagined a sense of betrayal and abandonment by her mother. She would stay awake at night on her divan in the other room, waiting eagerly to hear her parents' 'physical struggle' – that way she would feel somewhat shaken alive from her state of dejection, imagine being symbolically bodily close to her mother, thus feeling reassured and secured in her psychic middle position of infancy. I wonder if her later quivering voice found its seed in the night sounds that she yearned to hear from her parents' joint vocal spells which reassured her own secured middle position. At the same time, the symptom surreptitiously carried her own trembling anxiety in it. Thus, unknowingly she inherited that tremor within her (perhaps like the throbbing bodies, heavy breathing, and the intimate verbal exchanges of her parents), and did not want that lingering pulse of life in her to leave her. Was she caught, trapped, in that whispering/groaning from a past reality merged with her fantasy that she unconsciously carried within her even when she was speaking in general. On one hand, the 'symptom' itself resonated with an unsteady, shaky quality deep in her, while its consistent presence seemed to have acquired her imagined parental anchor in her.

By the time Dia was in her teens, she discovered her strong attraction to watching movies. She loved the late-night movies on TV when she would sneakily watch them in the dark sitting on her divan in the sitting room, almost compulsively. In sessions, she drew her own association of how this may have been a symbolic representation of her watching the 'night-shows' in her parents' bedroom. But at times she would be desperately drawn to her parents' bedroom to secretly watch her 'original night-shows.' She laughed aloud when she mentioned the phrase 'original night-shows,' but felt very guilty afterwards. It may be observed that it equally left her feeling excited and anxious. With such severe emotional unrest she at times felt very tired during the days when she was expected to get up to get ready for her school. Then she would wait for her mother's gentle physical touch and presence to calm her down. On such mornings, her mother would come to her and quietly just sit by her, touch her forehead, and try to make her laugh. She loved those tender moments, found them so peaceful, soothing down her edgy state. But the apprehensions of the nights scared her, and excited her, all at the same time – her ambivalent oscillation between yearning for maternal love, caring touch, nurturing sensuous moments, and her curiosity for sexual stimulation found words of gradual expression in our following sessions.

What disturbed Dia the most was her obsessive imaginings of parental sex that dominated her to date, even when she was involved with her husband in physical intimacy. Her growing years added elaborations to her fantasy of parental intimacy and left her wondering what was the reality of her parental intimacy that she witnessed and what was her own fantasy of it. She further wondered if those images were her own hidden sexual perversion that excited her to enjoy having sex with her husband, did she try to imitate those images in her own act of making love with her husband? Or, did they act as obstacles in her intimacy with her husband, as if she were being watched by parental omnipotence? All of this left her emotionally disturbed and consequently she could not enjoy having sex with her husband. What frightened her the most, and that's where she clearly articulated her immediate need for analytic intervention, was her growing visual of seeing herself as a child watching her parents in bed and often, unknowingly, having her son exchange position with that little girl in her mental imagery who stands watching her having sex with his father. She was terribly disturbed with her own fancies, and repressed desires and wanted to stop them somehow. She sounded like a desperate child who was seeking help to be saved by her mother/analyst – to free her from the seductive maternal sexual web.

The internalisation of the desired maternal in the analyst through transference helped Dia to imagine a loving maternal object relationship, free from its undue sexualised inundation. That holding gave her the reassurance to look deep into herself – she could not forgive herself for the horrible, disgusting, fantasy of hers in wanting to entice her son in her sexual excitement. She was further puzzled thinking if her mother also wanted the same with her, did she learn this from her mother? It gave us an enormous opportunity to examine Dia's sexual fantasies and travesties – which in addition took us to her own childhood fantasy of her 'ugly brother' who 'ousted' her of her 'middle position' to enjoy her rightful enjoyment of the parental bed and parental intimacy. She was left with the apprehension of whether he was then enjoying what once was her site of pleasure. This created further prospects for our analytic work to introspect the nuances of Dia's surreptitious jealousy of him, later her son, all camouflaged with maternal anxiety. All this takes us deeper into Dia's intrapsychic space where dwelt her terrible anger against her mother. Also, it further opened up avenues for us to perceive, at least to some extent, Dia's mother beyond her socially defined maternal role and her possible related feelings of oppression, conflict, and fantasies. The analytic journey unravelled the sexual gateway to Dia's own sexual desires, conflicts, and mental debauchery and to accept them over time. This identification helped her to seek emotional maturity to start thinking of 'forgiving' her mother, herself. The deeper her own contempt and aggression got worked through in the sessions the clearer she could see the extent of her own imagined sense of maternal betrayal and abandonment that she accused her mother of. In this process, the hysterical quiver in Dia's voice gradually gave way to a much clearer and more confident voice – she started enjoying taking her classes once again. She was finding her own voice. Her intimacy with her husband was more anxiety-free, and she was less dependent or haunted by her inner imageries of parental intimacy. She was engaged in creating her own sexual narratives of intimacy with her husband, an intimate embodiment of her self-body agency.

Case – 2

Ajit was brought for consultation by his father when he was 16 years old. He was alarmed by Ajit's increasing physical demands on his mother in the past year. The mother looked like a quiet lady, a little demure perhaps in nature, much smaller in size than her husband who was large with a loud voice. Ajit had a rough and unkempt look, perhaps echoing his youthful defiance as well as indirectly challenging our acceptance of his inner 'repulsive self' as his father referred him to be. His apparent aggressive attributes were threatening towards his parents. The mother reported that from childhood Ajit was aggressive and demanding. A way of calming him down was to hold him close to the mother's body. This became a natural pattern over time, and to fall asleep he would often take his mother's nipple in his mouth, like many children, and sleep peacefully. As Ajit was growing up, this habit was substituted by having his hand over his mother's naked breast. Initially both the parents did not mind this, and saw this as a child's harmless demand of playing with the mother's breast to get himself to sleep. The father slept in the same bed, next to the son while Ajit slept in between his parents, more importantly next to his mother.

However, by the time Ajit was about 12 years old the parents tried to change this habit of Ajit's since it seemed to them that he was becoming somewhat adamant about his mother. They tried to have him sleep in another room with his grandparents. But even in the middle of the night Ajit would keep coming back to his parents' room to sleep next to his mother with his hand over her naked breast. If the mother resisted this then Ajit would become very agitated until his father would intervene by forcing the mother to allow Ajit to do what he wanted to so that he could sleep through the night and be fresh for his office the next morning. Ajit enjoyed this powerful position where he had his father on his side to make his mother succumb to his demands. One would notice Ajit's early expressions of his manipulative, passive-sadistic ways of trying to control his mother. Over time the father started feeling a little uneasy about his son when Ajit started making further demands on his mother, almost persecuting her, and would not listen to any stopping of his persistence. It appeared that Ajit's sense of reality was getting merged with his desire in attempting to be like his father in his fantasy of acting out the 'nightly actions' claiming his mother's body. His fierce stimulation and possible identification with the masculine/the father (in bed in particular) from childhood may have invalidated his capacity to experience object relationships in other empathic receptive positions. In Ajit's mind, the distorting subjectivities were confusing and he was losing perspective in distinguishing reality boundaries and reality social roles. Equally perhaps the passive seductive feminine in the mother (who was by character a quiet-natured woman) excited his dominating fantasy of possessing the maternal object to pronounce his infantile feeble self with an omnipotent armour of virility. Also, it acted as his immediate armour against the aggressive patriarchal dominance of his father. Thus, over time the evolution of his authentic subjectivity became a fraught process.

In sessions, he would often make it clear how he was a good person, unlike what his father had been projecting him to be. At least he never wanted to physically hurt his mother, contrary to his father who would often hit his mother after coming back home drunk on some nights, which is why he had such a big stomach, followed by his command over his mother in bed. And then his mother would take Ajit in her arms, holding him tight against her chest, sobbing quietly – as if he were her sole comfort. He remembered how at such times his mother would take his small soft hand and place it on her soft breast before they both fell asleep. Perhaps for the mother the gentle benign touch of her son's innocent hand reassured her of the existence of love and care, which she missed from her husband. For Ajit this gesture became a complex symbol of him protecting his mother from his father, being gentle and caring of his mother when she would be crying, along with his erotic incitement of being close to his mother's body and touching her soft breast. Being drawn into Ajit's parental vacillating intimacy and their ugly fights left him emotionally baffled, which further affected his cognitive inference of reality as well as his daily functionality in reality (for example, his studies and school).

It was difficult for Ajit to understand why suddenly his mother too objected to his growing physical affinity towards her. He still used to love her the same way he used to when he was much younger, lying next to her comforting her with his gentle hand stroking her breast. He did not realise his reality shifted from that soft stroking hand to his commanding body/self over his mother. His capacity to distinguish a sensual touch from a sexual move was completely blurred by his infantile baffling experience of the maternal submissive seductive bodily invitation as well as his involvement in parental intimacy. While stating this in session it appeared that Ajit was almost drowsy and would doze off into his dreamworld as he did in his earlier days lying next to his mother with his hand on her breast. The difference in this context was that in the analytic situation it was next to me that he was lying down on the couch, indirectly inviting analytic intervention into his unconscious –

T: 'maybe you want to fall asleep here too, with me, like you used to sleep with your mother'

A: yes, it feels so gentle and quiet … (*implying without the sexual provocations?*) and safe … (*due to the physical distance?*)

T: 'just like how you wanted to feel with your mother. Maybe you too wanted to be the same with her, tender, soft, very different from your father. Like your softly touching her breast … Do you feel like protecting your mother like this, which no one seems to be understanding.'

A: 'even my mother doesn't understand that!'

T: 'perhaps you could explore other ways too that are your own ways of loving and caring for your mother other than your old childhood ways that you may have learnt from your father in bed. Maybe that will help your mother to understand you better.'

In later sessions, Ajit further explored his overpowering feelings of ambivalence against his mother especially when he was physically close to her. Initially, it was disturbing for him to accept this because he actually loved his mother very much, he could not understand why he felt like that. Somehow, he held his mother at fault for all that he was going through – he believed that only his mother could have 'saved' him but she did not bother to. How she deliberately failed him, betrayed him! It assisted the analytic process of delving into Ajit's whirlpool of accusations against his mother's cowardly role in the family, his imageries of parental coitus whose potential quality of love or aggression were all ambiguous and detesting to him. Those inciting images were constructed from both a reality provocation as well as a fantasy stimulation in him. He remembered how he hated his father's breath, and his bodily smell when he slept in the bed after drinking. It acted as a conflictual point of fixation in invoking ambivalence in him – he hated how he behaved with his mother then, and he felt furious with his mother for being such a 'doormat' to him. He could gradually see how he was drawn into it, stimulated by it but equally confused by it, leaving him with an altogether strong sense of disgust for both his parents. His point of crushing ambivalence and helplessness over decades was getting an opportunity to be dealt with in the sessions. Over time he could talk about how his mother failed him as a real mother who would guide him the right way. As for his father, he had no expectations, the paternal appeared only with toxic potential in his intrapsychic space. This had a direct impact on his own growing sense of masculinity. Gradually he could come to terms with the fact that it was possible for his parents to be flawed, aggressive and fighting with each other as well as to love each other enough to continue living together for so many decades. Just as much as his own initial resistance towards analysis/me could also turn into an affable quality. Equally, with time, he could begin to see his own coexistence of thoughts, and feelings towards his mother whom he could love and respect in totality but had his bitter feelings against her in context to a different situation when she failed to provide him with maternal protection. Needless to say, this entire *tour de force* demanded years of working together on his ambivalence revolving around his parental tryst. In terms of the transference situation the consistency of the object/analyst's benign self and the feeling of acceptance of his 'repulsive self,' which his father accused him of but on the contrary he found his father emitting more of that quality, helped Ajit to internalise a modified generous analytic reverie (Ogden, 1999). A firm yet loving maternal internalisation subsequently helped him to draw his experiences into the intersubjective space of the analytic pair, assisting in in-depth working through which successively nurtured him to begin cultivating a self-reliant subjectivity free from the captivity of his parental tryst.

Conclusion

It may be interesting to note an essential qualitative difference in response to the 'triadic in infancy' by Dia and Ajit, respectively. While Dia, a woman, felt 'prohibited' and guilty in her sexual fantasy and its related phantasy-pleasures in her life, Ajit as a man felt the 'right' to proclaim his sexual desires on his primal object, the maternal. Dia's approach to therapy was her own realisation and effort to overcome her triadic fantasies comprising her parental entanglement – from a possible dilemma arising out of her depressive inclination, while Ajit enjoyed his pleasurable omnipotent sexual position of the infantile fantasy and was introduced into the clinical situation by his parents. This is perhaps how the phallic construct works differently enticing mechanisms of maternal temptations upon its cultural upbringing of a girl-child who is dominated with sexual guilt, from a boy-child who is evoked with sexual desire. It would have been an interesting study to uncover Ajit's growing masculinity and sexual participation in his later adult life with his new love-objects.

The essence of the playful infantile merged with sexuality found in the many loving names given to the genitals in everyday language in the cultural context of Bengal (eastern India), for example, *shona* (meaning gold in Bengali) for vagina, or *pakhi* (meaning bird in Bengali) for penis as expressed in the clinical space (often used by both Dia and Ajit in this context), played a constructive provocative and impish role in the sessions. Such playful seductive locutions brought about amiable and mischievous associations in the patient in the clinical space which further helped in mitigating the violent tryst of parental alluring in being drawn into the 'state of threesome.' It appears to be accompanied by a salient internal somatic giddiness echoing its inherently intense intoxicating nature where one wishes to remain captivated in its magical frenzied whirlpool. A deliberate playful method in the analytic exercise helped in its articulation to open up this tornado of enchanted confinement. To indulge in analytic playful interactions, to develop qualities of mutual sharing and dependence assisted in rekindling the sensual connection and clarity between dyadic and triadic intersubjectivity. By attempting to open up the compelling orbit of a reality-merged-fantasy in its enthralling 'state of threesome in infancy' to another being (the analyst), it set in the process of freeing its subjectivity from the gripping parental pledge in the presence of the 'analytic third.' To be able to go beyond the external and internal prohibitions revolving around the 'state of threesome in infancy' in both the cultural and clinical contexts calls for an internal readiness as well as a ripe-enough time for the analysand/reader to negotiate its many cultural/intrapsychic complexities and resistances. To be able to feel independent from the parental incestuous web and maternal seduction embedded in the 'state of threesome in infancy' the child/growing adult needs a certain 'externality and objectivity from us analysts' (Chapter 9) who facilitates the containing process. The analyst's understanding of the complexity and the culturally shared phenomenon of the 'state of threesome in infancy' eventually creates the basis for the 'empathic third' in the clinical duo, and does not treat it as any anomaly. The dialectical interplay of the two subjectivities of the analyst–analysand in the clinical duo builds the abstract 'empathic third' that further assists in the internalisation of a mutated reverie for transformational developments in the evolving ego construction of the patient. The mystery and joy of being hidden (Winnicott, 1971) needs to be very gradually unravelled over a long period of time. As Okano says quoting Kitayama, a taboo to be broken in time (Okano, 2019). That may eventually prepare the evolving subjectivity to go beyond the prohibition of 'Don't Look' and 'uncover the ugliness and weakness in real human beings' (Okano, 2019) in order to claim its liberated, disenthralled position. That does not necessarily imply an opposition or exclusion to its fundamental enthralment that is embedded in its culture, but that which is not necessarily in any subjugation to that mesmerising oedipal realm and seeks its due independent entity in human love and sexuality.

References

Ambrosio, Giovanna (2005). *On Incest: Psychoanalytic Perspectives*. London: Karnac.

Basak, J. (2023). The enthrallment in the primal scene. *Journal of the Japan Psychoanalytic Society*, 5, 5–15.

Brickman, Celia (2018). *Race in Psychoanalysis: Aboriginal Populations in the Mind*. London: Routledge.

Bueskens, Petra (2021). *Nancy Chodorow and The Reproduction of Mothering: Forty Years On*. London: Palgrave Macmillan.

Doi, Takeo (1971). *The Anatomy of Dependence*. Tokyo: Kodansha International.

Doi, Takeo (2005). *Understanding Amae: The Japanese Concept of Need-Love*. Leiden: Global Oriental.

Freud, Sigmund (1913). Totem and Taboo. In *Standard Edition*, Vol. VIII. London: Hogarth Press.

Freud, Sigmund (1921). Group Psychology and the Analysis of the Ego. In *Standard Edition*, Vol. XVIII. London: Hogarth Press.

Green, A. (1986). The dead mother. In *On Private Madness* (pp. 142–173). London: Hogarth Press.

Kitayama, O. (1994). The wounded caretaker and Japanese folk tragedies. *Journal of Morita Therapy*, 5 (1), 43–46.

Kitayama, Osamu (2010). *Prohibition of Don't Look*. Tokyo: Iwasaki Gakujutsu Shuppansha.

Kitayama, Osamu (2023). Becoming drawn into a primal scene. *The Journal of the Japan Psychoanalytic Society*, 5, 22–31.

Klein, M (1975). *Love, Guilt and Reparation and Other Works 1921–1945*. Los Angeles: The Free Press.

Kosawa, Haisaku (2022). Two kinds of guilt feelings: The Ajase complex. *The Journal of The Japan Psychoanalytic Society*, 4, 18–25.

Lichtenberg, J. D. (2008). *Sensuality and Sexuality across the Divide of Shame*. Psychoanalytic Inquiry Book Series, Vol. 25. Wilmington: The Analytic Press.

Muni, Bharat. (1951). *Natya Shastra*, Trans. Manomohan Ghosh. Kolkata: Asiatic Society of Bengal.

Nishizono, M. (1998). *Child Rearing in Japan in Transition in Japanese Contributions in Psychoanalysis*, Vol. 1. Tokyo: Japan Psychoanalytical Society, 2004.

Ogden, Thomas (1999). *Reverie and Interpretation, Sensing Something Human*. London: Routledge.

Okano, Kenichiro (2019). Passivity, non-expression and the Oedipus in Japan. *Int. J. Psycho-Anal.*, 99 (6), 1353–1365.

Okonogi, Keigo (1979). The Ajase complex of the Japanese. *Japan Echo*, VI (1).
Perelberg, Rosine J. (Ed.) (2018). *Psychic Bisexuality*. London: Routledge.
The Journal of The Japan Psychoanalytic Society (*JJPS*), Vol. 4. Special Issue (2022). *Ajase Complex*. Tokyo: The Japan Psychoanalytic Society.
Winnicott, D. W. (1971). *Playing and Reality*. London: Routledge, 2005.

Part 3

An interface – 'listening to Asian female voices'

Chapter 12

Jhuma Basak interviews Osamu Kitayama

Jhuma Basak and Osamu Kitayama

JB: *Reflecting now on your theoretical development of the prohibition of 'Don't Look,' I feel there is a process of unfolding over time in its many layers of interpretations – did you see that when you first conceived of the theory?*

OK: First, I was moved by those stories. A sort of initial involvement in my childhood was reading or listening to these stories. I was moved, so surely there was identification with the characters in the stories. So I had Izanami–Izanagi inside me, Yohyo and the crane-wife too. It was not an intellectual encounter, it was emotional, a bodily physical involvement with the stories during my youth. To theorise about the development of these understandings I had to analyse myself which was the most difficult part because we can't objectify our personal and emotional experiences easily. So, I had to be slow and patient.

Although an intellectual interpretation was possible – obviously, it's a story of a primal scene, mother and father making love, sexual development, or emotional involvement … but, again they have to be carefully separated from the case studies, which are really tragic. Now, it is easier to see this from a distance, intellectually. Above all, clinical material was needed, to discuss it openly and theorise about it. For clinical theorisation, some patients have nothing to do with my personal experience of the stories. So, I had to try not to project my personal experiences onto those patients. We all enjoy being involved in the development of those stories. However, we all have to be careful to pick up material appropriately, because theorisation and interpretation are always selective, they don't cover everything. We have to drop something to pick up some other parts. Well, that is the problem with the prohibition of 'Don't Look' – we always want to see something, but we always substitute something else. That's why it took me 40 or 50 years, or maybe 60 or 70 years, including my childhood experiences to formulate the theory.

The reason why I use the word 'depth-psychology' or 'depth-psychological view' is because I want to stress the importance of the 'surface.' Although we can live and think superficially, we always insist that something deep beneath the surface is very important. Psychoanalysis is the

DOI: 10.4324/9781003501930-15

uncovering method, while conversely, in Japanese culture, the surface is most important in everyday life even when the content is empty. We need to respect the surface, so, in this unfolding process, we may find something empty, with nothing inside in spite of the beautiful surface, which can be an equally enjoyable journey.

I would like to say something more – language is my teacher. Language is my master because language is very insightful; although it causes many problems, it provides solutions too. That's why it is always difficult to move out of one's culture. There may be problems too in the superficiality of culture, we can become neurotic because of language. If we didn't have language then we wouldn't have to worry about anything. We could be carefree. Because we have developed language, we have to listen to it all the time because the answers are also formulated in it. To that extent, I depend on the language, and I'm also depending on the culture.

In English, culture has biological meanings – it is a medium for cultivation, the medium where we are living, and the soil where we grow up. In that context, Japanese culture is my home. I am a part of it. So, here are two family images for me – language is my father and culture is my mother. And they are always making love. I was born because of that. In this triadic fantasy, I am being fed, and playing, I am able to survive because of the culture and the language combined in me. I feel that way …

I have to tell you about an important traumatic memory – my aunt was my ophthalmologist and the elder sister of my father. I was born just after the Second World War, and she was already a medical doctor. I received a lot of help and care from her because I had eye problems. I suffered from diplopia, I had double vision – that was tiring for me because I had to always concentrate on only one object in order to read and become successful at school. At the same time, when I relaxed and released the tension between my eyes I could really listen to music. I enjoyed what I was listening to, not seeing. So, it was like swinging between two poles, listening and seeing. You may see this swing tendency in my papers, in these chapters; it's something that I always experience, this swing – both auditorily and visually. So, music was my mother and listening to medicine's logical ideas was my father.

Coming back to my aunt, she told me once that she had kept poison in her pocket after Japan was defeated. She was really afraid that American soldiers who came to Japan would rape her. It was possible as such incidents did happen to some extent. I was shocked by this story. The young female doctor who greatly helped me but who was afraid of dying.

My mother, who grew up in the countryside, was basically a cheerful person, and musical too. She was very young when they got married in wartime. A few months after atomic bombs were dropped on Hiroshima and Nagasaki, I was biologically conceived in the middle of this chaos – when fear and worry were everywhere. However, Kyoto avoided the bombing, because of the historical monuments, temples and shrines, our heritage ... She had a difficult time adjusting to the powerful traditions of Kyoto partly because of her strict mother-in-law. Growing up watching her struggle, even as the eldest son, I must have felt sorry for her devotion and felt compelled to protect and comfort her.

My father suffered from survivor's guilt, I also suffered very much from their traumatic experiences right after the war. This is the historical side of the beginning of my life story. I hated Japan but I also loved Japan so much. Being defeated and weak, while being strong and surviving – I could see both sides. Double vision again. I could see all this right in front of me, in front of Kyoto Station where I grew up. And this is the culture into which I was born and survived. This may not be directly related to your question, but I had to tell you this.

JB: *Did your background as a musician play a role in your interest in the cultural aspect of psychoanalysis?*

OK: Thank you very much for asking that question – actually I have reviewed my musical experiences in Chapter 10 of this book. Japanese music was initially so depressing to me, almost always lamenting, and melancholic because it was played by adults. As a young boy, who listened to that as adult music, it was very depressing. I longed for something more cheerful. As I wrote in Chapter 10, I followed an American jeep, asking for chocolates – 'give me chocolate' was the first English sentence that I uttered. Through their nearby hotel and on the radio, American culture was conveyed, and I enjoyed it very much. American music was alive and very stimulating. So, you see there was both sadness and cheerfulness in contrast right in front of me. It was rather an ambivalent time and I had to integrate that ambivalence towards cultures in me. It was the time of *baby boomers* – wherever you went there were a lot of young people on the streets, in the stations, and we all got together to hang out, a very natural tendency for young people. This was happening all over the world. Somebody started singing, and somebody else started playing music, on a guitar or a piano. That was how our ensemble got started, and we formed a music group as schoolboys. I was lucky because I was surrounded by a lot of talented people. Although very sadly some of these people killed themselves toward the end of their lives, the starting point was full of happiness, and cheerfulness and we could express that through songs ... I am getting nostalgic about the past. Musically, I belong to the time of folk songs, Western folk songs. Among them, Bob Dylan had become the most famous, and he has been one of my heroes. And they were rather intellectual, they were not just singers but they were folklorists, singing about lives and living – Pete Seeger was my hero too. He was a very intellectual person. They explained well what they were doing. So, I needed a keen intellect as well as playfulness to enjoy them as a whole, so we were educated players. We needed both – emotional involvement and profound thinking. And we all were singing songs about our own lives and living, not living for music. This was the lifestyle of folk singers. I liked this way of living.

Then I started to compare Japanese folk songs with American folk songs, and I was surprised to find many cultural differences. This was my first encounter with a sharp cultural difference which was seriously shocking to me. What was most insightful to me was the difference between the West and East in 'travelling songs,' or songs for travellers. Travelling is a metaphor for living, life is a journey and a journey is a metaphor for living. In Western songs, they tend to find a destination of the whole journey, such as heaven, home, or meeting God, a very definite destination. But in Japan, we have many more travelling songs where we just wander. As you know Basho, the haiku poet, in his essay says 'the passing months and days are the travellers of over a hundred generations, and the years that come and go are also travellers.' So, we are just travelling together through months, years, and over time. We have no destination, as long as we live by just travelling. Even in the songs that I created for travelling, I didn't mention a destination. We just pass through this world, and I still believe in this view of life. In other words, the future is a blank screen. We, folk singers, leave the destination to the audience. Maybe when I die, I might leave this land singing but you will never hear me singing about my last trip. I can't describe the content in that world because I have never taken that last journey to my destination yet. That is the feeling shared by most Japanese people about death and the afterlife. Our destination is blank, uncertain, and maybe ambiguous.

Let me quote that song I touched on in Chapter 10, that made me famous in Japan – in the song, we use the concept of heaven but the hero/drunkard was expelled from heaven, and the first line of the song is 'I ended up dying' – the song was a rather empty song from the start if I say so, where we have no destination, we're just travelling. And I wanted to convey that feeling from Japan. Do you see that?

JB: *Yes, I actually see that. This idea of eternal travel also resonates with your concept of transience, it's like life passing through.*

OK: That's very true. Thank you very much for understanding. I insist on this sharp cultural difference on this point. Of course, I have learnt a lot from the West – musically, linguistically, politically, and intellectually. My humble policy of not mentioning heaven in my musical creation is very psychological and culture-oriented too. Freud was described as 'a godless Jew,' and he was scientific about this too – he was godless, and in this way, he was very psychoanalytical. In Japan, we have 8 million gods and goddesses at one time, too many to have one God.

JB: A little like India …

OK: So, we don't have anything absolute. The promised land afterlife, after death, is always uncertain. This feeling needs to be shared among our readers.

JB: *In Chapter 9, 'Being drawn into a primal scene' you mention 'death while engaging in a sexual act' in reference to the crane-wife – how do you think the women of today's Japan respond to this aspect of the woman dying during sexual engagement in the myth of the crane-wife?*

OK: A very good question – as I mentioned when you were in Japan, you know it is not only women but also men who say 'I am dying' or 'I am going' during orgasmic experiences. While in sexual engagement our superficial self dies, like Winnicott says about the 'false self.' Maybe, that's why we say I am dying, we are going, as we disappear from reality. Possibly, we become empty. It may be similar to the Lacanian concept of self; he theorised about the superficial self with the true self dying in order to adapt ourselves to society or reality; we are like an 'automata' according to him. But from my personal point of view, I prefer Winnicott because his real self still survives possibly inside us. And this is not just a matter for women but also for men experiencing sexual orgasm in this way, and calling it dying. A small disappearance, a small death, a temporary death of the 'false self' or the 'adapting self,' or the 'adult self.' At that time we become 'amphibian-like.' We jump into the bed, or water (like a frog) – and that's the place where we meet the crane-wives, snake-wives, and frog-kings, together in our shared amphibian lives. We live in both worlds – underwater and in our land-based reality. As long as we live realistically outside, we can always go back to the water.

Changing the subject, 'Godzilla' is a frightening creature produced by Japanese movie directors and producers; he lives underwater and come to Japan from out of the sea. He is the most famous amphibian monster from Japan, created by Japan. There are many kinds of Godzillas inside women too, and we may become Godzilla in the middle of sexual engagement. In the Japanese language we differentiate between 'voiced' and 'unvoiced' sounds, like a 'clean sound' and a 'dirty sound,' and Godzilla has the 'dirtiest sound' from that perspective. And both sexes can share this experience.

I want to add one more point about sexual activities – sex is enjoyable but it has realistic consequences, sometimes undesirable consequences such as sexually transmitted diseases, abortions, and real death, etc. And in Japanese culture, abortion is very well known. These consequences are mostly a burden for women – as in the stories where men do not take any responsibilities at all. Although times are changing and women are abandoning irresponsible men, the 'hierarchy of love' (Kitayama, 1997) is still there.

JB: *Do you think cultural understanding and its nuances are important for psychoanalysis across the world? What impact does it have on the clinical work?*

OK: I have addressed this before in several of these chapters, but I want to stress language and child-rearing here because our experience is very different from Western styles. Theoretically, child-rearing is very important in psychoanalysis, and language is equally important in the psychoanalytic practice too. For example, to make interpretations which make insights possible. So, when language and child-rearing are different in some cultures then psychoanalysis can be very different too in those cultures. That's why we have to learn about the Japanese language, nature and content of child-rearing to practice psychoanalysis in Japan. That's what Doi Takeo insisted on, almost 50–60 years ago when I was just a beginner in psychoanalysis. I was so impressed by his contention, and his way of writing papers, I liked and respected him very much. *Amae* is such a beautiful concept that he talked about. Speaking internationally about this difference can be unique in Japan, but it can also be insightful for Westerners when regarding their way of life because of the differences.

In the sexual aspect of Japanese culture, transience is most important to us because sexual pleasure is basically transient. In Tokyo, which was called Edo, the Edo culture was very sexually involved – it looks beautiful but the people are floating. Just like a sexual experience, it is transient and soon passes. In the end one may experience emptiness or disillusionment … which is the most enjoyable part of the whole process, based on my observation. We should include this emptiness in life too. And that is not pathological at all, it is part of life.

JB: *In your clinical experience do patients freely discuss the 'threesome in infancy' or 'participation-type' of primal scene that you mention in Chapter 9, 'Being drawn into a primal scene'? What may the resistances be?*

OK: Japan is a 'shame culture,' so, of course, shame resistance is possible. It is part of our sense of beauty because we think sexuality is animalistic, 'amphibian' – we become like a frog, tortoise or snake. So, patients don't want to talk about it in their initial contact. Though people say that young people are changing I still don't see much difference. Japanese are really Japanese all the time! Some people may want to talk about it but it takes time, so gradual unfolding is much better. I think I mentioned this in Chapters 6 and 10, sexual expression can be verbalised in a way through onomatopoeia, like *zubu-zubu, gucha-gucha, gusho-gusho* – all natural sounds. Those 'voiced,' 'dirty,' and unclean words like Godzilla are so expressive, sexually, metaphorically, and phonetically. That may be true in almost every culture.

JB: *Yes, we have it in our culture and language too.*

OK: Yes, yes. In this way, it is easy for us to talk about sex. This may be a unique culturally Japanese way to express it, though not really talking about it. For infants, 'triadic experiences' are very common, a part of everyday life in early infancy. We experience them onomatopoeically, auditorily, and olfactorily, we experience vibrations of adult sexual activities while sleeping. We experience 'triadic experiences' in this way. The children may enjoy the bodily vibrations, physical proximity, its closeness while maybe sleeping in the middle. It's also a sense of safety that can be produced with this 'co-sleeping,' which is a more neutral word than 'threesome.' It is not pathological at all to us. It's our home, we feel safe, close, and intimate, maybe we even feel sexually excited, all of this can be part of our normal life. This is experienced as a mass – all aspects of life are there, adult and infant, front and back, sexual and non-sexual intimacy, body and emotion, and male and female which are not separated, maybe even making love to conceive, so they are often in a 'threesome with me.' Sometimes it is 'unfathomable,' you can't think about it but you may feel safe sharing the threesome way of thinking, while for some it can be traumatic. This practice of sexual activity combined with the prohibition of 'Don't Look' is very important, but it is often the responsibility of the mother to take care of everything in bed including the time for sex, and that could be very troublesome and tiring for Japanese women to enjoy the whole process.

JB: *How do you think the West may view this 'threesome infancy'?*

OK: I have presented this in papers in the West and usually they think our way of sleeping is quite different from theirs. That's why we may appear strange and sometimes frightening because of the unfathomable difference. As I mentioned in certain chapters in this book, it is something not understandable, something unfathomable because of the multi-layered meanings of our co-sleeping habit. In a way, I feel we really have to introduce this aspect too, as we need to explain the background, and the basic mental structure related to this. That's what I am trying to do now, with you. As I said to you before, I am very happy to make myself understood in this way, it's really a great joy. So, by sharing this joy through introduction, we are better understood in their language. Psychoanalysis can be a rather universal tool which we can utilise mutually to introduce ourselves. I am trying to do my best, but what is your response?

JB: *I think that you, as an experienced analyst who has worked on this for over 50 years, are showing us the path in a way. It is difficult to express in language, so there may be certain resistances from the 'outside.' Your work makes it easier for us, so it is needed for us.*

OK: One more aspect about this primary 'triadic sleeping,' or 'co-sleeping' – it might look or could seem just promiscuous to people from the outside. So, we have to explain it in terms of a 'compromise formation,' as in the psychoanalytic terms, which I am trying to use. I should say we Japanese people are good at making compromises, taking the middle road between two extremes. And the threesome way of thinking can be sophisticated in our own way.

JB: *When you mention that the Japanese are good at making compromises, would you also mean it in the political domain?*

OK: As a psychoanalyst, or as a musician in Japan, we are not politically powerful at all. We cannot be strong influencers because we are treating minorities, and we are a minority. We treat individuals in separate forbidden chambers – so, we may look very small from the outside. My personal intention is not to become powerful outside, as we have to be very significant inside. This internal significance is the most important. We have to be neutral outside to be significant inside. When I was a part-time musician as a student, the idea of 'young revolution' which was described as 'youthquake,' a journalistic term of our generation impressed me a lot. We may have idealised the idea of a student revolution, but in a way we failed due to our immaturity as a group. So, I decided to treat people individually, but not try omnipotently to change the larger group. This is my personal history. I gave up the idea of changing the outside rapidly. We have to first be on good terms with our individual existences.

JB: *How does the rearing practice of the 'threesome in infancy' impact the future adult sexuality and their choice of sexualities? Does it have different kinds of developmental processes for men, women and others? What may be the complexities associated with it?*

OK: The first thing that comes to my mind concerning this question, is that it can be a serious burden on women. They are becoming independent now and they want to work outside. We all have to share this burden, both men and women have to share this responsibility. Now is the time to change as the Japanese population is rapidly declining. In other words, we may not have a chance to continue this practice of 'triadic sleeping' in the future, so we really need something new. New ways and new ideas regarding practices of co-sleeping, may be equally difficult to think up. In Japan this 'threesome sleeping' arrangement has been possible mainly because of female sacrifice, which is often mentioned in the stories … tell me what you think of 'triadic sleeping'?

JB: *You are right about this being a burden on women, and today's women want a different narrative for themselves. We may have to set them free from these kinds of traditional bindings. But keeping in mind the Indian context, this is so deeply rooted culturally, as well as the difficulty of socio-economic limitations, that this 'co-sleeping,' or 'triadic sleeping,' or sharing the parental bed, that it may not evaporate just like that. Of course, it may change but perhaps over a very long time. At least in the Indian context, it will probably linger in the background.*

OK: Right, but we are not prophets, right?

JB: *Absolutely!*

OK: We have to follow the people, we have to follow the changing times. We have to wait for them to come to us, we are not social leaders. Let's see what will happen in the future.

JB: *Given the very volatile political condition of the world, and the growing political climate of coercive control over critical minds, what is your perception of the current position of psychoanalysis in the world, in Japan, and in the East? What should be the stance of psychoanalysis/psychoanalysts in such settings?*

OK: A very important point, that I think I have partially answered earlier. As I mentioned we must be politically outside, therefore we have to try to be neutral. So, we don't have to be politically involved in public. But, we should show the psychoanalytic benefits to the outside, as Freud did, we have to write books, just like we are doing now. We have to express ourselves culturally, it's a big challenge for us. That's what I have been doing, trying to do my best. In Japan, I have many books on Japanese culture and making use of psychoanalytic knowledge to show our purpose and ideals. That is freedom of thought. This freedom of thought may be our God which we should share. Writing books for the general audience is the best way to show our existence. As this time I am enjoying doing this with you. We as analysts are good at using language and making good compromises between the unconscious and the conscious. In this way we are significant. We can produce meanings useful to people outside. That is my way. We have to see what we are good at, and what we are not good at. We have limitations too, along with advantages.

JB: *Do you have any specific expectations from the next generation of analysts (from the East)? What could be their point of strength to move forward?*

OK: As a university professor, I have taught so many students, including you when you were younger! It is not just a matter of passing knowledge from one generation to the next. It is my contention that identification can be the most useful part of education. Students should identify themselves with us, their teachers. They are watching us in the classroom. If they can identify themselves with us then education can become very successful. In other words, it depends a lot on how we behave, how we think, how we talk, how we sing … They are watching us. Whenever we do something in front of them, it is part of their education, it's teaching. So, we have to take walks together with them by the sea, we have to go to karaoke with them, we have to drink together, we have to eat together, and then we have to read books together. So, it's a matter of identification with me as well as my colleagues … I have been a teacher even to my family members, but we have to ask them if I have been successful or not! Because of this, we have been fortunate enough to have many students from Kyushu University in the Institute of Psychoanalysis in Japan. You may remember Mr Shinpei Kudo from the graduate school of Kyushu University, he is a candidate to become a psychoanalyst. Ms Minako Nishi, now a psychoanalyst, is from the university and has been working at Kyoto University together with Professor Takahashi, my colleague at the university (you may remember her too) who is now a psychoanalytic psychotherapist.

JB: *Yes, I do remember Mr Kudo-san, Professor Takahashi ...*

OK: Mr Koji Toyokawa, went to medical college after he graduated from Kyushu University's Department of Education, and now he is a candidate too. Ms Yuko Fujimoto has also just become a candidate. There are many others who are coming up from among our students. They may be our followers in a way, although we are not trying hard to lead them. I have been singing, and talking, and eating, living, all in front of them. That's the only way of influencing students in education. I feel this way. It's an unconscious process. We cannot seduce them into our practice, and we cannot seduce patients, clients, or anybody. We are doing just what we are doing now, and waiting patiently and neutrally. That is the most difficult part of our practice. Writing papers, writing books, and speaking in front of them is the most effective way of showing our way to freedom of thought. But again, we are not prophets and we don't know what will happen in the future. The idea of psychoanalysis is still a brand new idea in Japan, there is a lot of resistance against it but it's worth the challenge.

JB: *Though you may have touched upon this point in your previous answers, this is of personal interest to me – would you like to elaborate on how your artistic sensibility has complemented your psychoanalytic thoughts/works, and, of course, vice-versa?*

OK: Certainly, I will be happy to touch on that again ... In the West, the poet can be ranked high, maybe at the top of the cultural hierarchy. Poetry is classified as a highly valued practice of human beings in the West. Also, musicians can be placed prominently in their cultural hierarchy. But in Japan, we are not like that. That's why I use the term 'riverbank beggar,' because we musicians, and maybe we psychoanalysts too, sell something invisible. We don't sell concrete things. It's all invisible, invisible knowledge, an invisible future, an invisible way of thinking. We can be praised sometimes and devalued at other times. In America there is a well-known word, 'shrink' – they are valued but at the same time devalued, praised and looked down on alternatingly in quick succession. Like amphibians who live underwater but on land too, we live in between. I see this clearly as between-ness, I appreciate myself being in between. But in the West, they tend to dislike this because of its ambiguity, because of the undifferentiated-ness. This is the most important part of our practice in our minds. Theoretically, we have to help the people to integrate themselves, and their ambivalence. As a parent, we have to be idealistic, but at the same time we have to accept being devalued, being blamed by the young people. So we have to be swinging in the middle, but maybe we have to get a little better than exactly in the middle – which really means, being 'neutral enough,' somewhere in the better middle. I live in this middle position like this although we have to be more or less the target of the public's ambivalence.

This is also a chance for you to integrate yourself, or integrate your images of me – I have bad aspects and good aspects, and I can show you a good future and a bad future at the same time. Don't you think that that can be a sort of fluctuating movement between two extremes, and this in the middle is the place for our practice to show our freedom of thought? This is our method. And I am lucky to have found this job, thanks to Freud! This is a very unique place to be. That's why I am not afraid of being described as a 'riverside beggar' an elusive artist, a depth-psychological performer communicating fully with people. I can understand how they are frightened of being looked down on by their patients, students, by the people – but I am tolerant of being the target of their ambivalence. Ambivalence can imply two values, 'ambi' means both, and 'valence' can mean values – it's a place for two values. Two extreme values. This is a very delicate part of our job. Of course, I feel uncomfortable with their fluctuating emotional expressions towards us. But we also sometimes feel happy about it because they go back to the other pole, so we can wait. It takes time, and time is a valuable factor for human development. That's my hope, my belief. It's a very difficult job, but it's worth doing.

JB: *On a lighter note, to conclude, I just thought that all your students (including me) can create a band which will be called 'Riverside Beggars.'*

OK: Oh yes! But 'Riverside Godzilla' is better. And psychoanalytically, we are helping those patients, particularly female patients, who have been told by their mothers, 'I picked you up by the river, under the bridge,' so we have to be there as a 'riverbank beggar' for them. We just can't be on the bridge, we may have to appear from deep in the muddy river. That's what I am thinking inside in Japanese, but it is difficult, even for me, to speak like this even here in Japan.

Reference

Kitayama, O. (1997). *Amae and its Hierarchy of Love. In: Prohibition of Don't Look* (pp. 68–79). Tokyo: Iwasaki Gakujutsu Shuppansha, 2010.

Chapter 13

Osamu Kitayama interviews Jhuma Basak

Osamu Kitayama and Jhuma Basak

OK: *Could you introduce your cultural and social background?*

JB-A: Let me begin with my family background a little – I come from a family of second-generation immigrants where both my parents were born in Bangladesh (East Pakistan) in its pre-independence era, in two different districts speaking two distinct dialects. Both my paternal and maternal grandparents came to India during colonial rule (pre-1947) – they came in search of a 'better life,' far from the political unrest then in Bangladesh ignited between Hindus and Muslims leading to the division of land. The majority of Hindus from Bangladesh were compelled to flee to India where the colonial fury of 'divide and rule' was equally tearing apart its people between the two religious polarities of Hindus and Muslims. This political fire in both countries (two Bengals) continued to burn homes for decades until the formation of independent Bangladesh (1971), resulting in mass displacement that also carried my grandparents to India.

In this perspective, my growing up has been very political with a multi-lingual background. In those times any 'middle-class educated Bengali family' was invariably inclined towards leftist ideology and Tagore literature. While on the other hand, my grandparents were 'Vaishnav' religious practitioners (that religious sector that worships Lord Vishnu, Krishna, as the preserver of the world). In my early years, I noticed the conflict between my father's ideological position as an atheist, and communist, who was actively involved in the Bengal leftist politics, and my grandfather's religious dogmatic beliefs. But we all lived together under the same roof in a joint family – it was like a miniature scenario of the Indian panorama of 'unity in diversity.' Living with differences, the 'this and that' state instead of the 'this or that' state, is a socio-cultural and political reality for India, for me in my home.

My mother was a professional dancer, both a classical and a folk performer, who had by-then travelled all across the world as an Indian delegate representing India in various cultural performances that the Indian government used to send in those days during the Indian post-independence era as part of their political strategy for developing cultural

DOI: 10.4324/9781003501930-16

relationships with many different countries (like Russia, Afghanistan, Syria, Iran, Iraq). Having travelled widely she developed an aptitude for different languages – like, Hindi, Punjabi, Russian. She was part of the national IPTA movement (the Indian People's Theatre Association), which was an all-India artists' cultural movement as an extension of the national freedom movement. That is where she met my father which led to their love-marriage – something that was not very common in those days. She was not very well accepted by my grandparents because it was not considered very respectable for women in those days to be professional dancers. The only reason they finally accepted my mother was because she came from a Brahmin family, the 'highest caste,' while my father was from a 'lower-caste.'

As you can well imagine it was quite a diverse familial climate that I grew up in. My artistic interests in life were introduced at an early age by my mother, leading to my learning different classical dance forms (Odissi, Bharatnatyam, Kathakali), and other pursuits in the arts in general. So, my interest in arts and culture definitely comes from my mother, much later leading to my postgraduate degree in comparative literature. While my father's engrossed professional commitment as an independent lawyer fascinated me as a child – I would often land up in his chamber full of books on the mezzanine floor of our house and do my homework while he would be writing his lawyer's briefs on those uncountable green blank pages.

It was at my university where I first came encountered psychoanalysis, more as a theoretical discipline rather than a clinical application, that introduced me to character analysis in novels, film analysis, and so on. I was absolutely thrilled to discover such a field as psychoanalysis that embraced arts, culture, social sciences, and critical political ideologue all in one discipline! And that was the beginning of my psychoanalytic journey – in my mid-20s. Now, you can understand from where my specific interest in culture and gender in psychoanalysis comes. It was actually my mother wanting me to go for higher education that led me to seek psychoanalysis in depth and to pursue my PhD – something that eventually led me to you, to Japan.

OK: *So, we share 'this and that' thinking but you often say Japan is clean while India is chaotic. They seem to be two sides of the same coin. Could you touch upon Indian cleansing and purification against shame or dirt?*

JB: I prefer to hold a 'psycho-social and cultural' framework of psychoanalytic enquiry as my theoretical grounding in psychoanalysis, and my response to this would be from that model of perception. When I first came to Japan in 2009, I was struck by the visible 'order' of the country, its cleanliness, and discipline, in contrast to the 'chaos' of my country, India, where I grew up. Both countries run very different 'systems-of-order,' that appear to be just the two sides of the same coin as you so rightly mentioned. Both aspects of 'order' and 'chaos' get manifested through cleanliness and dirt, expressing the consuming point of fixation inherent in compulsive motives and behaviour. To put it from a psycho-analytic perspective, these seemingly opposite characteristics in the two different cultures seem to share a similar psychoanalytic explanation in their reading of obsessive pathology – one expressed through retention and the other through expulsion. While one embraces 'mysophobia,' the other perhaps enfolds 'mysophilia' – the former is an extreme fear of germs and contamination, and the latter may be a compelling interest, engagement with dirt and filth. However, it is important to understand that both these aspects work only at the manifest level. The seed of this manifestation may take us deeper into the socio-cultural and political histories of the two countries where we may find much similar grounds in both the countries. In order to truly appreciate such cultural specificities and diversities it is important to see them against the backdrop of their individual national socio-cultural and political chronicles.

Both countries are preoccupied with specific aspects of their environment to the point where it has a dominant influence on individual habits and collective cultural practices. Whether gripped in maintaining cleanliness or dwelling in the dirt, the underlying compulsion remains fundamentally connected. The ritualistic purification by water, *misogi*, runs deep in the cultural rites of both countries. Both signify equal religious inheritance and notions of 'purity' and 'impurity' that drive its cultural rites and people's belief systems. At the apparent level, it may be interesting to note that while Japan as a country may be noted for its nature of order and cleanli-ness, India on the contrary may be charged with dirt and chaos. But, at the latent level, both convey a similar employment of aggressive and coarse ambivalence in reaction to their own national socio-political and cultural history. Such shame-based cultures, like India and Japan, may often coun-ter-prompt the subjectivity to seek narcissistic solutions for its survival against its sense of inner denigration and inflicted humiliation. The envir-onment gets charged with an overt paradoxical, yet simultaneous, existence of the 'true self' and the 'false self' in everyday living. Thereby, generating a very complex cultural and human communication mechanism with a multi-layered medium of deliberation.

In the Indian cultural imagination, cleansing and purification practices hold significant cultural, spiritual, and religious importance. A determin-ing aspect of Indian cleansing and purification rituals revolves around the concept of shame or contamination that finds its ancient inheritance buried in the caste division in socio-cultural reality along with in the human psyche for centuries (which I have written about here in Chapter 8). Hindu spiritual purification processes and physical cleansing through bathing, ablution, and chanting, all serve as a powerful cultural mechan-ism in restoring its sense of purity for the soul, body and mind. The ele-ment of water plays a very important role in this purification process, for example, the water of the *Holy Ganges* of India is considered to be sacred for every socio-religious practice be it worshipping of deities, to marriages, birth, and death. The soul's purity, its sanctity is very crucial in the Indian imagination – perhaps a very unique quality from the Western perception of purity. The infinite soul connects one to the higher cosmic infinitude giving rise to the concept of life after death, to an eternal flow of life. In important cultural rites like birth, marriage, and death within Hindu rituals, cleansing of the body and soul is a necessary ceremonial performance of the entire occasion – the act symbolically emphasises the eternal vow undertaken by individuals which further reflects its interminable cultural relevance.

In conservative orthodox settings in the Indian site, the woman's psychobiological experiences of bodily discharges and fluids (like menstruation, postpartum discharge, and lactation period) are treated with even added quality of shame due to patriarchal taboos on the female body, on the feminine, and its sexuality. In this sense, the environment of mysophilia may find its direct correlate to the female body that emits such a potent imagination comprising a conjoined element of both attraction and revulsion of the female body – the derivation of which may lead us to the gory and violent treatment of the 'mother earth' throughout the innumerable foreign invasions in the country along with its colonial history. Its colonial ambivalence with the 'mother earth' finds contradictory significance against a belief system that equally worships nature. That way you can say that India is a site of paradoxes – another salient common feature with Japan.

The devaluation and objectification of women's bodies by the patriarchate machinery only reinforces the denigration of femininity in society and family. Perhaps this holds a further foundational root to the surreptitious 'culture of violence' against women that may be found alarmingly increasing in the Indian site. In the Indian cultural site, the maternal is worshipped, as we see in the overwhelming rituals of the worshipping of Hindu goddesses, but sadly enough femininity suffers much disgrace and condemnation in the private psychic plane. The construction of the male gaze within the larger phallic order makes the female body, her femininity, a seductive object of desire that is used only for male pleasurable consumption (Chapter 7), or used as a utility product for the purpose of reproductive mechanism. However, perhaps traditional patriarchal morals along with our colonial legacy may have undermined certain gender dynamics that may have been more egalitarian in the indigenous regional community environment in the pre-colonial era. Nonetheless, women are still fighting socio-cultural and economic conformities to voice their worth and autonomous subjectivity in society.

OK: *Oh, you have explained our differences with a lot of 'earthy' similarities. Learning from each other, we are all interested in female passivity and maternal vulnerability, which should be acknowledged everywhere. Do you imagine any possibility that early involvement in parental heterosexual activities can lead to a clear differentiation between male sadism and female masochism in a later stage?*

JB: In Chapter 11 here on 'Enthralled infancy in a bed of parental tryst' I have attempted to exemplify through my clinical illustrations how in the case of early exposure and involvement of children in parental hetero-sexual activities it may create probable ground for premature onset of sexual stimulation, both erotically and in fantasy, for the child. It may be overtly simplistic to directly link early engagement in parental hetero-sexual activities as a singular causality for the later development of spe-cific sexual preferences or other anomalies in sexual behaviour (like sadism or masochism) in adult life. Because 'early involvement in par-ental heterosexual activities' does not imply direct erotic participation in parental sexual activities, but as an indirect, passive, receptive engage-ment (in the form of auditory, olfactory employment of the infant/child), which equally involves non-sexual promptings as well. Thereby, it may be confusing for the growing child, but it does not necessarily indicate a direct derivative per se of a 'pathological' development.

Whether one would respond with male sadism or female masochism equally depends heavily on the identification of the child with its parental masculine or feminine qualities, along with their play of gender roles in regular life. Similarly other significant familial members or cultural representations as well have an imprint on the imagination of the child that adds further to its development of aggressive masculine sadistic qualities or passive feminine masochistic potentials. Both men and women can exhibit sadistic or masochistic tendencies, depending upon their active–passive identifications and cultural impact, and these pre-ferences can manifest regardless of one's sex but more on its identification with feminine and masculine traits. However, the pathogenesis of its manifestation may highly depend on unresolved conflicts during its psy-chosexual development, including its early exposure, involvement and response to parental heterosexual activities (particularly as experienced in the 'site of parental tryst,' the parental bed, in its triadic engagement), and its unconscious desires and defences that it imbibes for survival. Culture more often plays a dominant, yet covert, role in shaping our gender roles and behaviour, determining masculine aggressivity or femi-nine submissiveness, in an individual. In cultures with traditional gender roles, like in the case of India to some extent, the predominance of het-eronormative practices tends to override and create a taboo on all other forms of sexualities, and sexual preferences. However, it is a changing time now and one hopes for human progression towards civility and thus, more cultural integration of such sexual variances.

It appears that both the Indian and Japanese cultures direct a masochistic quality of 'inexhaustible giving' on its women which may often act as a guise to the underlying sadism of society that covertly forces the other to love the subject from an internal harbouring of a sense of guilt. In this way, the subject enjoys its lost dominance in reality through the employment of masochistic omnipotent fantasies. Needless to say, such cultural leanings will have added complexity prompting the elevation of masochistic investments in cultural imagination of the feminine. And this may be a characteristic that spreads across Asia at large.

OK: *Lastly, could you tell us your thoughts on the possibility that our culturist/ psychoanalyst combination can be a powerful container for clients' and patients' projections locally?*

JB: In 1907 Freud in 'Obsessive actions and religious practices' addressed human culture by drawing parallels between private ritualistic, obsessional practices of an individual and the ceremonial religious customs of their society. The personal obsessional neurosis of an individual was accompanied by a collective traditional religious views. While the individual obsessional practice had its own associated distinctive expression, the religious ceremonials were a collective stereotypical structure accompanying the individual's symptomatic formation. Freud's conviction of cultural relevance in psychoanalysis runs throughout his philosophy of work and is not necessarily confined to *Totem and Taboo* (1912), *The Future of an Illusion* (1927), *Civilisation and its Discontents* (1930).

Culture is deeply intertwined with symbolic representations as found in religious beliefs/practices, mythological narratives, and traditional values of civilisation. And so is the unconscious structured with such symbols of the collective. Similarly, language which is the crux of culture itself, is the symbolic representation of such a collective cultural design that the individual psychic construct carves out, and organises according to its own scheme. And in psychoanalysis, we emphasise the importance of symbols in the unconscious mind that create our dreams, fantasies, desires, conflicts, and so on and so forth. As a psychoanalyst from India, which has such a rich cultural reference, I would like to be attuned to how cultural norms and values shape our clients'/patients' introjections and projections into themselves, others, as well as the analyst in the transference situation. In Indian Hindu culture, symbols such as the lotus flower, the cow, or the colour red carry deep symbolic significance, representing concepts such as purity, fertility, and auspiciousness (subliminally interweaving the feminine in a culturally imaginative composition). These symbols are further woven into religious practices, folklores, and everyday life – as well as knitted with political colours – those shape individual beliefs in both subtle and primaeval ways. Further, notions of familial duty, honour, and social hierarchy in Indian society (maybe applicable to Japan too, and other Asian countries also to some extent) can significantly impact how individuals perceive themselves and others in their specific cultural environment. Patients may project idealised or demonised versions of cultural archetypes into their therapists or significant others, reflecting deeper conflicts and unresolved issues within themselves. As much as patients carry all these compound symbolic representations in their intrapsychic space into the clinical space, we analysts also bring these aspects into the dyadic dynamism in our clinical engagement. Integrating cultural specificities into psychoanalytic applications creates the foundation for understanding different cultural determinants, its oedipal constellations, its human attachment designs, sexualities, and so on in the evolution of varied societies, and human development. Further, by having a shared cultural idiom the analyst can provide a powerful framework of identification in facilitating patients to explore their projections in the context of their cultural background. That way the possibility of clinical resistance gets narrowed down significantly and its defensive mechanism may even act in favour of an ego-syntonic evolution within the analytic dyad. By engaging with the symbolic embedded in a specific cultural imagination, the analytic dyad gains familiar ground, bringing about identification and working through the unconscious for the patient (as we see in Case – 2, Ajit, in Chapter 11 'Enthralled infancy in a bed of parental tryst'). The shared cultural well of allegory helps the dyad to identify its non-articulable, layered symbolic language that adds to the foundational trust within the transferential dyad enabling collective unconscious connect and psychoanalytic work possible. The shared professional, clinical language of psychoanalysis may be universal but that universality finds contextual significance when seen through the specificity of different cultural nuances. In this sense, we may all sing songs in our different languages, and from different cultures, but its musical melody, its inherent rhythm, moves us all in related harmony. So, that way, the universe embraces contextual relevance, and the contextual seeks universal connectedness – a dual fuelling process that interconnects each other.

OK: *Thank you, Jhuma! I enjoyed knowing about how our earthy and earthly atmospheres are both deep-seated. I wish we could continue like this but …*

Index

For Product Safety Concerns and Information please contact our EU
representative GPSR@taylorandfrancis.com
Taylor & Francis Verlag GmbH, Kaufingerstraße 24, 80331 München, Germany

www.ingramcontent.com/pod-product-compliance
Lightning Source LLC
Chambersburg PA
CBHW050635280326
41932CB00015B/2659

9 781032 752044